The Unwomanly Face of War

'Magnificent . . . Alexievich doesn't just hear what these women say; she cares about how they speak . . . It's a mark of her exceptional mind that she tries to retain the incomprehensible in any human story'
Gaby Wood, *Daily Telegraph*, Books of the Year

'An astonishing book, harrowing and life-affirming. It deserves the widest possible readership' Paula Hawkins, author of *The Girl on the Train*

'Magnificent . . . After decades of the war being remembered by "men writing about men," she aims to give voice to an ageing generation of women who found themselves dismissed not just as storytellers but also as veterans, mothers and even potential wives . . . a literary excavation of memory itself' Rebecca Reich, *The New York Times Book Review*

'This is an oral history of women who fought in the Second World War. And it's brilliant' Kamila Shamsie, *Guardian*, Books of the Year

'Nothing can quite prepare the reader for the shattering force of Svetlana Alexievich's oral history of Soviet women in the Second World War'
Geoff Dyer, *Observer*, Books of the Year

'As with her other books, terrifying documentation meets great artfulness of construction' Julian Barnes

'Alexievich's "documentary novels" are crafted and edited with a reporter's cool eye for detail and a poet's ear for the intricate rhythms of human speech. Reading them is like eavesdropping on a confessional. This is history at its rawest and most uncomfortably intimate . . . The book is not merely a corrective to male-centred accounts of conflict; it is a shattering and sometimes overwhelming experience' Andrew Dickson, *Evening Standard*

'Much more than a historical harvest, this is a polyphonic book, superbly orchestrated . . . a mark of her exceptional mind'
Anthony Cummins, *Daily Telegraph*, Books of the Year

'These accounts fight our ingrained ideas about what makes a war story' *Vanity Fair*

'Refusing to pass judgment, crediting all, she listens, suffers and brings to life . . . It took years and many miles of traveling to find and capture all the testimonies here . . . We still end up feeling that we have been sitting at her side. With her, we hear the memories of partisans, guerrilla fighters trapped behind the lines' *Wall Street Journal*

'A revelation . . . Alexievich's text gives us precious details of the kind that breathe life into history . . . more than a historical document – it is the stuff of history itself' Lyuba Vinogradova, *Financial Times*

'A profoundly humbling, devastating book, it should be compulsory reading for anyone wishing to understand the experience of the war and its haunting legacy in the former Soviet Union' Daniel Beer, *Literary Review*

'We hear the testimony of Soviet women as they rush to the front to in serve a wide range of roles, from nurses to snipers, in the battle against the invading fascists. This book was initially published in Russia in the 1980s, but with a great deal of the explicit detail scrubbed out by anxious authorities. Now with the full text restored and expanded, the book has appeared in a brilliant English translation by Richard Pevear for the first time' Kathryn Hughes, *Guardian*, Books of the Year

'One of the most heart-breaking books I have ever read . . . I urge you to read it' Julian Evans, *Daily Telegraph*

'Women did everything – this book reminds and reveals. They learned to pilot planes and drop bombs, to shoot targets from great distances . . . Alexievich has turned their voices into history's psalm' *Boston Globe*

'Alexievich did an enormous service, recovering these stories . . . *The Unwomanly Face of War* tells the story of these forgotten women, and its great achievement is that it gives credit to their contribution but also to the hell they endured' Washington Post

'In a post-truth era when journalism is under pressure – susceptible to propaganda, sensationalism, and "alternative facts" – the power of documentary literature stands out more clearly than ever . . . Listen to Alexievich' *The Atlantic*

'One of the most gifted writers of her generation' *Economist*, Books of the Year

'A remarkable collection of testimonies . . . Sitting at kitchen tables, Alexievich coaxes out of the women stories that describe a reality vastly different from the officially sanctioned version. . . . They speak guardedly but vividly of fleeting encounters, deep relationships, unexpressed feelings' *New Yorker*

ABOUT THE AUTHOR

Svetlana Alexievich was born in Ivano-Frankivsk in 1948 and has spent most of her life in the Soviet Union and present-day Belarus, with prolonged periods of exile in Western Europe. Starting out as a journalist, she developed her own, distinctive non-fiction genre which brings together a chorus of voices to describe a specific historical moment. Her works include *The Unwomanly Face of War* (1985), *Last Witnesses* (1985), *Boys in Zinc* (1991), *Chernobyl Prayer* (1997) and *Second-Hand Time* (2013). She has won many international awards, including the 2015 Nobel Prize in Literature for 'her polyphonic writings, a monument to suffering and courage in our time'.

Richard Pevear and Larissa Volokhonsky have translated works by Tolstoy, Dostoevsky, Chekhov, Gogol, Bulgakov and Pasternak. They were twice awarded the PEN/Book-of-the-Month Club Translation Prize (for Dostoevsky's *The Brothers Karamazov* and Tolstoy's *Anna Karenina*). They are married and live in France.

SVETLANA ALEXIEVICH

The Unwomanly Face of War

Translated by Richard Pevear and Larissa Volokhonsky

PENGUIN BOOKS

PENGUIN CLASSICS

UK | USA | Canada | Ireland | Australia
India | New Zealand | South Africa

Penguin Books is part of the Penguin Random House group of companies
whose addresses can be found at global.penguinrandomhouse.com.

First published in Russian as *У войны не женское лицо* by Mastatskaya Litaratura,
Minsk 1985
First published in English as *War's Unwomanly Face* by Progress Publishers, Moscow 1988
This translation first published in the United States by Random House, an imprint and
division of Penguin Random House LLC 2017
This translation first published in Great Britain by Penguin Classics 2017
This edition published in Penguin Classics 2018
001

Printed and bound in Great Britain by Clays Ltd, Elcograf S.p.A.

A CIP catalogue record for this book is available from the British Library

ISBN: 978–0–141–98353–0

www.greenpenguin.co.uk

MIX
Paper from
responsible sources
FSC
www.fsc.org   FSC® C018179

Penguin Random House is committed to a
sustainable future for our business, our readers
and our planet. This book is made from Forest
Stewardship Council® certified paper.

CONTENTS

———

FROM A CONVERSATION
WITH A HISTORIAN

—*At what time in history did women first appear in the army?*

—Already in the fourth century B.C. women fought in the Greek armies of Athens and Sparta. Later they took part in the campaigns of Alexander the Great.

The Russian historian Nikolai Karamzin* wrote about our ancestors: "Slavic women occasionally went to war with their fathers and husbands, not fearing death: thus during the siege of Constantinople in 626 the Greeks found many female bodies among the dead Slavs. A mother, raising her children, prepared them to be warriors."

—*And in modern times?*

—For the first time in England, where from 1560 to 1650 they began to staff hospitals with women soldiers.

—*What happened in the twentieth century?*

—The beginning of the century . . . In England during World War I women were already being taken into the Royal Air Force. A Royal

---

* The Russian poet and writer Nikolai Karamzin (1766–1826) was the author of a masterful twelve-volume *History of the Russian State*.

Auxiliary Corps was also formed and the Women's Legion of Motor Transport, which numbered 100,000 persons.

In Russia, Germany, and France many women went to serve in military hospitals and ambulance trains.

During World War II the world was witness to a women's phenomenon. Women served in all branches of the military in many countries of the world: 225,000 in the British army, 450,000 to 500,000 in the American, 500,000 in the German . . .

About a million women fought in the Soviet army. They mastered all military specialties, including the most "masculine" ones. A linguistic problem even emerged: no feminine gender had existed till then for the words "tank driver," "infantryman," "machine gunner," because women had never done that work. The feminine forms were born there, in the war . . .

A HUMAN BEING IS
GREATER THAN WAR

Millions of the cheaply killed
Have trod the path in darkness . . .

—OSIP MANDELSTAM[*]

FROM THE JOURNAL OF THIS BOOK

1978–1985

I am writing a book about war . . .

I, who never liked to read military books, although in my child-hood and youth this was the favorite reading of everybody. Of all my peers. And that is not surprising—we were the children of Victory. The children of the victors. What is the first thing I remember about the war? My childhood anguish amid the incomprehensible and frightening words. The war was remembered all the time: at school and at home, at weddings and christenings, at celebrations and wakes. Even in children's conversations. The neighbors' boy once asked me: "What do people do under the ground? How do they live there?" We, too, wanted to unravel the mystery of war.

It was then that I began to think about death . . . And I never

---

[*]   Osip Mandelstam (1891–1938) was one of the greatest Russian poets of the twentieth cen-tury. The epigraph comes from "Lines on the Unknown Soldier" (1937–1938). Mandelstam died in transit to one of Stalin's hard-labor camps.

stopped thinking about it; it became the main mystery of life for me.

For us everything took its origin from that frightening and mysterious world. In our family my Ukrainian grandfather, my mother's father, was killed at the front and is buried somewhere in Hungary, and my Belorussian grandmother, my father's mother, was a partisan* and died of typhus; two of her sons served in the army and were reported missing in the first months of the war; of three sons only one came back. My father. The Germans burned alive eleven distant relations with their children—some in their cottage, some in a village church. These things happened in every family. With everybody.

For a long time afterward the village boys played "Germans and Russians." They shouted German words: *Hände hoch! Zurück! Hitler kaputt!*

We didn't know a world without war; the world of war was the only one familiar to us, and the people of war were the only people we knew. Even now I don't know any other world and any other people. Did they ever exist?

———

THE VILLAGE OF MY postwar childhood was a village of women. Village women. I don't remember any men's voices. That is how it has remained for me: stories of the war are told by women. They weep. Their songs are like weeping.

In the school library half of the books were about the war. The same with the village library, and in the nearby town, where my father often drove to get books. Now I know the reason why. Could it have been accidental? We were making war all the time, or preparing for war. Remembering how we made war. We never lived any other way, and probably didn't know how. We can't imagine how to live differently, and it will take us a long time to learn, if we ever do.

---

* A participant in a voluntary resistance movement fighting a guerrilla war against the Germans during World War II.

At school we were taught to love death. We wrote compositions about how we would like to die in the name of . . . We dreamed . . .

But the voices outside shouted about other more alluring things.

For a long time I was a bookish person, both frightened and at-tracted by reality. My fearlessness came from an ignorance of life. Now I think: If I were a more realistic person, could I throw myself into that abyss? What caused it all—ignorance? Or the sense of a path? For the sense of a path does exist . . .

I searched for a long time . . . What words can convey what I hear? I searched for a genre that would correspond to how I see the world, how my eye, my ear, are organized.

Once a book fell into my hands: *I Am from a Burning Village,* by A. Adamovich, Ya. Bryl, and V. Kolesnik.* I had experienced such a shock only once before, when I read Dostoevsky. Here was an un-usual form: the novel was composed from the voices of life itself, from what I had heard in childhood, from what can be heard now in the street, at home, in a café, on a bus. There! The circle was closed. I had found what I was looking for. I knew I would.

Ales Adamovich became my teacher . . .

————

FOR TWO YEARS I was not so much meeting and writing as thinking. Reading. What will my book be about? Yet another book about war? What for? There have been a thousand wars—small and big, known and unknown. And still more has been written about them. But . . . it was men writing about men—that much was clear at once. Every-thing we know about war we know with "a man's voice." We are all captives of "men's" notions and "men's" sense of war. "Men's" words. Women are silent. No one but me ever questioned my grandmother.

* The novel *I Am from a Burning Village* (also known in English as *Out of the Fire*), by the Be-lorussian writers Ales Adamovich (1927–1994), Yanka Bryl (1917–2006), and Vladimir Kolesnik (1922–1994), chronicles the Nazi destruction of Belorussian villages during World War II. Ad-amovich was a novelist, critic, and philosopher who had fought as a partisan in 1942–1943 and became a forceful antiwar activist.

My mother. Even those who were at the front say nothing. If they suddenly begin to remember, they don't talk about the "women's" war but about the "men's." They tune in to the canon. And only at home or waxing tearful among their combat girlfriends do they begin to talk about their war, the war unknown to me. Not only to me, to all of us. More than once during my journalistic travels I witnessed, I was the only hearer of, totally new texts. I was shaken as I had been in childhood. The monstrous grin of the mysterious shows through these stories . . . When women speak, they have nothing or almost nothing of what we are used to reading and hearing about: How certain people heroically killed other people and won. Or lost. What equipment there was and which generals. Women's stories are different and about different things. "Women's" war has its own colors, its own smells, its own lighting, and its own range of feelings. Its own words. There are no heroes and incredible feats, there are simply people who are busy doing inhumanly human things. And it is not only they (people!) who suffer, but the earth, the birds, the trees. All that lives on earth with us. They suffer without words, which is still more frightening.

But why? I asked myself more than once. Why, having stood up for and held their own place in a once absolutely male world, have women not stood up for their history? Their words and feelings? They did not believe themselves. A whole world is hidden from us. Their war remains unknown . . .

I want to write the history of that war. A women's history.

––––––

AFTER THE FIRST ENCOUNTERS . . .

Astonishment: these women's military professions—medical assistant, sniper, machine gunner, commander of an antiaircraft gun, sapper—and now they are accountants, lab technicians, museum guides, teachers . . . Discrepancy of the roles—here and there. Their memories are as if not about themselves, but some other girls. Now they are surprised at themselves. Before my eyes history "humanizes" itself, becomes like ordinary life. Acquires a different lighting.

I've happened upon extraordinary storytellers. There are pages in their lives that can rival the best pages of the classics. The person sees herself so clearly from above—from heaven, and from below—from the ground. Before her is the whole path—up and down—from angel to beast. Remembering is not a passionate or dispassionate retelling of a reality that is no more, but a new birth of the past, when time goes in reverse. Above all it is creativity. As they narrate, people create, they "write" their life. Sometimes they also "write up" or "rewrite." Here you have to be vigilant. On your guard. At the same time pain melts and destroys any falsehood. The temperature is too high! Simple people—nurses, cooks, laundresses—behave more sincerely, I became convinced of that . . . They, how shall I put it exactly, draw the words out of themselves and not from newspapers and books they have read—not from others. But only from their own sufferings and experiences. The feelings and language of educated people, strange as it may be, are often more subject to the working of time. Its general encrypting. They are infected by secondary knowledge. By myths. Often I have to go for a long time, by various roundabout ways, in order to hear a story of a "woman's," not a "man's" war: not about how we retreated, how we advanced, at which sector of the front . . . It takes not one meeting, but many sessions. Like a persistent portrait painter.

I sit for a long time, sometimes a whole day, in an unknown house or apartment. We drink tea, try on the recently bought blouses, discuss hairstyles and recipes. Look at photos of the grandchildren together. And then . . . After a certain time, you never know when or why, suddenly comes this long-awaited moment, when the person departs from the canon—plaster and reinforced concrete, like our monuments—and goes on to herself. Into herself. Begins to remember not the war but her youth. A piece of her life . . . I must seize that moment. Not miss it! But often, after a long day, filled with words, facts, tears, only one phrase remains in my memory (but what a phrase!): "I was so young when I left for the front, I even grew during the war." I keep it in my notebook, although I have dozens of yards of tape in my tape recorder. Four or five cassettes . . .

What helps me? That we are used to living together. Communally. We are communal people. With us everything is in common—both happiness and tears. We know how to suffer and how to tell about our suffering. Suffering justifies our hard and ungainly life. For us pain is art. I must admit, women boldly set out on this path . . .

———

HOW DO THEY RECEIVE ME?

They call me "little girl," "dear daughter," "dear child." Probably if I was of their generation they would behave differently with me. Calmly and as equals. Without joy and amazement, which are the gifts of the meeting between youth and age. It is a very important point, that then they were young and now, as they remember, they are old. They remember across their life—across forty years. They open their world to me cautiously, to spare me: "I got married right after the war. I hid behind my husband. Behind the humdrum, behind baby diapers. I wanted to hide. My mother also begged: 'Be quiet! Be quiet! Don't tell.' I fulfilled my duty to the Motherland, but it makes me sad that I was there. That I know about it . . . And you are very young. I feel sorry for you . . ." I often see how they sit and listen to themselves. To the sound of their own soul. They check it against the words. After long years a person understands that this was life, but now it's time to resign yourself and get ready to go. You don't want to, and it's too bad to vanish just like that. Casually. In passing. And when you look back you feel a wish not only to tell about your life, but also to fathom the mystery of life itself. To answer your own question: Why did all this happen to me? You gaze at everything with a parting and slightly sorrowful look . . . Almost from the other side . . . No longer any need to deceive anyone or yourself. It's already clear to you that without the thought of death it is impossible to make out anything in a human being. Its mystery hangs over everything.

War is an all too intimate experience. And as boundless as human life . . .

Once a woman (a pilot) refused to meet with me. She explained on the phone: "I can't . . . I don't want to remember. I spent three years at war . . . And for three years I didn't feel myself a woman. My organism was dead. I had no periods, almost no woman's desires. And I was beautiful . . . When my future husband proposed to me . . . that was already in Berlin, by the Reichstag . . . He said: 'The war's over. We're still alive. We're lucky. Let's get married.' I wanted to cry. To shout. To hit him! What do you mean, married? Now? In the midst of all this—married? In the midst of black soot and black bricks . . . Look at me . . . Look how I am! Begin by making me a woman: give me flowers, court me, say beautiful words. I want it so much! I wait for it! I almost hit him . . . I was about to . . . He had one cheek burned, purple, and I see: he understood everything, tears are running down that cheek. On the still-fresh scars . . . And I myself can't believe I'm saying to him: 'Yes, I'll marry you.'

"Forgive me . . . I can't . . ."

I understood her. But this was also a page or half a page of my future book.

Texts, texts. Texts everywhere. In city apartments and village cottages, in the streets and on the train . . . I listen . . . I turn more and more into a big ear, listening all the time to another person. I "read" voices.

———

A HUMAN BEING IS greater than war . . .

Memory preserves precisely the moments of that greatness. A human being is guided by something stronger than history. I have to gain breadth—to write the truth about life and death in general, not only the truth about war. To ask Dostoevsky's question: How much human being is in a human being, and how to protect this human being in oneself? Evil is unquestionably tempting. Evil is more artful than good. More attractive. As I delve more deeply into the boundless world of war, everything else becomes slightly faded, more ordinary than the ordinary. A grandiose and predatory world. Now I understand the solitude of the human being who comes back from there. As if from another planet or from the other world. This human being has a knowledge that others do not have, that can be obtained only there, close to death. When she tries to put something into words, she has a sense of catastrophe. She is struck dumb. She wants to tell, the others would like to understand, but they are all powerless.

They are always in a different space than the listener. They are surrounded by an invisible world. At least three persons participate in the conversation: the one who is talking now, the one she was then, at the moment of the event, and myself. My goal first of all is to get at the truth of those years. Of those days. Without sham feelings. Just after the war this woman would have told of one war; after decades, of course, it changes somewhat, because she adds her whole life to this memory. Her whole self. How she lived those years, what she read, saw, whom she met. Finally, whether she is happy or unhappy. Do we talk by ourselves, or is someone else there? Family? If it's friends, what sort? Friends from the front are one thing, all the rest are another. My documents are living beings; they change and fluctuate together with us; there is no end of things to be gotten out of them. Something new and necessary for us precisely now. This very moment. What are we looking for? Most often not great deeds and heroism, but small, human things, the most interesting and intimate for us. Well, what would I like most to know, for instance, from the life of ancient Greece? From the history of Sparta? I would like to read how people talked at home then and what they talked about. How they went to war. What words they spoke on the last day and the last night before parting with their loved ones. How they saw them off to war. How they awaited their return from war . . . Not heroes or generals, but ordinary young men . . .

History through the story told by an unnoticed witness and participant. Yes, that interests me, that I would like to make into literature. But the narrators are not only witnesses—least of all are they witnesses; they are actors and makers. It is impossible to go right up to reality. Between us and reality are our feelings. I understand that I am dealing with versions, that each person has her version, and it is from them, from their plurality and their intersections, that the image of the time and the people living in it is born. But I would not like it to be said of my book: her heroes are real, and no more than that. This is just history. Mere history.

I write not about war, but about human beings in war. I write not the history of a war, but the history of feelings. I am a historian of the soul. On the one hand I examine specific human beings, living in a specific time and taking part in specific events, and on the other hand I have to discern the eternally human in them. The tremor of eternity. That which is in human beings at all times.

They say to me: Well, memories are neither history nor literature. They're simply life, full of rubbish and not tidied up by the hand of an artist. The raw material of talk, every day is filled with it. These bricks lie about everywhere. But bricks don't make a temple! For me it is all different . . . It is precisely there, in the warm human voice, in the living reflection of the past, that the primordial joy is concealed and the insurmountable tragedy of life is laid bare. Its chaos and passion. Its uniqueness and inscrutability. Not yet subjected to any treatment. The originals.

I build temples out of our feelings . . . Out of our desires, our disappointments. Dreams. Out of that which was, but might slip away.

ONCE AGAIN ABOUT THE same thing . . . I'm interested not only in the reality that surrounds us, but in the one that is within us. I'm interested not in the event itself, but in the event of feelings. Let's say— the soul of the event. For me feelings are reality.

And history? It is in the street. In the crowd. I believe that in each of us there is a small piece of history. In one half a page, in another two or three. Together we write the book of time. We each call out our truth. The nightmare of nuances. And it all has to be heard, and one has to dissolve in it all, and become it all. And at the same time not lose oneself. To combine the language of the street and literature. The problem is also that we speak about the past in present-day language. How can we convey the feelings of those days?

———

A PHONE CALL IN the morning: "We're not acquainted . . . But I've come from Crimea, I'm calling from the train station. Is it far from you? I want to tell you my war . . ."

Really?!

And I was about to go to the park with my little girl. To ride the merry-go-round. How can I explain to a six-year-old what it is I do? She recently asked me: "What is war?" How do I reply? . . . I would like to send her out into this world with a gentle heart, and I teach her that one shouldn't simply go and pick a flower. It's a pity to crush a ladybug, to tear the wing off a dragonfly. So how am I to explain war to the child? To explain death? To answer the question of why people kill? Kill even little children like herself. We, the adults, are as if in collusion. We understand what the talk is about. But what of children? After the war my parents somehow explained it to me, but I can't explain it to my child. Can't find the words. We like war less and less; it's more and more difficult to find a justification for it. For us it's simply murder. At least it is for me.

I would like to write a book about war that would make war sickening, and the very thought of it repulsive. Insane. So that even the generals would be sickened . . .

My men friends (as opposed to women) are taken aback by such "women's" logic. And again I hear the "men's" argument: "You weren't in the war." But maybe that's a good thing: I don't know the passion of hatred; my vision is normal. Unwarlike, unmanly.

There is a concept in optics called "light-gathering power"—the greater or lesser ability of a lens to fix the caught image. So, then, women's memory of the war is the most "light-gathering" in terms of strength of feelings, in terms of pain. I would even say that "women's" war is more terrible than "men's." Men hide behind history, behind facts; war fascinates them as action and a conflict of ideas, of interests, whereas women are caught up with feelings. And another thing: men are prepared from childhood for the fact that they may have to shoot. Women are not taught that . . . They are not prepared to do that work . . . And they remember other things, and remember differently. They are capable of seeing what is closed to men. I repeat once more: their war has smell, has color, a detailed world of existence: "They gave us kit bags and we made skirts out of them"; "I went into the recruiting office through one door wearing a dress, and came out through the other wearing trousers and an army shirt, with my braid cut off, and only a little lock left on my forehead . . ."; "The Germans gunned down the village and left . . . We came to the place: trampled yellow sand, and on top of it one child's shoe . . ." I had been warned more than once (especially by male writers): "Women are going to invent a pile of things for you. All sorts of fiction." But I'm convinced that such things cannot be invented. Who could they be copied from? If that can be copied, it's only from life; life alone has such fantasy.

Whatever women talk about, the thought is constantly present in them: war is first of all murder, and then hard work. And then simply ordinary life: singing, falling in love, putting your hair in curlers . . .

In the center there is always this: how unbearable and unthinkable it is to die. And how much more unbearable and unthinkable it is to kill, because a woman gives life. Gives it. Bears it in herself for a long time, nurses it. I understood that it is more difficult for women to kill.

———

MEN . . . THEY reluctantly let women into their world, onto their territory.

At the Minsk tractor factory I was looking for a woman who had served in the army as a sniper. She had been a famous sniper. The newspapers from the front had written about her more than once. Her Moscow girlfriends gave me her home phone number, but it was old. And the last name I had noted down was her maiden name. I went to the factory where I knew she worked in the personnel department, and I heard from the men (the director of the factory and the head of the personnel department): "Aren't there enough men? What do you need these women's stories for? Women's fantasies . . ." The men were afraid that women would tell about some wrong sort of war.

I visited a family . . . Both husband and wife had fought. They met at the front and got married there: "We celebrated our wedding in the trench. Before the battle. I made a white dress for myself out of a German parachute." He had been a machine gunner, she a radio operator. The man immediately sent his wife to the kitchen: "Prepare something for us." The kettle was already boiling, and the sandwiches were served, she sat down with us, but the husband immediately got her to her feet again: "Where are the strawberries? Where are our treats from the country?" After my repeated requests, he reluctantly relinquished his place, saying: "Tell it the way I taught you. Without tears and women's trifles: how you wanted to be beautiful, how you wept when they cut off your braid." Later she whispered to me: "He studied *The History of the Great Patriotic War* with me all last night. He was afraid for me. And now he's worried I won't remember right. Not the way I should."

That happened more than once, in more than one house.

Yes, they cry a lot. They shout. Swallow heart pills after I am gone. Call an ambulance. But even so they beg me: "Come. Be sure to come. We've been silent so long. Forty years . . ."

I realize that tears and cries cannot be subjected to processing, otherwise the main thing will be not the tears and cries, but the processing. Instead of life we're left with literature. Such is the material, the temperature of this material. Permanently off the charts. A human being is most visible and open in war, and maybe also in love. To the depths, to the subcutaneous layers. In the face of death all ideas pale, and inconceivable eternity opens up, for which no one is prepared. We still live in history, not in the cosmos.

Several times women sent back my transcribed text with a post-script: "No need for small details ... Write about our great Victory ..." But "small details" are what is most important for me, the warmth and vividness of life: a lock left on the forehead once the braid is cut; the hot kettles of kasha and soup, which no one eats, because out of a hundred persons only seven came back from the battle; or how after the war they could not go to the market and look at the rows of red meat ... Or even at red cloth ... "Ah, my good girl, forty years have already gone by, but you won't find anything red in my house. Ever since the war I've hated the color red!"

———

I LISTEN TO THE pain ... Pain as the proof of past life. There are no other proofs, I don't trust other proofs. Words have more than once led us away from the truth.

I think of suffering as the highest form of information, having a direct connection with mystery. With the mystery of life. All of Russian literature is about that. It has written more about suffering than about love.

And these women tell me more about it ...

———

WHO WERE THEY—RUSSIANS OR Soviets? No, they were Soviets—and Russians, and Belorussians, and Ukrainians, and Tajiks ...

Yet there was such a thing as Soviet people. I don't think such people will ever exist again, and they themselves now understand that. Even we, their children, are different. We want to be like everybody else. Not like our parents, but like the rest of the world. To say nothing of the grandchildren ...

But I love them. I admire them. They had Stalin and the Gulag,* but they also had the Victory. And they know that.

I received a letter recently: "My daughter loves me very much; I am a heroine for her. If she reads your book, she will be greatly disappointed. Filth, lice, endless blood—that's all true. I don't deny it. But can the memory of it possibly engender noble feelings? Prepare one for a great deed . . . ?"

More than once I've realized:

. . . our memory is far from an ideal instrument. It is not only arbitrary and capricious, it is also chained to time, like a dog.

. . . we look at the past from today; we cannot look at it from anywhere else.

. . . they, too, are in love with what happened to them, because it is not only war, but also their youth. Their first love.

———

I LISTEN WHEN THEY speak . . . I listen when they are silent . . . Both words and silence are the text for me.

—This isn't for print, it's for you . . . The older people . . . they sat on the train deep in thought . . . Sad. I remember how one major began talking to me during the night, when everybody was asleep, about Stalin. He had drunk a lot and became bold; he confessed that his father had already spent ten years in the camps without the right of correspondence.† Whether he was alive or not, no one knew. This major spoke terrible words: "I want to defend the Motherland, but I don't want to defend that traitor of the revolution—Stalin." I had

* Gulag is the Russian acronym for "Main Administration of Camps," i.e., the system of "corrective" forced labor camps instituted in the Soviet Union beginning in 1918.

† In Soviet legal terminology the phrase "without the right of correspondence" usually meant the prisoner had been executed.

never heard such words . . . I was frightened. Fortunately, by morning he disappeared. Probably got off . . .

—I'll tell you in secret . . . I was friends with Oksana, she was from
Ukraine. It was from her that I first heard of the horrible hunger in
Ukraine. Golodomor.* You couldn't even find a frog or a mouse—
everything had been eaten. Half the people in her settlement died. All
her younger brothers, her father and mother died, but she saved herself
by stealing horse dung at the kolkhoz† stable by night and eating it. Nobody could eat it, but she did: "When it's warm it's disgusting, but you
can eat it cold. Frozen is the best, it smells of hay." I said, "Oksana, Comrade Stalin is fighting. He destroys the saboteurs, but there are many."
"No," she said, "you're stupid. My father was a history teacher, he said
to me, 'Someday Comrade Stalin will answer for his crimes . . . '"

   At night I lay there and thought: What if Oksana is the enemy? A
spy? What am I to do? Two days later she was killed in combat. She
had no family left, there was no one to send the death notice to . . .

I touch upon this subject carefully and rarely. They are still paralyzed
not only by Stalin's hypnosis and fear, but also by their former faith.
They cannot stop loving what they used to love. Courage in war and
courage of thought are two different courages. I used to think they
were the same.

———

THE MANUSCRIPT HAS BEEN lying on the desk for a long time . . .
   For two years now I've been getting rejections from publishers.

---

*   Golodomor ("holodomor" in Ukrainian) means "death by hunger." The term refers to the
deliberately created famine of 1932–1933 in Ukraine, which cost many millions of lives.

†   The Soviet acronym for "collective farm."

Magazines don't reply. The verdict is always the same: war is too terrible. So much horror. Naturalism. No leading and guiding role of the Communist Party. In short, not the right kind of war . . . What is the right kind? With generals and a wise generalissimo? Without blood and lice? With heroes and great deeds? But I remember from childhood: my grandmother and I are walking beside a big field, and she tells me: "After the war nothing grew in this field for a long time. The Germans were retreating . . . And there was a battle here, it went on for two days . . . The dead lay next to each other like sheaves. Like railroad ties. The Germans' and ours. After rain they all had tear-stained faces. Our whole village spent a month burying them."

How can I forget that field?

I don't simply record. I collect, I track down the human spirit wherever suffering makes a small man into a great man. Wherever a man grows. And then for me he is no longer the mute and traceless proletarian of history. With a torn-off soul. What then is my conflict with the authorities? I understood—a great idea needs a small human being, not a great one. A great one is superfluous and inconvenient for it. Hard to process. And I look for them. I look for small great human beings. Humiliated, trampled upon, insulted—having gone through Stalin's camps and treachery, these human beings came out victorious. They performed a miracle.

But the history of the war had been replaced by the history of the victory.

They themselves will tell about it . . .

SEVENTEEN YEARS LATER

2002–2004

I'M READING MY OLD journal . . .

I'm trying to remember the person I was when I was writing this book. That person is no more, just as the country in which we then lived is no more. Yet it is that country that had been defended and in whose name people had died in the years '41 to '45. Outside the window everything is different: a new millennium, new wars, new ideas, new weapons, and the Russian (more exactly, Russian-Soviet) man changed in a totally unexpected way.

Gorbachev's perestroika began . . . * My book was published at once, in an astonishing printing—two million copies. This was a time when many startling things were happening, when we again furiously tore off somewhere. Again into the future. We still did not know (or else forgot) that revolution is always an illusion, especially in our history. But that would come later, and at the time everybody was drunk with the air of freedom. I began to receive dozens of letters daily, my folders were swelling. People wanted to talk . . . to finish talking . . . They became more free and more open. I had no doubt that I was doomed to go on writing my books endlessly. Not rewriting, but writing. A full stop immediately turns into an ellipsis . . .

———

I THINK THAT TODAY I would probably ask different questions and hear different answers. And would write a different book—not entirely different, but still different. The documents (the ones I deal with) are living witnesses; they don't harden like cooled clay. They don't grow mute. They move together with us. What would I ask more about now? What would I like to add? I would be interested in . . . I'm hunting for the word . . . the biological human being, not just the human being of time and ideas. I would try to delve deeper into human nature, into the darkness, into the subconscious. Into the mystery of war.

I would write about my visit to a former partisan fighter. A heavyset but still beautiful woman. She told me how her group (she was the oldest, plus two adolescents) went on a scouting mission and accidentally captured four Germans. They circled about in the forest with

* Gorbachev's perestroika: The "restructuring" begun in 1986 under Mikhail Gorbachev (1933–), the last General Secretary of the Communist Party and head of state until the dissolution of the Soviet Union in 1991.

them for a long time. Ran into an ambush. It became clear that they would not be able to break through with the captives and get away, and she made a decision—to dispose of them. The adolescents would not have been able to kill them; they had been wandering together in the forest for a few days, and when you spend that much time with a person, even a stranger, you get used to him, he becomes close—you know how he eats, how he sleeps, what kind of eyes and hands he has. No, the adolescents couldn't do it. That became clear to her at once. So she had to kill them. She recalled how she did it. She had to deceive her own people and the Germans. She supposedly went to fetch water with one German and shot him from behind. In the head. She took another to gather brushwood . . . I was shocked to hear her tell it so calmly.

Those who were in the war remember that it took three days for a civilian to turn into a military man. Why are three days enough? Or is that also a myth? Most likely. A human being in war is all the more unfamiliar and incomprehensible.

I read in all the letters: "I didn't tell you everything then, because it was a different time. We were used to keeping quiet about many things . . ." "I didn't confide everything to you. Not long ago it was impossible to speak about it. Or embarrassing." "I know the doctors' verdict: my diagnosis is terrible . . . I want to tell the whole truth . . ."

And recently this letter came: "For us old people life is hard . . . But not because our pensions are small and humiliating. What wounds us most of all is that we have been driven from a great past into an unbearably small present. No one invites us anymore to appear at schools, in museums, we are not needed anymore. In the newspapers, if you read them, the fascists become more and more noble, and the Red soldiers become more and more terrible."

Time is also the Motherland . . . But I love them as before. I don't love their time, but I do love them.

———

Everything can become literature . . .

In my archives I was interested most of all in the notebooks where I wrote down the episodes crossed out by the censors. And my conversations with the censors as well. I also found there pages that I had thrown out myself. My self-censorship, my own ban. And my explanation— why I had thrown them out. Many of these and other things have been restored in the book, but I would like to give these few pages separately— they also make a document. My path.

FROM WHAT THE CENSORS
THREW OUT

—I just woke up in the night . . . It's as if somebody's . . . crying nearby . . . I'm at the front . . .

We're retreating . . . Beyond Smolensk some woman gives me her dress, and I manage to change my clothes. I'm alone . . . among men. I was wearing trousers, but now I march in a summer dress. Suddenly I begin to have my . . . woman's thing . . . It started early, probably from the agitation. From being nervous, upset. There was nowhere to find what I needed. I was embarrassed! So embarrassed! People slept under bushes, in ditches, on stumps in the forest. There were so many of us, there was no room in the forest for everybody. We went on bewildered, deceived, trusting nobody anymore . . . Where was our air force, where were our tanks? Everything that flew, drove, rumbled—was all German.

In that state I was captured. On the last day before I was captured, both of my legs got broken . . . I lay there and peed under myself . . . I don't know where I found strength to crawl away by night to the forest . . . The partisans chanced to pick me up.

I'm sorry for those who will read this book, and for those who won't . . .

———

—I was on night duty . . . Went to the ward of the badly wounded. There was a captain there . . . The doctors warned me before I started my shift that he would die during the night. Wouldn't make it till morning . . . I ask him: "How are things? Anything I can do for you?" I'll never forget it . . . He suddenly smiled, such a bright smile on his haggard face: "Unbutton your coat . . . Show me your breast . . . I haven't seen my wife for so long . . ." I was totally at a loss, I'd never even been kissed before. I gave him some answer. I ran away and came back an hour later.

He lay dead. And still had that smile on his face . . .

—Near Kerch . . . We went on a barge at night under shelling. The bow caught fire . . . The fire crept along the deck. Our store of ammunition exploded . . . a powerful explosion! So violent that the barge tilted on the right side and began to sink. The bank wasn't far away, we knew the bank was somewhere close by, and the soldiers threw themselves into the water. There was machine-gun fire from the bank. Shouts, moans, curses . . . I was a good swimmer, I wanted to save at least one of them. At least one wounded man . . . This was in the water, not on dry land—a wounded man perishes at once. Goes to the bottom . . . I heard somebody next to me come up to the surface, then sink down again. Up—then down. I seized the moment and grabbed hold of him . . . Something cold, slimy . . . I decided it was a wounded man, and his clothes had been torn off by the explosion. Because I was naked myself . . . Just in my underwear . . . Pitch dark. Around me: "Ohh! Aiie!" and curses . . . I somehow made it to the bank with him . . . Just then there was the flash of a rocket, and I saw that I was holding a big wounded fish. A big fish, the size of a man. A white sturgeon . . . It was dying . . . I fell down beside it and ripped out some sort of well-rounded curse. I wept from rancor . . . And from the fact that everybody was suffering . . .

———

—We were trying to get out of an encirclement . . . Wherever we went, there were Germans. We decided that in the morning we would fight our way through. We were going to die anyway, it was better to die with dignity. In combat. There were three girls with us. They came during the night to each of us who could . . . Of course, not everybody was able to. Nerves, you understand. That sort of thing . . . Each of us was preparing to die . . .

A few of us survived till morning . . . Very few . . . Well, maybe seven men, and we had been fifty, if not more. The Germans cut us down with machine-gun fire . . . I remember those girls with gratitude. In the morning I didn't find a one of them among the living . . . Never ran into them again . . .

FROM A CONVERSATION
WITH THE CENSOR

—Who will go to fight after such books? You humiliate women with a primitive naturalism. Heroic women. You dethrone them. You make them into ordinary women, females. But our women are saints.

—*Our heroism is sterile, it leaves no room for physiology or biology. It's not believable. War tested not only the spirit but the body, too. The material shell.*

—Where did you get such thoughts? Alien thoughts. Not Soviet. You laugh at those who lie in communal graves. You've read too much Remarque . . . * Remarquism won't get you anywhere with us. A Soviet woman is not an animal . . .

———

—Somebody betrayed us . . . The Germans found out where the camp of our partisan unit was. They cordoned off the forest and the

* The German novelist Erich Maria Remarque (1898–1970) is best known for his novel *All Quiet on the Western Front* (1928), about the harsh experiences of German soldiers during World War I. His works were banned and publicly burned by the Nazis in 1933.

approaches to it on all sides. We hid in the wild thickets, we were saved by the swamps where the punitive forces didn't go. A quagmire. It sucked in equipment and people for good. For days, for weeks, we stood up to our necks in water. Our radio operator was a woman who had recently given birth. The baby was hungry . . . It had to be nursed . . . But the mother herself was hungry and had no milk. The baby cried. The punitive forces were close . . . With dogs . . . If the dogs heard it, we'd all be killed. The whole group—thirty of us . . . You understand?

The commander makes a decision . . .

Nobody can bring himself to give the mother his order, but she figures it out herself. She lowers the swaddled baby into the water and holds it there for a long time . . . The baby doesn't cry anymore . . . Not a sound . . . And we can't raise our eyes. Neither to the mother nor to each other . . .

—We took prisoners, brought them to the detachment . . . We didn't shoot them, that was too easy a death for them; we stuck them with ramrods like pigs, we cut them to pieces. I went to look at it . . . I waited! I waited a long time for the moment when their eyes would begin to burst from pain . . . The pupils . . .

What do you know about it?! They burned my mother and little sisters on a bonfire in the middle of our village . . .

—I don't remember any cats or dogs during the war, I remember rats. Big . . . with yellow-blue eyes . . . There were huge numbers of them. When I recovered from a wound, I was sent back to my unit from the hospital. The unit was stationed in the trenches near Stalingrad. The commander ordered: "Take her to the girls' dugout." I entered the dugout and first of all was surprised that there was nothing in it. Empty beds of fir branches and that's all. They didn't warn me . . . I left my knapsack in the dugout and stepped out. When I came back half an hour later I didn't find my knapsack. Not a trace of anything, no hair comb, no pencil. It turned out the rats instantly devoured everything . . .

In the morning they showed me the gnawed hands of the badly wounded . . .

Not even in the most horrible film did I see how the rats leave before the bombing of a town. This wasn't at Stalingrad . . . This was already near Vyazma . . . In the morning swarms of rats went through the town, heading for the fields. They sensed death. There were thousands of them . . . Black, gray . . . People watched this sinister spectacle in horror and pressed against the houses. And precisely at the moment when the rats disappeared from sight, the bombing began. Planes came flying. Instead of houses and basements only rubble was left . . .

—There were so many people killed at Stalingrad that horses stopped being afraid. Usually they're afraid of the dead. A horse will never step on a dead man. We gathered our own dead, but there were Germans lying about everywhere. Frozen . . . Icy . . . I was a driver, I transported crates of artillery shells, I heard their skulls crack under the wheels . . . the bones . . . And I was happy . . .

FROM A CONVERSATION
WITH THE CENSOR

—Yes, we paid heavily for the Victory, but you should look for heroic examples. There are hundreds of them. And you show the filth of the war. The underwear. You make our Victory terrible . . . What is it you're after?

—*The truth.*

—You think the truth is what's there in life. In the street. Under your feet. It's such a low thing for you. Earthly. No, the truth is what we dream about. It's how we want to be!

———

—We advance . . . The first German villages . . . We're young. Strong. Four years without women. There's wine in the cellars. Food. We'd catch German girls and . . . Ten men violated one girl . . . There weren't enough women, the population fled before the Soviet army, we found very young ones. Twelve or thirteen years old . . . If she cried, we'd beat her, stuff something into her mouth. It was painful for her, but funny for us. Now I don't understand how I could . . . A boy from a cultivated family . . . But I did it . . .

The only thing we were afraid of was that our own girls would find out about it. Our nurses. We were ashamed before them . . .

—We were encircled . . . We wandered in the forests, over the swamps. Ate leaves, tree bark. Some sort of roots. There were five of us, one a very young boy, just called up for the army. At night my neighbor whispers to me: "The boy's half dead, he'll die anyway. You get me . . ." "What do you mean?" "An ex-convict once told me . . . When they escaped from the labor camp, they purposely took a young man with them . . . Human flesh is edible . . . That's how they stayed alive . . ."

I didn't have strength enough to hit him. The next day we ran into some partisans . . .

—In the afternoon the partisans rode into the village on horseback. They led the village headman and his son out of their house. They beat them on the head with iron rods till they fell down. And finished them off on the ground. I sat by the window. I saw everything . . . My older brother was among the partisans . . . When he came into our house and wanted to embrace me—"Sister dear!"—I shouted: "Don't come near me! Don't come near me! You're a murderer!" Then I went dumb. Couldn't speak for a month.

My brother was killed . . . What would have happened if he had stayed alive? And come back home . . .

—In the morning the punitive forces set fire to our village . . . Only those who fled to the forest survived. They fled with nothing, empty-handed, didn't take even bread. No eggs or lard. During the night Aunt Nastya, our neighbor, beat her daughter because she cried all the time. Aunt Nastya had her five children with her. Yulechka, my friend, was the weakest. She was always sick . . . And the four boys, all of them little, also asked to eat all the time. And Aunt Nastya went crazy: "Ooo . . . Ooo . . ." And in the night I heard . . . Yulechka begged, "Mama, don't drown me. I won't . . . I won't ask to eat any-more. I won't . . ."

In the morning there was no Yulechka to be seen . . .

Aunt Nastya . . . We went back to the embers of the village . . . It had burned down. Soon Aunt Nastya hanged herself from the charred apple tree in her garden. She hung very, very low. Her children stood around her asking to eat . . .

FROM A CONVERSATION
WITH THE CENSOR

—This is a lie! This is slander against our soldiers, who liberated half of Europe. Against our partisans. Against our heroic people. We don't need your little history, we need the big history. The history of the Victory. You don't love our heroes! You don't love our great ideas. The ideas of Marx and Lenin.

—*True, I don't love great ideas. I love the little human being . . .*

FROM WHAT I THREW OUT MYSELF

—1941 ... We were encircled. With our political instructor, Lunin ... He read us the order, that Soviet soldiers do not surrender to the enemy. With us, as Comrade Stalin said, there are no prisoners, there are only traitors. The boys drew their pistols ... The political instructor ordered: "Don't. Go on living, boys, you're young." And he shot himself ...

And now it's 1943 ... The Soviet army is advancing. We're moving through Belorussia. I remember a little boy. He ran out to us from somewhere under the ground, some basement, and shouted, "Kill my mama ... Kill her! She loved a German ..." His eyes were round from fear. An old woman in black ran after him. All in black. She was running and crossing herself: "Don't listen to the child. The child's gone crazy ..."

—I was summoned to school ... A teacher who had just returned from evacuation talked to me:

"I want to transfer your son to another class. In my class I have the best pupils."

"But my son has high grades."

"That doesn't matter. The boy lived under the Germans."

"Yes, it was hard for us."

"That's not the point. All those who were in occupied territories ... They are under suspicion ..."

"What? I don't understand ..."

"He tells other children about the Germans. And he stutters."

"That's because he was frightened. The German officer who was billeted with us gave him a beating. He didn't like how my son polished his boots."

"You see ... You yourself admit ... You lived alongside the enemy ..."

"And who let that enemy get as far as Moscow? Who left us here with our children?"

I was in hysterics . . .

For two days I was afraid the teacher would denounce me. But she kept my son in her class . . .

—During the day we were afraid of the Germans and the *polizei*[*] and during the night of the partisans. The partisans took my last cow, I had only a cat left. The partisans were starved, angry. They took my cow, and I followed them . . . I walked about seven miles. I begged them to give it back. I left three hungry children at home by the stove. "Go back, woman!" they threatened. "Or else we'll shoot you."

Try finding a good man during the war . . .

People turned against each other. The children of the kulaks[†] came back from exile. Their parents had been killed, and they served the German forces. They took their revenge. One of them shot an old teacher in his cottage. Our neighbor. This neighbor had once denounced his father and had taken part in dispossessing him. He was a fervent Communist.

At first the Germans disbanded the kolkhozes and gave people the land. People breathed more freely after Stalin. We paid quitrent . . . Paid it accurately . . . And then they began to burn us. Us and our houses. They drove the livestock away and burned the people . . .

Aie, daughter dear, I'm afraid of words. Words are scary . . . I saved myself by doing good, I didn't wish evil on anyone. I pitied them all . . .

—I went with the army as far as Berlin . . .

I came back to my village with two Medals of Honor and some

---

[*] German for "police," but the term was also applied to Russian collaborators.

[†] Originally a term for wealthy independent peasant farmers; under the Soviets it became a derogatory label for any peasants who resisted the forced collectivization of agriculture. Kulaks were arrested and either shot or sent to hard labor in Siberia.

decorations. I spent three days there, and on the fourth my mother got me up early, while everybody was asleep: "Daughter dear, I've prepared a bundle for you. Go away . . . Go away . . . You have two younger sisters growing up. Who will marry them? Everybody knows you spent four years at the front, with men . . ."

Don't touch my soul. Write, as the others do, about my decorations . . .

—War is war. It's not some kind of theater . . .

They had our unit form up in a clearing; we stood in a ring. In the middle were Misha K. and Kolya M.—our boys. Misha was a brave scout, he played the accordion. And nobody sang better than Kolya . . .

They spent a long time reading the sentence: in such-and-such village they had demanded two bottles of moonshine, and at night . . . raped their host's two daughters . . . And in such-and-such village they robbed a peasant of an overcoat and a sewing machine . . . which they went and exchanged for drink at the neighbors' . . .

They were sentenced to be shot . . . The sentence was final and without appeal.

Who will do the shooting? The unit is silent . . . Who? We're silent . . . The commander himself carried out the sentence . . .

—I was a machine gunner. I killed so many . . .

For a long time after the war I was afraid to have children. I gave birth to a child when I calmed down. Seven years later . . .

But I still haven't forgiven anything. And I won't . . . I was glad when I saw German prisoners. I was glad that they were pitiful to look at: footwraps on their feet instead of boots, footwraps on their heads . . . They were led through the villages and they asked, *"Mother, give brot . . . Brot . . ."* I was astonished that peasants came out of their cottages and gave them—one a piece of bread, another a potato . . .

Boys ran after the column and threw stones . . . But the women wept . . .

It seems to me that I've lived two lives: one a man's, the other a woman's . . .

—After the war . . . Human life was worthless. I'll give you an example . . . I'm riding on a bus after work; suddenly there's shouting: "Stop thief! Stop thief! My purse . . ." The bus stops . . . A crowd forms at once. A young officer takes a boy outside, puts his arm on his knee and—whack!—breaks it in two. Jumps back on the bus . . . And we go on . . . Nobody defended the boy, nobody called a policeman. A doctor. The officer had his whole chest covered with combat decorations . . . I was getting off at my stop, he hopped down and gave me his hand: "Allow me, Miss . . ." Such a gallant one . . .

I've just remembered it . . . At the time we were all still people of the war, we lived by the laws of wartime. Are they human at all?

—The Red Army came back . . .

We were allowed to dig up the graves, to search for where our families had been shot. By an old custom you have to wear white next to death—a white kerchief, a white shirt. I'll remember it to my last breath! People went with white embroidered towels . . . Dressed all in white . . . Where did they get it?

We dug . . . Whatever we found and recognized we took. One brought an arm in a wheelbarrow, another a head in a cart . . . A man doesn't stay whole in the ground for long, they were all mixed up together. With clay, with sand.

I didn't find my sister, but I thought that a scrap of a dress was hers, it looked familiar . . . Grandfather also said, "Take it, there'll be something to bury." We put this piece of a dress into a little coffin . . .

We got a notice that my father was "missing in action." Others got something for those who had been killed, but my mother and I got a scare in the village council: "You're not entitled to any aid. It may be he's living in clover with some German Frau. An enemy of the people."

I began to look for my father under Khrushchev.* Forty years later, under Gorbachev, I received an answer: "Not listed in the records . . ." But his regimental comrade wrote to me and I found out that my father had died a hero. He had thrown himself with a grenade under a tank at Mogilev† . . .

It's a pity my mother didn't live to get this news. She died branded as the wife of an enemy of the people. A traitor. There were many like her. They didn't live to learn the truth. I went to mother's grave with this letter. Read it . . .

—Many of us believed . . .

We thought that after the war everything would change . . . Stalin would trust his people. But the war was not yet over, and the troop trains were already going to Magadan.‡ Troop trains with the victors . . . Those who had been captured, those who had survived the German camps, those whom the Germans had taken along to work for them—all those who had seen Europe—were arrested. Those who could tell how people there lived. Without Communists. What kind of houses they had and what kind of roads. And that there were no kolkhozes . . .

After the Victory everybody became silent. Silent and afraid, as before the war . . .

* Nikita Khrushchev (1894–1971), who became First Secretary of the Communist Party in 1953, at Stalin's death, and later served as premier, instituted the process of "de-Stalinization" of the Soviet Union, beginning with the 20th Party Congress in 1956.

† Mogilev, an old city in Belorussia, was taken by the Nazis in 1941 and retaken by the Soviets in 1944. Its large Jewish population was exterminated.

‡ A city and territory in the far east of Russia, which became the center for a vast labor-camp system established by Stalin in 1932.

———

—I'm a history teacher . . . Within my memory the history textbook has been rewritten three times. I taught children with three different textbooks . . .

Ask us while we're alive. Don't rewrite afterward without us. Ask . . .

Do you know how hard it is to kill a human being? I worked in the underground. After six months I was sent on a mission—to take a job as a waitress in a German officers' mess . . . I was young, beautiful . . . They hired me. I was supposed to put poison into the soup cauldron and leave for the partisans the same day. I had already grown used to them; they were the enemy, but I saw them every day, they said, "*Danke schön . . . Danke schön . . .*" It was hard . . . To kill is hard . . . To kill is more terrible than to die . . .

I've taught history all my life . . . And I never knew how to tell about that . . . In what words . . .

———

I HAD MY OWN war . . . I went a long way together with my heroines. Just like them, for a long time I did not believe that our Victory had two faces—one beautiful and the other terrible, all scars—unbearable to look at. "In hand-to-hand combat, when you kill a man, you look him in the eye. It's not like throwing bombs or shooting from a trench," they told me.

Listening to how a person killed or died is the same—you look him in the eye . . .

THE

UNWOMANLY

FACE

OF WAR

"I DON'T WANT
TO REMEMBER . . ."

———

An old three-story house on the outskirts of Minsk, one of those built hastily just after the war and, as it then seemed, not meant to last, now cozily overgrown with old jasmine bushes. With it began a search that went on for seven years, seven extraordinary and tormenting years, during which I was to discover for myself the world of war, a world the meaning of which we cannot fully fathom. I would experience pain, hatred, temptation. Tenderness and perplexity . . . I would try to understand what distinguishes death from murder and where the boundary is between the human and the inhuman. How does a human being remain alone with the insane thought that he or she might kill another human being? Is even obliged to? And I would discover that in war there is, apart from death, a multitude of other things; there is everything that is in our ordinary life. War is also life. I would run into countless human truths. Mysteries. I would ponder questions the existence of which I had never suspected. For instance, why is it that we are not surprised at evil, why this absence in us of surprise in the face of evil?

A road and many roads . . . Dozens of trips all over the country, hundreds of recorded cassettes, thousands of yards of tape. Five hundred meetings, after which I stopped counting; faces left my memory, only voices remained. A chorus resounds in my memory. An enormous chorus; sometimes the words almost cannot be heard, only the weeping. I confess: I did not always believe that I was strong enough for this path, that I could make it. Could reach the end. There were moments of doubt and fear, when I wanted to stop or step aside, but I no longer could. I fell captive to evil, I looked into the abyss in order to understand something. Now I seem to have acquired some knowledge, but there are still more questions, and fewer answers.

But then, at the very beginning of the path, I had no suspicion of that . . .

What led me to this house was a short article in the local newspaper about a farewell party given at the Udarnik automobile factory in Minsk for the senior accountant Maria Ivanovna Morozova, who was retiring. During the war, the article said, she had been a sniper, had eleven combat decorations, and her total as a sniper was seventy-five killings. It was hard to bring together mentally this woman's wartime profession with her peacetime occupation. With the routine newspaper photograph. With all these tokens of the ordinary.

. . . A small woman with a long braid wound in a girlish crown around her head was sitting in a big armchair, covering her face with her hands.

"No, no, I won't. Go back there again? I can't . . . To this day I can't watch war movies. I was very young then. I dreamed and grew, grew and dreamed. And then—the war. I even feel sorry for you . . . I know what I'm talking about . . . Do you really want to know that? I ask you like a daughter . . ."

Of course she was surprised.

"But why me? You should talk to my husband, he likes to remember . . . The names of the commanders, the generals, the numbers of units—he remembers everything. I don't. I only remember what happened to me. My own war. There were lots of people around, but you were always alone, because a human being is always alone in the face of death. I remember the terrifying solitude."

She asked me to take the tape recorder away.

"I need your eyes in order to tell about it, and that will hinder me."

But a few minutes later she forgot about it . . .

Maria Ivanovna Morozova (Ivanushkina)

CORPORAL, SNIPER

This will be a simple story . . . The story of an ordinary Russian girl, of whom there were many then . . .

The place where my native village, Diakovskoe, stood is now the Proletarian District of Moscow. When the war began, I was not quite eighteen. Long, long braids, down to my knees . . . Nobody believed the war would last, everybody expected it to end any moment. We would drive out the enemy. I worked on a kolkhoz, then finished accounting school and began to work. The war went on . . . My girl-friends . . . They tell me: "We should go to the front." It was already in the air. We all signed up and took classes at the local recruitment office. Maybe some did it just to keep one another company, I don't know. They taught us to shoot a combat rifle, to throw hand grenades. At first . . . I'll confess, I was afraid to hold a rifle, it was unpleasant. I couldn't imagine that I'd go and kill somebody, I just wanted to go to the front. We had forty people in our group. Four girls from our village, so we were all friends; five from our neighbors'; in short—some from each village. All of them girls . . . The men had all gone to the war already, the ones who could. Sometimes a messenger came in the middle of the night, gave them two hours to get ready, and they'd be carted off. They could even be taken right from the fields. (*Silence.*) I don't remember now—whether we had dances; if we did, the girls danced with girls, there were no boys left. Our villages became quiet.

Soon an appeal came from the central committee of Komsomol[*] for the young people to go and defend the Motherland, since the Germans were already near Moscow. Hitler take Moscow? We won't allow it! I wasn't the only one . . . All our girls expressed the wish to go to the front. My father was already fighting. We thought we were the only ones like that . . . Special ones . . . But we came to the re-

---

[*] Soviet acronym for "League of Communist Youth."

cruitment office and there were lots of girls there. I just gasped! My heart was on fire, so intensely. The selection was very strict. First of all, of course, you had to have robust health. I was afraid they wouldn't take me, because as a child I was often sick, and my frame was weak, as my mother used to say. Other children insulted me because of it when I was little. And then, if there were no other children in a household except the girl who wanted to go to the front, they also refused: a mother should not be left by herself. Ah, our darling mothers! Their tears never dried . . . They scolded us, they begged . . . But in our family there were two sisters and two brothers left—true, they were all much younger than me, but it counted anyway. There was one more thing: everybody from our kolkhoz was gone, there was nobody to work in the fields, and the chairman didn't want to let us go. In short, they refused us. We went to the district committee of Komsomol, and there—refusal. Then we went as a delegation from our district to the regional Komsomol. There was great inspiration in all of us; our hearts were on fire. Again we were sent home. We decided, since we were in Moscow, to go to the central committee of Komsomol, to the top, to the first secretary. To carry through to the end . . . Who would be our spokesman? Who was brave enough? We thought we would surely be the only ones there, but it was impossible even to get into the corridor, let alone to reach the secretary. There were young people from all over the country, many of whom had been under occupation, spoiling to be revenged for the death of their near ones. From all over the Soviet Union. Yes, yes . . . In short, we were even taken aback for a while . . .

By evening we got to the secretary after all. They asked us: "So, how can you go to the front if you don't know how to shoot?" And we said in a chorus that we had already learned to shoot . . . "Where? . . . How? . . . And can you apply bandages?" You know, in that group at the recruiting office our local doctor taught us to apply bandages. That shut them up, and they began to look at us more seriously. Well, we had another trump card in our hands, that we weren't alone, there were forty of us, and we could all shoot and give first aid. They told us: "Go and wait. Your question will be decided in the affirmative." How happy we were as we left! I'll never forget it . . . Yes, yes . . .

And literally in a couple of days we received our call-up papers . . .

We came to the recruiting office; we went in one door at once and were let out another. I had such a beautiful braid, and I came out without it . . . Without my braid . . . They gave me a soldier's haircut . . . They also took my dress. I had no time to send the dress or the braid to my mother . . . She very much wanted to have something of mine left with her . . . We were immediately dressed in army shirts, forage caps, given kit bags and loaded into a freight train—on straw. But fresh straw, still smelling of the field.

We were a cheerful cargo. Cocky. Full of jokes. I remember laughing a lot.

Where were we going? We didn't know. In the end it was not so important to us what we'd be. So long as it was at the front. Everybody was fighting—and we would be, too. We arrived at the Shchelkovo station. Near it was a women's sniper school. It turned out we were sent there. To become snipers. We all rejoiced. This was something real. We'd be shooting.

We began to study. We studied the regulations: of garrison service, of discipline, of camouflage in the field, of chemical protection. The girls all worked very hard. We learned to assemble and disassemble a sniper's rifle with our eyes shut, to determine wind speed, the movement of the target, the distance to the target, to dig a foxhole, to crawl on our stomach—we had already mastered all that. Only so as to get to the front the sooner. In the line of fire . . . Yes, yes . . . At the end of the course I got the highest grade in the exam for combat and noncombat service. The hardest thing, I remember, was to get up at the sound of the alarm and be ready in five minutes. We chose boots one or two sizes larger, so as not to lose time getting into them. We had five minutes to dress, put our boots on, and line up. There were times when we ran out to line up in boots over bare feet. One girl almost had her feet frostbitten. The sergeant major noticed it, reprimanded her, and then taught us to use footwraps. He stood over us and droned: "How am I to make soldiers out of you, my dear girls, and not targets for Fritz?" Dear girls, dear girls . . . Everybody loved us and pitied us all the time. And we resented being pitied. Weren't we soldiers like everybody else?

Well, so we got to the front. Near Orsha . . . The 62nd Infantry Division . . . I remember like today, the commander, Colonel Borodkin, saw us and got angry: "They've foisted girls on me. What is this, some sort of women's round dance?" he said. "Corps de ballet! It's war, not a dance. A terrible war . . ." But then he invited us, treated us to a dinner. And we heard him ask his adjutant: "Don't we have something sweet for tea?" Well, of course, we were offended: What does he take us for? We came to make war . . . And he received us not as soldiers, but as young girls. At our age we could have been his daughters. "What am I going to do with you, my dears? Where did they find you?" That's how he treated us, that's how he met us. And we thought we were already seasoned warriors . . . Yes, yes . . . At war!

The next day he made us show that we knew how to shoot, how to camouflage ourselves in the field. We did the shooting well, even better than the men snipers, who were called from the front for two days of training, and who were very surprised that we were doing their work. It was probably the first time in their lives they saw women snipers. After the shooting it was camouflage in the field . . . The colonel came, walked around looking at the clearing, then stepped on a hummock—saw nothing. Then the "hummock" under him begged: "Ow, Comrade Colonel, I can't anymore, you're too heavy." How we laughed! He couldn't believe it was possible to camouflage oneself so well. "Now," he said, "I take back my words about young girls." But even so he suffered . . . Couldn't get used to us for a long time.

Then came the first day of our "hunting" (so snipers call it). My partner was Masha Kozlova. We camouflaged ourselves and lay there: I'm on the lookout, Masha's holding her rifle. Suddenly Masha says: "Shoot, shoot! See—it's a German . . ."

I say to her: "I'm the lookout. You shoot!"

"While we're sorting it out," she says, "he'll get away."

But I insist: "First we have to lay out the shooting map, note the landmarks: where the shed is, where the birch tree . . ."

"You want to start fooling with paperwork like at school? I've come to shoot, not to mess with paperwork!"

I see that Masha is already angry with me.

"Well, shoot then, why don't you?"

We were bickering like that. And meanwhile, in fact, the German officer was giving orders to the soldiers. A wagon arrived, and the soldiers formed a chain and handed down some sort of freight. The officer stood there, gave orders, then disappeared. We're still arguing. I see he's already appeared twice, and if we miss him again, that will be it. We'll lose him. And when he appeared for the third time—it was just momentary; now he's there, now he's gone—I decided to shoot. I decided, and suddenly a thought flashed through my mind: he's a human being; he may be an enemy, but he's a human being— and my hands began to tremble, I started trembling all over, I got chills. Some sort of fear . . . That feeling sometimes comes back to me in dreams even now . . . After the plywood targets, it was hard to shoot at a living person. I see him in the telescopic sight, I see him very well. As if he's close . . . And something in me resists . . . Something doesn't let me, I can't make up my mind. But I got hold of myself, I pulled the trigger . . . He waved his arms and fell. Whether he was dead or not, I didn't know. But after that I trembled still more, some sort of terror came over me: I killed a man?! I had to get used even to the thought of it. Yes . . . In short—horrible! I'll never forget it . . .

When we came back, we started telling our platoon what had happened to us. They called a meeting. We had a Komsomol leader, Klava Ivanova; she reassured me: "They should be hated, not pitied . . ." Her father had been killed by the fascists. We would start singing, and she would beg us: "No, don't, dear girls. Let's first defeat these vermin, then we'll sing."

And not right away . . . We didn't manage right away. It's not a woman's task—to hate and to kill. Not for us . . . We had to persuade ourselves. To talk ourselves into it . . .

A few days later Maria Ivanovna would call and invite me to see her war friend Klavdia Grigoryevna Krokhina. And once again I would hear . . .

Klavdia Grigoryevna Krokhina
FIRST SERGEANT, SNIPER

The first time is frightening . . . Very frightening . . .

We were in hiding, and I was the lookout. And then I noticed one German poking up a little from a trench. I clicked, and he fell. And then, you know, I started shaking all over, I heard my bones knocking. I cried. When I shot at targets it was nothing, but now: I—killed! I killed some unknown man. I knew nothing about him, but I killed him.

Then it passed. And here's how . . . It happened like this . . . We were already on the advance. We marched past a small settlement. I think it was in Ukraine. And there by the road we saw a barrack or a house, it was impossible to tell, it was all burned down, nothing left but blackened stones. A foundation . . . Many of the girls didn't go close to it, but it was as if something drew me there . . . There were human bones among the cinders, with scorched little stars among them; these were our wounded or prisoners who had been burned. After that, however many I killed, I felt no pity. I had seen those blackened little stars . . .

. . . I came back from the war gray-haired. Twenty-one years old, but my hair was completely white. I had been badly wounded, had a concussion, poor hearing in one ear. Mama met me with the words: "I believed you'd come back. I prayed for you day and night." My brother had fallen at the front.

Mama lamented: "It's all the same now—to give birth to girls or boys. But still he was a man, he had to defend the Motherland, but you're a girl. I asked one thing of God, that if they disfigure you, better let them kill you. I went to the train station all the time. To meet the trains. Once I saw a girl soldier there with a burned face . . . I shuddered—you! Afterward I prayed for her, too."

In the Chelyabinsk region, where I was born, they were doing some sort of mining not far from our house. As soon as the blasting began—it was always during the night for some reason—I instantly jumped out of the bed and grabbed my coat first thing—and ran, I had to run somewhere quickly. Mama would catch me, press me to her, and talk to me: "Wake up, wake up. The war is over. You're home." I would come to my senses at her words: "I'm your mama. Mama . . ." She spoke softly. Softly . . . Loud talk frightened me . . .

The room is warm, but Klavdia Grigoryevna wraps herself in a heavy plaid blanket—she is cold. She goes on:

We quickly turned into soldiers . . . You know, there was no real time to think. To dwell on our feelings . . .

Our scouts took a German officer prisoner, and he was extremely surprised that so many soldiers had been killed at his position, and all with shots in the head. Almost in the same spot. A simple rifleman, he insisted, would be unable to make so many hits to the head. That's certain. "Show me," he asked, "the rifleman who killed so many of my soldiers. I received a large reinforcement, but every day up to ten men fell." The commander of the regiment says: "Unfortunately, I cannot show you. It was a girl sniper, but she was killed." It was our Sasha Shliakhova. She died in a snipers' duel. And what betrayed her was her red scarf. She liked that scarf very much. But a red scarf is visible against white snow. When the German officer heard that it was a girl, he was staggered, he didn't know how to react. He was silent for a long time. At the last interrogation before he was sent to Moscow (he turned out to be a bigwig), he confessed: "I've never fought with women. You're all beautiful . . . And our propaganda tells us that it's hermaphrodites and not women who fight in the Red Army . . ." So he understood nothing. No . . . I can't forget . . .

We went in pairs. It's very hard to sit alone from sunup to sundown; your eyes get tired, watery, your hands lose their feeling, your whole body goes numb with tension. It's especially hard in spring. The snow melts under you; you spend the whole day in water. You float in it; sometimes you freeze to the ground. We started out at daybreak and came back from the front line when it got dark. For twelve hours or more we lay in the snow or climbed to the top of a tree, onto the roof of a shed or a ruined house, and there camouflaged ourselves, so that the enemy wouldn't see where we were observing them from. We tried to find a position as close as possible: seven or eight hundred, sometimes only five hundred yards separated us from the trenches where the Germans sat. Early in the morning we could even hear their talk. Laughter.

I don't know why we weren't afraid . . . Now I don't understand it.

We were advancing, advancing very quickly . . . And we ran out of steam, our supplies lagged behind: we ran out of ammunition, out of provisions, and the kitchen was demolished by a shell. For three days we ate nothing but dry crusts; our tongues were so scraped we couldn't move them. My partner was killed, and I went to the front line with a "new" girl. And suddenly we saw a colt on "no man's land." Such a pretty one, with a fluffy tail . . . Walking about calmly, as if there wasn't any war. And I heard the Germans make some stir, having seen him. Our soldiers also started talking among themselves.

"He'll get away. Could make a nice soup . . ."

"You can't hit him with a submachine gun at such a distance . . ."
They saw us.

"The snipers are coming. They'll get him straight off . . . Go on, girls!"

I had no time to think; out of habit I took aim and fired. The colt's legs buckled under him; he collapsed on his side. It seemed to me—maybe it was a hallucination—but it seemed to me that he gave a thin, high whinny.

Only then did it hit me: why had I done it? Such a pretty one, and I killed him, I put him into a soup! I heard someone sob behind me. I turned; it was the "new" girl.

"What's the matter?" I asked.

"I'm sorry for the colt . . ."—and her eyes were full of tears.

"Oh, oh, what a sensitive nature! And we've gone hungry for a whole three days. You're sorry because you haven't buried anyone yet. Go and try marching twenty miles a day with a full kit, and hungry to boot. First drive Fritz out and later we can get emotional. We can feel sorry. Later . . . Understand, later . . ."

I look at the soldiers who just now had egged me on, shouted. Asked me. Just now . . . A few minutes ago . . . Nobody looks at me, as if they don't notice me; each of them drops his eyes and goes about his own business. Smokes, digs . . . One is sharpening something . . . And I can do as I like. Sit down and cry. Howl! As if I'm some sort of a butcher, who doesn't mind killing just like that. But I had loved all living creatures since childhood. We had a cow—I was already going to school—and it got sick and had to be slaughtered. I cried for two days. Couldn't calm down. And here—bang!—I shot a defenseless colt. What can I say . . . It was the first colt I'd seen in two years . . .

In the evening supper was served. The cooks: "Well, young sniper! Tonight we've got meat in the pot . . ." They set down the pots and left. And my girls sat and didn't touch the supper. I understood what it was about, burst into tears, and ran out of the dugout . . . The girls ran after me, started comforting me. Then quickly grabbed their pots and began to eat . . .

Yes, that's how things were . . . Yes . . . I can't forget . . .

At night we talked, of course. What did we talk about? Of course, about home, each told about her own mother, and the father or brothers who were fighting. And about what we would do after the war. And how we would get married, and whether our husbands would love us. Our commanding officer laughed.

"Eh, you girls! You're good all around, but after the war men will be afraid to marry you. You've got good aim; you'll fling a plate at his head and kill him."

I met my husband during the war. We were in the same regiment. He was wounded twice, had a concussion. He went through the whole war, from beginning to end, and was in the military all his life afterward. Was there any need for me to explain to him what war was? Where I had come back from? How I was? Whenever I raise my voice, he either pays no attention or holds his peace. And I forgive him, too. I've also learned. We raised two children; they've both finished university. A son and a daughter.

What else can I tell you . . . So I was demobilized, came to Moscow. And to get home from Moscow I had to ride and then go several miles on foot. Now there's a subway, but then it was old cherry orchards and deep ravines. One ravine was very big, and I had to cross it. It was already dark when I got to it. Of course, I was afraid to go across that ravine. I stood there, not knowing what to do: either go back and wait for dawn, or pluck up my courage and risk it. Remembering it now, it's quite funny. I had the war behind me, what hadn't I seen, corpses and all the rest—and here I was afraid to cross a ravine. I remember to this day the smell of the corpses, mingled with the smell of cheap tobacco . . . But then I was still a young girl. Riding on the train . . . We were coming home from Germany . . . A mouse ran out of somebody's knapsack, and all our girls jumped up; the ones on the upper bunks came tumbling down, squealing. And there was a captain traveling with us; he was surprised: "You're all decorated, and you're afraid of mice."

Luckily for me, there was a truck passing by. I thought: I'll hitch a ride.

The truck stopped.

"I need to go to Diakovskoe," I shouted.

"I'm going to Diakovskoe myself." The young fellow opened the door.

I got into the cabin, he put my suitcase into the back, and off we went. He sees I'm in uniform, with decorations. He asks: "How many Germans did you kill?"

I say to him: "Seventy-five."

He says a bit mockingly: "Come on, you probably didn't lay eyes on a single one."

Then I recognized him: "Kolka Chizhov? Is it you? Remember, I helped you tie your red neckerchief?"

Before the war I had worked for a time as a Pioneer leader in my school.*

"Maruska, it's you?"

"Me . . ."

"Really?" He stopped the truck.

"Take me home! What are you doing stopping in the middle of the road?" There were tears in my eyes. And in his, too, I could see. Such a meeting!

We drove up to my house, he ran with my suitcase to my mother, danced across the courtyard with this suitcase.

"Come quick, I've brought you your daughter!"

I can't forget . . . O-oh . . . How can I forget it?

I came back, and everything had to start over from the beginning. I had to learn to wear shoes; I'd spent three years at the front wearing boots. We were used to belts, always pulled tight, and now it seemed that clothes hung baggy on us, we felt somehow awkward. I looked at skirts with horror . . . at dresses . . . We didn't wear skirts at the front, only trousers. We used to wash them in the evening and sleep on them—that counted as ironing. True, they weren't quite dry, and they would freeze stiff in the frost. How do you learn to walk in a skirt? It was like my legs got tangled. I'd go out in a civilian dress and

---

* The All-Union Pioneer Organization, for Soviet children from ten to fifteen years old, was founded in 1922. It was similar to Scout organizations in the West.

shoes, meet an officer, and involuntarily raise my hand to salute him. We were used to rationing; everything was provided by the state, so I'd go to a bakery, take as much bread as I needed, and forget to pay. The salesgirl knew me, understood why, she was embarrassed to remind me, so I wouldn't pay, I'd take it and leave. Then I'd be ashamed of myself; the next day I'd apologize, take something else, and pay for it all together. I had to learn ordinary things over again. To remember ordinary life. Normal! Who could I confide in? I'd go running to a neighbor . . . To mama . . .

I also think this . . . Listen . . . How long was the war? Four years. Very long . . . I don't remember any birds or flowers. They were there, of course, but I don't remember them. Yes, yes . . . Strange, isn't it? Can they make a color film about war? Everything was black. Only the blood was another color, the blood was red . . .

Just recently, about eight years ago, we found our Mashenka Alkhimova. The commander of the artillery division was wounded; she crawled to save him. A shell exploded right in front of her . . . The commander was killed, she didn't make it to him, and both her legs were so mangled that we were barely able to bandage her. We had a hard time with her . . . We carried her to the first-aid station, and she kept asking: "Dear girls, shoot me dead . . . I don't want to live like this . . ." She begged and pleaded . . . So! They sent her to the hospital, and we went on advancing. When we started looking for her . . . the trail was already lost. We didn't know where she was, what had become of her. For many years . . . We wrote everywhere, and nobody could tell us. The "pathfinders" of Moscow's School No. 73 helped us. Those boys, those girls . . . They found her in a veterans' home, somewhere in Altai,* thirty years after the war. So far away. All those years she had been traveling from one invalid home to another, from one hospital to another, undergoing dozens of surgeries. She didn't even tell her mother she was alive . . . She hid from every-

* The mountainous Altai region is in central Asia, on the border of Russia, China, and Kazakhstan.

body . . . We brought her to our reunion. We were all bathed in tears. Then we brought her together with her mother . . . They met thirty years after the war . . . Her mother almost lost her mind. "I'm so happy that my heart didn't break from grief before now. So happy!" And Mashenka repeated: "Now I'm not afraid to meet people. I'm already old." Yes . . . In short . . . That's war . . .

I remember lying at night in the dugout. I am not asleep. Somewhere there is artillery fire. Our cannons are shooting . . . I really didn't want to die . . . I gave an oath, a military oath, that if need be I'd give my life, but I really didn't want to die. Even if you come home alive, your soul will hurt. Now I think: it would be better to be wounded in an arm or a leg. Then my body would hurt, not my soul . . . It's very painful. We were so young when we went to the front. Young girls. I even grew during the war. Mama measured me at home . . . I grew four inches . . .

Saying goodbye, she awkwardly reaches her hot arms out and embraces me:
    Forgive me . . .

"GROW UP, GIRLS . . .
YOU'RE STILL GREEN . . ."

———

Voices . . . Dozens of voices . . . They descended upon me, revealing the unaccustomed truth, and that truth did not fit into the brief formula familiar from childhood—we won. An instant chemical reaction took place: pathos dissolved in the living tissue of human destinies; it turned out to be a very short-lived substance. Destiny—is when there is something else beyond the words.

What do I want to hear decades later? How things were in Moscow or Stalingrad, descriptions of military operations, the forgotten names of captured heights and hillocks? Do I need stories about the movements of sites and fronts, about advances and retreats, about the number of blown-up troop trains and partisan raids—about all that has already been written in thousands of volumes? No, I am seeking something else. I gather what I would call knowledge of the spirit. I follow the traces of inner life; I make records of the soul. For me the path of a soul is more important than the event itself. The question of "how it was" is not so important, or not the most important; it does not come first. What disturbs and frightens me is something else: What happened to human beings? What did human beings see and understand there? About life and death in general? About themselves, finally? I am writing a history of feelings . . . A history of the soul . . . Not the history of a war or a state and not the lives of heroes, but the history of small human beings, thrown out of ordinary life into the epic depths of an enormous event. Into great History.

The girls of 1941 . . . The first thing I want to ask: Where did their kind come from? Why were there so many? How is it they decided to take up arms on a par with men? To shoot, mine, blow up, bomb—kill?

Pushkin asked himself this same question in the nineteenth century, publishing in his magazine The Contemporary *an excerpt from the notes of Cavalry Maiden Nadezhda Durova,* who took part in the war with Napoleon: "What were the reasons that made a young girl from a good aristocratic family leave her ancestral home, renounce her sex, take on labors and duties that even frighten men, and turn up on the battlefield—and what a battlefield! Napoleon's. What prompted her? Secret griefs of the heart? Inflamed imagination? An inborn irrepressible inclination? Love?"*

Well, so—what?! A hundred and some years later, the same question . . .

OF OATHS AND PRAYERS

Natalya Ivanovna Sergeeva
PRIVATE, NURSE-AIDE

I want to speak . . . to speak! To speak it all out! Finally somebody wants to hear us. For so many years we said nothing, even at home we said nothing. For decades. The first year, when I came back from the war, I talked and talked. Nobody listened. So I shut up . . . It's good that you've come along. I've been waiting all the while for somebody, I knew somebody would come. Had to come. I was very young then. Absolutely young. Too bad. You know why? I didn't even know how to remember . . .

A few days before the war my girlfriend and I were talking about the war; we were certain there wouldn't be any war. We went to the movies, there was a newsreel before the film: Ribbentrop and Molo-

---

* The daughter of a Russian officer, Nadezhda Durova (1783–1866) disguised herself as a man and served in the Russian cavalry during the Napoleonic Wars, for which she was much decorated. Her memoirs, entitled *The Cavalry Maiden*, were published in 1836.

tov were shaking hands.* The words of the narrator stamped themselves on my memory: Germany is the faithful friend of the Soviet
Union.

Before the month was out German troops were already near Moscow . . .

We were eight children in our family, the first four were all girls, I
was the oldest. Papa once came home from work and wept: "I used to
be happy that we had girls first . . . Brides-to-be. But now in every
family someone is going to the front, and we have nobody . . . I'm too
old, they won't take me; you're all girls, and the boys are still little."
In our family this was keenly felt.

Courses for nurses were organized, and my father took me and my
sister there. I was fifteen, my sister fourteen. He said: "This is all I can
offer for our victory . . . My girls . . ." There was no other thought
then.

A year later I wound up at the front . . .

Elena Antonovna Kudina
PRIVATE, DRIVER

During the first days . . . Total confusion in town. Chaos. Icy fear.
Everybody was catching some sort of spies. People said to each other:
"Don't believe provocations." Nobody could accept even the thought
that our army had suffered a catastrophe, that it had been crushed in a
few weeks. We had been told that we'd make war on other countries'
territory. "We won't surrender an inch of our land . . ." And we were
retreating . . .

Before the war there were rumors that Hitler was preparing to attack the Soviet Union, but such talk was strictly forbidden. Certain
organizations saw to that . . . You know what I mean? The NKVD . . .

---

* The Molotov-Ribbentrop Pact, named for the foreign ministers of the Soviet Union and
Germany, was a nonaggression pact signed in August 1939. It was broken by the German invasion of eastern Poland in June 1941.

The Chekists . . . * If people whispered, it was at home, in the kitchen, and in the communal apartments—only in their own room, behind closed doors, or in the bathroom with water running. But when Stalin began to speak . . . He addressed us: "Brothers and sisters . . ." Then everybody forgot their grievances . . . We had an uncle sitting in a labor camp, mama's brother, a railroad worker, an old Communist. He had been arrested at work . . . You know who arrested him? The NKVD . . . Our beloved uncle, and we knew he wasn't guilty of anything. We believed it. He was decorated after the Civil War . . .† But after Stalin's speech mama said: "We'll defend the Motherland and sort it out later." Everybody loved the Motherland.

I ran to the recruiting office at once. I had angina, I still had a high temperature. But I couldn't wait . . .

Antonina Maximovna Knyazeva
JUNIOR SERGEANT, LIAISON

Our mother had no sons . . . There were five daughters. The announcement came: "War!" I had an excellent musical ear. Dreamed of studying at the conservatory. I decided that my ear would be of use at the front, that I'd be a liaison.

We were evacuated to Stalingrad. And when Stalingrad was besieged, we volunteered to go to the front. All together. The whole family: mother and five daughters; my father was already fighting by then . . .

---

* NKVD is the abbreviation for People's Commissariat for Internal Affairs, a police agency that by the 1930s had become a vast internal security force, responsible for running the Gulag, among other things. The Cheka was the early secret political police force of the Bolsheviks.

† The Russian Civil War (1917–1922) was fought between various pro- and antirevolutionary factions, loosely known as the Reds and the Whites.

Tatyana Efimovna Semyonova
SERGEANT, TRAFFIC CONTROLLER

Everybody had one wish: to get to the front . . . Scary? Of course it was scary . . . But all the same . . . We went to the recruiting office, and they told us: "Grow up, girls . . . You're still green . . ." We were sixteen or seventeen years old. But I insisted and they took me. My friend and I wanted to go to sniper school, but they said: "You'll be traffic controllers. There's no time to teach you."

Mama waited at the station for several days to see us transported. She saw us going to the train, gave me a pie and a dozen eggs, and fainted . . .

Efrosinya Grigoryevna Breus
CAPTAIN, DOCTOR

The world changed all of a sudden . . . I remember the first days . . . Mama stood by the window in the evening praying. I never knew that my mother believed in God. She looked and looked in the sky . . .

I was mobilized; I was a doctor. I went out of a sense of duty. My papa was happy that his daughter was at the front. Defending the Motherland. Papa went to the recruiting office early in the morning. He went to get my papers, and he went early in the morning on purpose, so that everybody in the village could see that his daughter would be at the front . . .

Lilya Mikhailovna Butko
SURGICAL NURSE

Summer. The last day of peace . . . The evening before, we went to a dance. We were sixteen. We went around in a group; together we took one home, then another. We still hadn't broken up into separate couples. So we went, say, six boys and six girls.

And just two days later these boys, tank-school students, who had taken us home from the dance, were brought back crippled, bandaged. It was dreadful! Dreadful! If I heard someone laugh, I couldn't forgive it. How could anybody laugh, how could anybody be joyful, when such a war was going on?

Soon my father went to join the militia. Only my little brothers and I remained at home. My brothers were born in '34 and '38. And I told mama that I would go to the front. She cried, and I, too, cried that night. But I ran away from home . . . I wrote to mama from my unit. There was no way she could fetch me back from there . . .

Polina Semyonovna Nozdracheva
MEDICAL ASSISTANT

The command: Fall in . . . We lined up by height; I was the smallest. The commander comes, looks. Walks up to me: "What sort of Thumbelina is this? What are you going to do? Maybe you should go back to your mother and grow up a little?"

But I no longer had a mother . . . My mother had been killed during a bombing . . .

The strongest impression . . . For my whole life . . . It was during the first year, when we were retreating . . . I saw—we were hiding in the bushes—I saw one of our soldiers rush at a German tank with his rifle and beat the armor with the rifle butt. He beat, and shouted, and wept till he fell. Till a German submachine gun shot him. During the first year we fought with rifles against tanks and "Messers" . . . *

---

*   Messerschmitts, German fighter aircraft.

Evgenia Sergeevna Sapronova
SERGEANT OF THE GUARDS, AIRPLANE MECHANIC

I begged my mama . . . I pleaded with her: only you mustn't cry . . .
This didn't happen at night, but it was dark, and there was constant
howling. They didn't cry, the mothers who were seeing their daughters off, they howled. But my mama stood as if made of stone. She
controlled herself; she was afraid I would start crying. I was my
mother's daughter; they pampered me at home. Now my hair was cut
like a boy's, they left only a small lock in the front. She and my father
didn't want me to go, but I lived for one thing only: To the front, to
the front! To the front! These posters we now see in the museums—
"The Motherland is calling!," "What have you done for the front?"—
affected me very strongly. They were before our eyes all the time.
And the songs? "Arise, vast country . . . Arise, for mortal combat . . ."

As we rode along, we were struck that dead people lay right on the
platforms. The war was already there . . . But youth holds its own,
and we sang songs. Even something merry. Some sort of silly couplets.

By the end of the war our whole family had taken part in it. Father, mama, sister—they all became railroad workers. They followed
the frontline units and restored the tracks. And each of us got a medal
"For victory": father, mama, sister, and I . . .

Galina Dmitrievna Zapolskaya
TELEPHONE OPERATOR

Before the war I worked as an army telephone operator . . . Our unit
was stationed in the town of Borisov, where the war came during the
first weeks. The head of the unit had us all line up. We were not in the
service, we weren't soldiers, we were hired workers.

He says to us: "A cruel war is beginning. It will be very difficult for you, girls. Before it's too late, whoever wants to can go back home. Those who wish to stay at the front, step forward . . ."

And all the girls, all of them, stepped forward. There were about twenty of us. We were all ready to defend our Motherland. Before the war I didn't even like books about war. I liked to read about love. And now!

We sat at the telephones all the time, around the clock. Soldiers brought us pots, we'd have a bite, doze off for a bit right there by the telephones, and then put our earphones on again. I had no time to wash my hair, so I asked: "Girls, cut off my braids . . ."

Elena Pavlovna Yakovleva
SERGEANT MAJOR, NURSE

We went to the recruiting office time after time . . .

And when we came yet again, after I don't know how many times, the commissar almost threw us out: "If you had at least some profession. If you were nurses, drivers . . . What are you able to do? What will you do at the front?" But we didn't understand him. This question had never presented itself to us: what will we do? We wanted to go to war, that's all. It never dawned on us that to make war one had to be able to do something. Something specific. He took us unawares with his question.

I and several more girls went to nursing school. We were told that we had to study for six months. We decided: no, that's too long, it doesn't suit us. There was another school where the studies took three months. True, we reckoned three months was also long. But the program there was just about to end. We asked to be allowed to take the exams. There was one month of studies left. At night we got practical training in the hospitals, and during the day we studied. Altogether, we studied for a little over a month . . .

We were sent not to the front, but to a hospital. This was at the end of August '41 . . . Schools, hospitals, clubs were overcrowded with the wounded. But in February I left the hospital, you might say I ran away, deserted, it can't be called anything else. Without any documents, with nothing, I ran away on a hospital train. I left a note: "Not coming for my shift. Leaving for the front." That was all . . .

Vera Danilovtseva
SERGEANT, SNIPER

I had a rendezvous that day . . . I flew there on wings . . . I thought that day he would confess to me: "I love you." But he came all sad: "Vera, it's war! We're being sent from school straight to the front." He studied in a military school. Well, so I, of course, at once imagined myself in the role of Joan of Arc. Only to the front and only with a rifle in my hands. We had to be together. Only together! I ran to the recruiting office, but they cut me off sternly: "For now only medics are needed. And you have to study six months." Six months—that's completely crazy! I was in love . . .

They somehow persuaded me that I had to study. All right, I'll study, but not to be a nurse . . . I want to shoot! To shoot like he does. Somehow I was ready for that. The heroes of the Civil War and those who fought in Spain often came to our school. Girls felt equal to boys; we weren't treated differently. On the contrary, we had heard since childhood and at school: "Girls—at the wheel of the tractors!," "Girls—at the controls of a plane!" Well, and there was love as well! I even imagined we'd be killed together. In the same battle . . .

I had studied at the theater institute. Dreamed of becoming an actress. My ideal was Larissa Reisner.* A woman commissar in a leather jacket . . . I liked her because she was beautiful . . .

---

* Larissa Reisner (1895–1926) was a pro-Bolshevik Russian journalist and, after the revolution, a political commissar.

Anna Nikolaevna Khrolovich

NURSE

My friends, who were all older than me, were taken to the front . . . I cried terribly, because I was left alone, I wasn't taken. They told me: "You must study, little girl."

But my studies didn't last long. Soon our dean made an announcement: "Once the war is over, you'll finish your studies, girls. Now it's necessary to defend the Motherland . . ."

Our patrons from the factory saw us off to the front.* It was summertime. I remember the whole train was decorated with greenery, flowers . . . They gave us presents. I got some delicious homemade cookies and a pretty sweater. On the platform I danced a Ukrainian *gopak* with such enthusiasm!

We rode for many days . . . At some station we girls got off the train with a bucket, to fetch some water. We looked around and gasped: there were trains passing by one after another with nothing but girls in them. They were singing. They waved to us—some with scarves, some with forage caps. It became clear: there weren't enough men, they had all been killed . . . Or taken prisoner. Now we were to replace them.

Mama wrote a prayer for me. I put it into a locket; maybe it helped—I did come back home. Before combat I used to kiss that locket . . .

Antonina Grigoryevna Bondareva

LIEUTENANT OF THE GUARDS, SENIOR PILOT

I was a pilot . . .

When I was still in the seventh grade, a plane came flying to us. It

---

* Factories in the Soviet Union offered "patronage" to schools and orphanages, helping to train young people, sending them to summer camps, and so on.

was years ago, imagine, in 1936. Then it was a great novelty. And just then a slogan appeared: "Girls and boys—to the airplanes!" As a Komsomol member I was, of course, among the first. I signed up for the flying club at once. My father, to tell the truth, was categorically against it. Up to then in our family they had all been metallurgists, several generations of blast-furnace metallurgists. And my father thought that metallurgy was a woman's work, and piloting wasn't. The director of the flying club learned about it and allowed me to take my father for a flight in a plane. So I did. My father and I went up in the air together, and after that day he kept mum. He liked it. I graduated from the club with honors, I was good at parachuting. Before the war I had time to get married and give birth to a girl.

From the first days of the war there were various reorganizations in our club: the men were taken, and we, the women, replaced them. We taught the cadets. There was a lot of work, we worked from morning till night. My husband was one of the first to leave for the front. All I had left was a photograph: he and I are standing together beside a plane in pilot's helmets . . . I now lived together with my daughter; we lived all the time in the camps. How did we live? I would lock her up early in the morning, give her some porridge, and at four in the morning we already started flying. I would come back in the evening, and she would have eaten or not eaten; she would be all covered with that porridge. She didn't cry, she just looked at me. She had big eyes, like my husband . . .

At the end of 1941 I received a death notice: my husband had been killed near Moscow. He was a flight commander. I loved my daughter, but I left her with his family. And I started requesting to be sent to the front . . .

The last night . . . I spent it kneeling by my daughter's little bed . . .

Serafima Ivanovna Panasenko

SECOND LIEUTENANT, PARAMEDIC OF
A MOTORIZED INFANTRY BATTALION

I've turned eighteen . . . I'm so happy; it's my birthday. And everybody around shouts: "War!!!" I remember how people wept. As many
as I met outside, they all wept. Some even prayed. It was unusual . . .
People in the street praying and crossing themselves. In school they
taught us that there was no God. But where were our tanks and our
beautiful planes? We always saw them during parades. We were proud!
Where were our commanders? Budenny . . . * There was, of course, a
moment of perplexity. And then we began to think about something
else: how to win the war.

I was a second-year student at the paramedical-obstetric school
in the city of Sverdlovsk. I immediately thought: "Since it's war, I
must go to the front." My papa was a longtime Communist; he had
been a political prisoner before the revolution. He had instilled in
us from childhood that the Motherland was everything, the Motherland must be defended. I didn't hesitate: if I don't go, who will? I've
got to . . .

Tamara Ulyanovna Ladynina

PRIVATE, FOOT SOLDIER

Mama came running to the train . . . My mama was strict. She never
kissed us, never praised us. If we did something good, she just gave us
a gentle look, that's all. But this time she came running, held my head
and kissed me, kissed me. And looked in my eyes . . . Looked . . . For

---

* Semyon Budenny (1883–1973) was a Russian cavalry officer during World War I, became
the leader of the Red Cavalry during the Civil War, served in various government positions,
and was a close ally of Stalin's. He was one of the first Marshals of the Soviet Union, the highest Soviet military rank.

a long time . . . I realized that I'd never see my mother again. I sensed it . . . I wanted to drop my kit bag and go back home. I felt sorry for everybody . . . My grandmother . . . And my little brothers . . .

Then music began to play . . . The command: "Fall out! Get on the train . . . !"

I kept waving for a long time . . .

Maria Semyonovna Kaliberda
SERGEANT MAJOR, LIAISON

I was assigned to a communications regiment . . . I would never have agreed to go into communications, because I didn't understand that that, too, meant fighting. A division commander came to us; we all lined up. Mashenka Sungurova was with us. This Mashenka Sungurova takes a step forward.

"Comrade General, allow me to address you."

He says: "Well, address me, then, address me, Soldier Sungurova."

"Private Sungurova requests to be relieved of service in communications and sent where the shooting is."

You understand, we were all in that state of mind. We had the idea that this communications thing was very puny; it even humiliated us. We just had to be on the front line.

The general's smile disappeared at once.

"My dear girls!" (And you should have seen how we looked then—without food, without sleep; in short, he spoke to us not as a commander, but as a father.) "You clearly don't understand your role at the front. You are our eyes and ears. An army without communications is like a man without blood."

Mashenka Sungurova was the first to give in.

"Comrade General! Private Sungurova is ready surefire to perform any task you give her!"

Afterward we called her "Surefire" till the end of the war.

. . . In June 1943 at the Kursk Bulge* we were handed the regimental banner, and our regiment, Detached Communications Regiment 129 of the 65th Army, consisted then of 80 percent women. And I want to tell you something, so that you get an idea . . . So that you understand . . . What was going on in our souls then. Because there probably will never again be such people as we were then. Never! So naïve and so sincere. With such faith! When the commander of the regiment received the banner and gave the command: "Regiment, before the banner! On your knees!"—we all felt so happy. We were trusted, we were now a regiment like all others, tank regiments, infantry regiments . . . We stood there and wept; we all had tears in our eyes. You won't believe me now, but my whole body had been so tense from the turmoil that I got sick, I came down with "night blindness." It was from lack of food, from nervous strain. But now my night blindness went away. You understand, the next day I was healthy, I got well, and it was because my whole soul was so shaken . . .

Xenia Sergeevna Osadcheva

PRIVATE, HOSPITAL MATRON

I just became an adult . . . On June 9, 1941, I turned eighteen, I became an adult. And two weeks later this cursed war began, even twelve days later. We were sent to build the Gagra-Sukhumi railroad. There were only young people. I remember the bread we ate. There was almost no flour in it, but all sorts of other things, mostly water. This bread lay on the table and left a little puddle of water. We used to lick it up.

In 1942 . . . I voluntarily applied to serve in Evacuation-Clearance Hospital No. 3201. It was a very big frontline hospital that belonged to the Trans- and North-Caucasian fronts and the separate Coastal Army. There were fierce battles, with a lot of wounded. I was as-

---

* A major battle took place in July-August 1943 at a salient ("bulge") around the city of Kursk, ending in a decisive Russian victory.

signed to distribute food—this was a round-the-clock duty; it would already be morning and time to serve breakfast, but we would still be handing out supper. Several months later I was wounded in the left leg—I hopped on the right one, but went on working. Then I was appointed to the post of matron, and also had to be there round the clock. I lived at work.

May 30, 1943 . . . At exactly one o'clock in the afternoon there was a massive airstrike in Krasnodar. I ran out of the building to see if the wounded had been sent off from the train station. Two bombs hit a shed where ammunition was stored. Before my eyes boxes flew up higher than a six-story building and exploded. I was thrown against a brick wall by the blast. I lost consciousness . . . When I came to it was already evening. I raised my head, tried to bend my fingers—they seemed to move. I cautiously unglued my left eye and went to my section, all covered with blood. In the corridor I met our head nurse, who did not recognize me at first and asked: "Who are you? Where from?" She came closer, gasped, and said: "Where have you been so long, Xenia? The wounded are hungry and you're not there." They quickly bandaged my head and my left arm above the elbow, and I went to fetch the supper. It was dark before my eyes; I was dripping sweat. I started serving supper and fell down. They brought me back to consciousness and all I heard was: "Quick! Hurry!" And again— "Quick! Hurry!"

A few days later they were still taking blood from me for the badly wounded. People were dying . . .

. . . I changed so much during the war that when I came home, mama didn't recognize me. People showed me where she lived, I went to the door and knocked.

There came an answer: "Yes, come in . . ."

I go in, greet her, and say: "Let me stay the night."

Mama was lighting the stove, and my two little brothers were sitting on the floor on a pile of straw, naked, they had no clothes. Mama didn't recognize me and said: "Do you see how we live, citizen? Go somewhere else before it gets dark."

I go up closer, and she again says: "Go somewhere else, citizen, before it gets dark."

I bend over her, embrace her, and murmur: "Mama, dear mama!"

Then they all just fell on me and burst out crying . . .

Now I live in Crimea . . . Here everything drowns in flowers, and every day I look out the window at the sea, but I'm worn out with pain, I still don't have a woman's face. I cry often, I moan all day. It's my memories . . .

OF THE SMELL OF FEAR AND A SUITCASE OF CANDY

Olga Mitrofanovna Ruzhnitskaya

NURSE

I was leaving for the front . . . It was a magnificent day. Clear air and a sprinkle of rain. So beautiful! I stepped out in the morning and stood there: can it be I won't come back here again? Won't see our garden . . . Our street . . . Mama wept, clutched me, and wouldn't let go. I had already left, she caught up with me, embraced me, and wouldn't let go . . .

Nadezhda Vasilyevna Anisimova
MEDICAL ASSISTANT IN A MACHINE-GUN COMPANY

To die . . . I wasn't afraid to die. Youth, probably, or whatever . . . There was death around, death was always close, but I didn't think about it. We didn't talk about it. It was circling somewhere nearby, but kept missing. Once during the night a whole company conducted a reconnaissance mission in our regiment's sector. Toward morning it pulled back, and we heard moaning in no-man's-land. A wounded man had been left behind. "Don't go there, you'll be killed," the soldiers held me back. "Look, it's already dawn."

I didn't listen to them and crawled there. I found the wounded man. It took me eight hours to drag him back, tied with a belt by the hand. He was alive when we finally made it. The commander of the regiment learned about it, had a fit, and was going to arrest me for five days for being absent without permission. The deputy commander's reaction was different: "She deserves to be decorated."

At nineteen I had a medal "For Courage." At nineteen my hair was gray. At nineteen in my last battle I was shot through both lungs, the second bullet went between two vertebrae. My legs were paralyzed . . . And they thought I was dead . . .

At nineteen . . . My granddaughter's age now. I look at her—and don't believe it. A child!

When I came home from the front, my sister showed me my death notice . . . They had already buried me . . .

Albina Alexandrovna Gantimurova
SERGEANT MAJOR, SCOUT

I don't remember my mama . . . Only vague shadows remain in my memory . . . Outlines . . . Her face or her body when she bent over me. Close to me. So it seemed afterward. I was three years old when she died. My father served in the Far East, a career officer. He taught me to ride a horse. That was the strongest impression of my childhood. My father didn't want me to grow up a sissy. I remember myself from the age of five living in Leningrad with my aunt. During the Russo-Japanese War* my aunt was a nurse. I loved her like my mama . . .

What kind of girl was I? I'd jump from the second floor of our school on a bet. I loved soccer; I was always goalkeeper for the boys. When the Finnish War began, I kept running away to the Finnish War.† In 1941 I had just finished seventh grade and had time to apply to a technical school. My aunt wept: "It's war!" But I was glad I would go to the front and fight. How could I know what blood is?

The 1st Guards Division of the people's militia was being formed, and several of us girls were accepted in a medical battalion.

I phoned my aunt: "I'm going to the front."

From the other end came the reply: "Come home at once! Dinner's already cold."

I hung up. Later I felt sorry for her, terribly sorry. The siege began, the dreadful siege of Leningrad,‡ when half the city died, and she was there alone. A little old woman.

I remember I got leave to go home. Before going to my aunt I stopped at the grocery store. Before the war I was awfully fond of candy.

I said: "Give me some candy."

The salesgirl looked at me as if I was crazy. I didn't understand: what are food coupons, what is a siege? Everybody in the line turned

---

* The Russo-Japanese War was fought between February 1904 and September 1905 over conflicting territorial ambitions in Manchuria and Korea, and ended with Russian defeat.

† The Russo-Finnish War, also known as the Winter War, was fought between the Soviet Union and Finland from November 1939 to March 1940, following a Soviet invasion of Finland to "reclaim" extensive border territory around Leningrad.

‡ The siege of Leningrad by the German army began in September 1941 and ended in January 1944, after 872 days, with a toll of some 1.5 million lives of Russian soldiers and civilians.

to me, and my rifle was bigger than I was. When they gave them out to us, I looked at it and thought: "When will I grow big enough for this rifle?"

And suddenly everybody, the whole line, begged: "Give her candy. Take our coupons."

And they gave me candy.

They were collecting aid for the front in the streets. Big trays lay on tables right in the square; people came and took off, one a golden ring, another earrings . . . They brought watches, money . . . Nobody noted anything down, nobody signed anything . . . Women took off their wedding rings . . .

These are pictures in my memory . . .

And there was Stalin's famous Order No. 227: "Not a step back!" If you turn back, you're shot! Shot right there. Or else court-martialed and sent to the specially created penal battalions. Those who wound up there were as good as dead. Those who escaped from encirclement or captivity were sent to the filtration camps. Behind us moved the retreat-blocking detachments . . . Our own shot at our own . . .

These are pictures in my memory . . .

An ordinary clearing . . . It's wet, muddy after rain. A young soldier is on his knees. In glasses. For some reason they keep falling off; he picks them up. After rain. A cultivated boy from Leningrad. They had already taken away his rifle. We are all lined up. There are puddles everywhere . . . We . . . hear him beg . . . He swears . . . He begs not to be shot; his mother is alone at home. He begins to cry. And they shoot him on the spot—right in the forehead. With a pistol. A show execution: this is what will happen to people who waver. Even for a single moment! A single moment . . .

This order turned me into an adult at once. This you couldn't . . . For a long time we didn't remember . . . Yes, we won the war, but at what cost! At what terrible cost!

We stayed awake round the clock, there were so many wounded. Once none of us slept for three days and three nights. I was sent to the hospital with a truckload of wounded. I handed over the wounded, and the truck went back empty, so I could sleep. I returned fresh as a daisy, and everybody was falling off their feet.

I ran into the commissar.

"Comrade Commissar, I'm ashamed."

"What's the matter?"

"I slept."

"Where?"

I told him how I took the wounded in a truck, came back empty, and had a nice sleep.

"So what? Good for you! At least one of us can be normal; the rest of them are falling off their feet."

But I was ashamed. And with that kind of conscience we lived through the whole war.

They treated me well in the medical battalion, but I wanted to be a scout. I said I'd run away to the front line if they didn't let me go. They wanted to expel me from Komsomol for that, for not obeying military regulations. But I ran away even so . . .

My first decoration was the medal "For Courage" . . .

A battle began. A barrage of gunfire. The soldiers lay cowering. The order came: "Forward! For the Motherland!" They just lay there. Again the order, again they just lay there. I took off my cap so they could see: a girl's standing up . . . And they all stood up and we went into battle . . .

They gave me the medal, and that same day we went on a mission. For the first time in my life I had . . . our . . . women's thing . . . I saw blood and howled: "I'm wounded . . ."

There was a paramedic in the scouts with us, an older man. He came to me.

"Where are you wounded?"

"I don't know where . . . But there's blood . . ."

He told me all about it, like a father . . .

After the war I went scouting for some fifteen years. Every night. And dreamed things like that my submachine gun refused to shoot, or we were surrounded . . . I'd wake up grinding my teeth. Trying to remember—where are you? There or here?

When the war ended I had three wishes: first—to ride on a bus, instead of crawling on my stomach; second—to buy and eat a whole loaf of white bread; and third—to sleep in white sheets and have them make crinkly noises. White sheets . . .

Liubov Arkadyevna Charnaya
SECOND LIEUTENANT, CRYPTOGRAPHER

I was expecting a second child . . . I had a two-year-old son, and I was pregnant. Then—the war . . . And my husband was at the front . . . I went to my parents and had . . . Well, you understand? An abortion . . . Though it was forbidden then . . . How could I give birth? Tears all around . . . War! How could I give birth in the midst of death?

I finished the course in cryptography. They sent me to the front. I wanted to take revenge for this child I couldn't give birth to. My girl . . . I had expected a girl . . .

I requested the front line. They kept me at headquarters . . .

Valentina Pavlovna Maximchuk
ANTIAIRCRAFT GUNNER

They were leaving town . . . Everybody was leaving . . . At noon on June 28, 1941, we, the students of Smolensk Pedagogical Institute, also assembled in the courtyard of the printing house. It was not a long assembly. We left the city by the old Smolensk road in the direction of the town of Krasnoe. Observing caution, we walked in separate groups. Toward the end of the day the heat subsided, walking became easier, we went more quickly, not looking back. We were afraid to look back . . . We reached a stopping place and only then looked to the east. The whole horizon was enveloped in a crimson glow. From a distance of thirty miles it seemed to fill the whole sky. It was clear that it was not ten or a hundred houses burning. The whole of Smolensk was burning . . .

I had a new chiffon dress with ruffles. My girlfriend Vera liked it. She tried it on several times. I promised to give it to her as a wedding present. She was going to get married. There was a nice guy.

And here suddenly was this war. We were leaving for the trenches. Our possessions were all given to the superintendent of the dormitory. What about the dress? "Take it, Vera," I said when we were leaving the city.

She didn't take it. Why, you promised it to me as a wedding present. It got burned up in that fire.

Now we walked and kept looking back. It felt as if our backs were being roasted. We walked all night without stopping and at dawn came to our work. Digging antitank ditches. A sheer wall seven yards long and three and a half yards deep. I was digging and my shovel burned like fire, the sand looked red. Before my eyes stands our house with flowers and lilac bushes . . . White lilacs . . .

We lived in hovels on a flood meadow between two rivers. Hot and humid. Myriads of mosquitoes. We used to smoke them out before going to bed, but at dawn they would get in anyway; it was impossible to sleep peacefully.

I was taken to the field hospital from there. We lay on the floor next to each other. Many of us got sick then. I had a high fever. Chills. I lay there—I cried. The door to the ward opened, the doctor says from the threshold (he couldn't get any further, the mattresses were lying so close to each other): "Ivanova has plasmodium in her blood." Me, that is. She didn't know that for me nothing could have been scarier than this plasmodium, ever since I read about it in a textbook back in the sixth grade. And at that moment the radio played: "Arise, vast country . . ." I heard this song for the first time then. "I'll recover," I thought, "and go to the front at once."

They brought me to Kozlovka, not far from Roslavl, unloaded me on a bench. I sat there, holding on with all my might so as not to fall over, and heard as if through sleep: "This one?"

"Yes," the paramedic says.

"Take her to the dining room. Give her something to eat first."

And then I was in a bed. You should understand what it was to sleep not on the ground by a fire, not on a tarpaulin under a tree, but in a hospital, in the warmth. With a sheet. I didn't wake up for seven days. They said the nurses roused me and fed me, but I don't remember it.

When I woke up by myself after seven days, a doctor came, examined me, and said: "Sturdy organism; you'll pull through."

And I plunged into sleep again.

. . . At the front my unit, for its part, immediately got encircled. The food norm was two dry crusts a day. There was no time to bury the dead; we simply scattered sand over them. The faces we covered with forage caps . . . "If we survive," the commander said, "I'll send you to the rear. I used to think that a woman couldn't live like this even for two days. I imagine my wife . . ." I was so hurt I burst into tears. For me to sit in the rear at such a time was worse than death. I could stand it all with my mind and my heart, but physically it was more than I could take. The physical load . . . I remember how we carried the shells, carried the guns through the mud, especially in Ukraine, where the ground after rain or in spring was so heavy, like dough. To dig a common grave and bury our comrades after we hadn't slept for three days . . . even that was hard. We no longer wept, because in order to weep you also need strength, but we wanted to sleep. To sleep and sleep.

On watch I used to walk back and forth without stopping and recite poetry out loud. Other girls sang songs, so as not to collapse and fall asleep . . .

Maria Vasilyevna Zhloba
UNDERGROUND FIGHTER

We were transporting the wounded out of Minsk . . . I wore high-heel shoes, because I was short and embarrassed by it. One heel broke just as they shouted: "Assault!" And I ran barefoot, the shoes in my hand; a pity, they were beautiful shoes.

When we were encircled and saw that we couldn't break through, the nurse-aide Dasha and I climbed out of the ditch, no longer hiding, and stood up tall: better to have your head torn off by a shell than to be captured and brutalized. The wounded, those who were able, also stood up . . .

When I saw my first fascist soldier, I couldn't say a word, I lost speech. And they walked along young, cheerful, smiling. And wherever they stopped, wherever they saw a water pump or a well, they washed themselves. They always had their sleeves rolled up. They wash and wash . . . Blood all around, screaming, and they wash and wash . . . Such hatred of them rose up in me . . . When I came back home, I changed blouses twice. Everything in me protested against them being here. I couldn't sleep nights. Wha-a-t?! Our neighbor, Aunt Klava, got paralyzed when she saw them walking on our land. In her house . . . She died soon, because she couldn't bear it . . .

Maria Timofeevna Savitskaya-Radiukevich
PARTISAN LIAISON

The Germans rode into the village . . . On big black motorcycles . . . I stared at them all eyes: they were young, cheerful. They laughed all the time. They guffawed! My heart stopped at the thought that they were here, on our land, and laughing.

I only dreamed of revenge. I imagined that I'd be killed, and some-one would write a book about me. My name would remain. Those were my dreams . . .

I gave birth to a baby girl in '43 . . . By then my husband and I had gone to the forest to join the partisans. I gave birth to her in a swamp, on a haystack. I dried the swaddling clothes on my body: I would put them in my bosom, warm them up, and swaddle the baby. Every-thing around us was burning, villages were burned down with people in them . . . They rounded people up in schools, in churches . . . Poured kerosene . . . My five-year-old niece listened to our conversa-tions and asked: "Aunt Manya, when I burn up, what will be left of me? Only rubber boots . . ." That's what our children asked us about . . .

I myself gathered the charred remains . . . I gathered my friend's family. We found little bones, and if there was a bit of clothing left, just some little scrap, we recognized who it was. Each of us looked for his own. I picked up a small piece, my friend said: "It's mama's jacket . . ." And fainted. Some gathered the bones in a sheet, some in a pillowcase. In whatever they had. My friend and I had a hand-bag; what we gathered filled less than half of it. And we put it all into a common grave. Everything was black, only the bones were white . . . and the bone ash . . . I already recognized it . . . White as could be . . .

After that, whatever mission they sent me to, I wasn't afraid. My baby was small, just three months old, I used to go on missions with her. The commissar would send me off, and weep himself . . . I used to bring medications, bandages, serums from town . . . I would apply it under her arms and between her legs, swaddle her, and carry her. There were wounded men dying in the forest. I had to go. I had to! There were German and police guard posts everywhere, nobody could pass except me. With the baby. I had her swaddled . . .

It's horrible to tell about it now . . . Oh, so hard! To give the baby a temperature and make her cry, I rubbed her with salt. She'd get all red then, covered with rash, scream her head off. I'd go up to the guard: "Typhus, sir . . . Typhus . . ." They'd shout at me: "Away! Away!" so as to send me off quickly. I rubbed her with salt and put in some garlic. The baby was small . . . I was still nursing her . . .

Once we got past the guards, I'd go into the forest and weep my heart out. I'd shout! I was so sorry for my baby. And in a day or two I'd go again . . .

Elena Fyodorovna Kovalevskaya
PARTISAN

I discovered what hatred was . . . For the first time I discovered that feeling . . . How can they walk on our land! Who are they? My temperature went up from those scenes. Why are they here?

A column of prisoners of war passes, and hundreds of corpses are left on the road . . . Hundreds . . . Those who fell down exhausted were shot on the spot. They were driven like cattle. There was no more wailing over the dead. It was impossible to bury them, there were so many. They went on lying on the ground. The living lived with the dead . . .

I met my half sister. Their village had been burned down.

She had three sons, but they were no more. Their house had been burned down with the children in it. She used to sit on the ground and rock from side to side, rocking her grief. She would get up and not know where to go. To whom?

We all left for the forest: papa, my brothers, and I. Nobody urged us, nobody forced us, we went on our own. Mama stayed alone with the cow . . .

Anna Semyonovna Dubrovina-Chekunova
FIRST LIEUTENANT OF THE GUARDS, PILOT

I didn't even think twice . . . I had a profession that was needed at the front. I didn't think, didn't hesitate for a second. In general I met few people then who wanted to sit out that time. Wait till it was over. I remember one . . . a young woman, my neighbor . . . She told me honestly: "I love life. I want to powder my nose and put makeup on, I don't want to die." I didn't see any more like that. Maybe they kept quiet, hid themselves. I don't know how to answer you . . .

I remember I took the plants from my room and asked the neighbors, "Please water them. I'll be back soon."

I came back four years later . . .

The girls who stayed home envied us, and the women wept. One of the girls who went with me stood there. Everybody is weeping, and she's not. Then she took some water and wetted her eyes. Once, twice. With a handkerchief. See, I'm embarrassed, everybody's weeping. How could we understand what war is? We were young . . . It's now that I wake up at night in fear, when I dream that I'm in the war . . . The plane takes off, my plane, gains altitude, and . . . falls . . . I realize that I'm falling. The last moments . . . And it's so terrifying, until you wake up, until the dream evaporates. An old person fears death, a young one laughs. He's immortal! I didn't believe I could die . . .

Maria Afanasyevna Garachuk
PARAMEDIC

I finished medical school . . . I came back home, my father was ill. And then—the war. I remember, it was morning . . . I learned this terrible news in the morning . . . The dew hadn't dried on the leaves of the trees yet, and they were already saying—war! And this dew that I suddenly saw on the grass and the trees, saw so clearly—I remembered at the front. Nature was in contrast with what was happening with people. The sun shone brightly . . . Daisies bloomed, my favorites, there were masses of them in the fields . . .

I remember us lying somewhere in a wheat field; it was a sunny day. The German submachine guns go rat-a-tat-tat—then silence. All you hear is the wheat rustling. Then again the German submachine guns go rat-a-tat-tat . . . And you think: will you ever hear again how the wheat rustles? This sound . . .

Liubov Ivanovna Liubchik
COMMANDER OF A MACHINE-GUN PLATOON

My mother and I were evacuated to the rear . . . To Saratov . . . Somewhere there I took a three-month course in metal turning. We would stand at the lathes for twelve hours on end. We were starving. Our only thought was to get to the front. There would be rations there. Rusks and tea with sugar. They'd give us butter. Someone told us so, I don't remember who. Maybe the wounded at the train station? To save ourselves from starvation, well, and also, obviously, we were Komsomol girls. My girlfriend and I went to the recruiting office. We didn't tell them we worked at the factory. In that case they wouldn't have taken us. And so we enlisted.

We were sent to the Ryazan Infantry School. We graduated as commanders of machine-gun units. A machine gun is heavy; you have to drag it with you. You feel like a horse. It's night. You stand watch and listen to every sound. Like a lynx. Wary of every rustle . . . In war they say you're half man and half beast. It's true. There's no other way to survive. If you're just a human being—you won't stay whole. You'll get bashed in the belfry! In war you have to remember something about yourself. Something . . . Remember something from when a man was not quite a man yet . . . I'm not very educated, I'm a simple accountant, but that I know.

I got as far as Warsaw . . . And all on foot . . . The infantry, as they say, is the wartime proletariat. We crawled on our stomachs . . . Don't ask me any more . . . I don't like books about war. About heroes . . . We went sick, coughing, sleepy, dirty, poorly dressed. Often hungry . . . But we won!

Ulyana Osipovna Nemzer
SERGEANT, TELEPHONE OPERATOR

My father had been killed, that I knew . . . My brother was dead. And to die or not to die no longer had any significance for me. I only pitied my mama. She had instantly turned from a beauty into an old woman, very embittered by her lot. She couldn't live without my papa.

"Why are you going to the war?" she asked.

"To avenge papa."

"Papa wouldn't stand seeing you with a rifle."

My papa used to do my braids when I was little. Tied the ribbons. He liked beautiful clothes more than mama did.

I served as a telephone operator in the unit. I remember best how our commander shouted into the receiver: "Reinforcements! I'm asking for reinforcements! I demand reinforcements!" The same every day . . .

Anna Iosifovna Strumilina
PARTISAN

I'm not a heroine . . . I used to be a pretty girl, I was pampered when I was little . . .

The war came . . . I didn't want to die. Shooting was scary, I never thought I'd shoot. Oh, lord! I was afraid of the dark, of the dense forest. Of wild animals, of course . . . Oh . . . I couldn't imagine how someone could meet a wolf or a wild boar. I was even afraid of dogs in my childhood; a big German shepherd bit me when I was little, and I was afraid of them. Oh, lord! That's how I was . . . But I learned everything with the partisans . . . I learned to shoot—with a rifle, a pistol, and a machine gun. And now, if need be, I can show you. I'll remember. We were even taught what to do if there's no other weapon than a knife or a shovel. I stopped being afraid of the dark. And of wild animals . . . But I would avoid a snake, I'm not used to snakes. At night she-wolves often howled in the forest. And we sat in our dugouts and didn't mind. The wolves were vicious, hungry. We had these small dugouts, like burrows. The forest was our home. The partisans' home. Oh, lord! I began to be afraid of the forest after the war . . . I never go to the forest now . . .

I thought I'd sit out the war at home with my mama. My beautiful mama. Mama was very beautiful. Oh, lord! I'd never have ventured . . . Myself, no. Never . . . But . . . They told us . . . The town had been taken by the Germans, and I discovered that I was Jewish. And before the war we all lived together: Russians, Tatars, Germans, Jews . . . We were the same. Oh, lord! I'd never even heard this word "yids," because I lived with papa, mama, and books. We became like lepers, we were driven out everywhere. People were afraid of us. Some of our acquaintances even stopped saying hello to us. Their children stopped. The neighbors said to us: "Leave us all your things, you don't need them anyway now." Before the war we used to be friends. Uncle Volodia, Aunt Anya . . . * Lord!

Mama was shot . . . This happened a few days before we were supposed to move to the ghetto. There were orders hanging all over town: Jews are not allowed—to walk on the sidewalks, to have haircuts in barber shops, to buy anything in the stores . . . Mustn't laugh, mustn't sing . . . Oh, lord! Mama couldn't get used to it; she was always absentminded. She probably didn't believe it . . . Maybe she

---

* Russians often use "uncle" and "aunt" as terms of endearment, with no reference to family relations.

went into a store? Or somebody said something rude, and she laughed. As a beautiful woman . . . Before the war she sang in the philharmonic, everybody loved her. Oh, lord! I imagine . . . If she hadn't been so beautiful . . . our mama . . . She would still have been with me or with papa. I think about it all the time . . . Strangers brought her to us at night, dead. Already without her coat and shoes. It was a nightmare. A terrible night! Terrible! Somebody had taken off her coat and shoes. Her gold wedding ring. Papa's gift . . .

We had no home in the ghetto; we were put in the attic of someone's house. Papa took a violin, our most valuable prewar thing. Papa wanted to sell it. I had a bad case of angina. I lay in bed . . . Lay in bed with a high fever, and I couldn't speak. Papa wanted to buy some food; he was afraid I might die. Die without mama . . . Without mama's words, mama's hands. I was so pampered . . . so loved . . . I waited for him for three days, until some acquaintances told me that papa had been killed . . . They said it was on account of the violin . . . I don't know how valuable it was. As he was leaving, papa said: "It will be good if they give me a pot of honey and some butter." Oh, lord! I was left—without mama . . . without papa . . .

I went looking for papa . . . I wanted to find him even if he was dead, so we could be together. I was blond, not dark-haired; my eyebrows and hair were light, so no one in the town touched me. I came to the market . . . I met papa's friend there, he lived in a village by then, with his parents. Also a musician, like my father. Uncle Volodia. I told him everything . . . He put me on his cart, under a cover. There were piglets squealing, chickens clucking in the cart. We drove for a long time. Oh, lord! Till evening. I slept, woke up . . .

That's how I wound up with the partisans . . .

Vera Sergeevna Romanovskaya

PARTISAN NURSE

There was a parade . . . Our partisan detachment merged with units of the Red Army, and after the parade we were told to surrender our weapons and go and work on restoring the city. But it just didn't make sense to us: the war was still going on, only Belorussia had been liberated, but we were supposed to surrender our weapons. Every one of us wanted to go on fighting. And we went to the recruiting office, all our girls . . . I said that I was a nurse and asked to be sent to the front. They promised me: "All right, we'll register you, and if there's a need, we'll summon you. Meanwhile go and work."

I waited . . . They didn't summon me . . . I went to the recruiting office again. I went many times . . . And finally they told me frankly that there was no need, they already had enough nurses. What was needed was sorting bricks in Minsk . . . The city was in ruins . . . What kind of girls did we have, you ask? We had Chernova; she was pregnant, and she carried a mine at her side, next to where her baby's heart was beating. So go and figure what sort of people they were. For us there was no need to figure, that's just how we were. We were brought up that we and the Motherland were one and the same. Or another friend of mine, she went around town with her little daughter, and under her dress her little body was wrapped in leaflets. The girl would raise her arms and complain: "Mama, I'm hot. Mama, I'm hot." And in the streets there were Germans everywhere. *Polizei*. It was possible to deceive a German, but not a *polizei*. He was one of us, he knew your life, your insides. Your thoughts.

And so even children . . . We took them into our detachment, but still they were children. How to save them? We decided to send them back across the front line. But they escaped from the children's centers and returned to the front. They were caught on the trains, along the roads. They would escape again, and again return to the front . . .

History will spend hundreds of years trying to understand: What was it? What sort of people were they? Where did they come from? Imagine, a pregnant woman walking with a mine . . . She was expecting a child, yes . . . She loved, she wanted to live. And, of course, she was afraid. But she went . . . Not for the sake of Stalin, but for the sake of her children. Their future life. She didn't want to live on her knees. To submit to the enemy . . . Maybe we were blind, and I won't even deny that there was much then that we didn't know or understand, but we were blind and pure at the same time. We were made of two parts, of two lives. You must understand that . . .

Maria Vasilyevna Tikhomirova
PARAMEDIC

Summer was beginning . . . I finished medical school. Received my diploma. War! They summoned me to the recruiting office at once. The order was: "You have two hours to get ready, we're sending you to the front." I packed everything in one small suitcase.

What did you take to the war?

Candy.

What?

A whole suitcase of candy. In the village I was sent to after training school, they gave me some relocation money. So there was money, and I spent it all on chocolate candy, a whole suitcaseful. I knew I wouldn't need money at the front. And on top of the candy I put my class picture, with all the girls. I came to the recruiting office. The commissar asks: "Where do you want to be sent?" I say: "And where are you sending my friend?" She and I came together to the Leningrad region; she worked in a village ten miles away. He laughs: "She asked the same question." He took my suitcase, to carry it to the truck that was to take us to the station. "What have you got that's so heavy?" "Candy. A whole suitcaseful." He said nothing. Stopped smiling. I saw he was embarrassed, even somehow ashamed. He was no longer a young man . . . He knew where I was going . . .

Tamara Illarionovna Davidovich

SERGEANT, DRIVER

My fate was decided at once . . .

An announcement hung in the recruiting office: "Drivers needed." So I took a driving course. Six months long . . . They didn't pay any attention to the fact that I was a teacher (I had studied to be a teacher before the war). Who needs teachers in wartime? It's soldiers that are needed. There were many of us girls, a whole auto battalion.

Once during a drill . . . For some reason I can't remember it without tears . . . It was in spring. We finished shooting and were going back. I picked some violets. A little bouquet. I picked it and tied it to my bayonet. And went on like that.

We returned to the camp. The commander had us all line up and asked me to step forward. I did . . . I forgot that I had violets tied to my rifle. He began to scold me: "A soldier should be a soldier, not a flower picker . . ." He found it incomprehensible that I could think about flowers in such circumstances. A man was unable to understand it . . . But I didn't throw those violets away. I took them off and put them in my pocket. I got three extra turns of duty for them . . .

Another time I was standing at my post. At two o'clock in the morning they came to relieve me, but I refused. I sent my replacement to sleep: "You'll stand during the day, and I'll stand now." I would accept to stand there all night till dawn, just to hear the birds sing. Only at night was there something reminiscent of the former life. Peaceful.

When we were leaving for the front, we walked down the street, and people stood all along it: women, old people, children. And they were all crying: "Girls are going to the front." We were a whole battalion of girls.

I'm at the wheel . . . We pick up the dead after the battle; they're scattered over the field. All young. Boys. And suddenly there's a young girl lying there. Killed . . . Everybody falls silent.

Vera Iosifovna Khoreva
ARMY SURGEON

How I prepared to go to the front . . . You won't believe . . . I thought it wouldn't be for long. We'll defeat the enemy soon! I took one skirt, my favorite one, two pairs of socks, one pair of shoes. We were retreating from Voronezh, but I remember going to a store and buying another pair of high-heeled shoes. I do remember that we were retreating, everything was black, smoky (but the store was open—a miracle!), and for some reason I felt like buying a pair of shoes. Such elegant little shoes, I remember as if it were today . . . I also bought some perfume . . .

It was hard to renounce all at once life as it had been up to then. Not only my heart but my whole body resisted. I remember how happy I was when I came running out of the store with those shoes. I was inspired. And there was smoke everywhere . . . Rumbling . . . I was already in the war, but I still didn't want to think about it. I didn't believe it.

And there was rumbling all around . . .

OF EVERYDAY LIFE
AND ESSENTIAL LIFE

Nonna Alexandrovna Smirnova
PRIVATE, ANTIAIRCRAFT GUNNER

We dreamed . . . We wanted to go to war . . .

We were assigned seats in a train car, and classes began. Everything was different from the way we had pictured it at home. We had to get up early, and run around all day. But the former life still lived in us. We were indignant when the section commander, Sergeant Gulyaev, who had a fourth-grade education, taught us the regulations and mispronounced certain words. We wondered: what can he teach us? But he taught us how not to perish . . .

After the quarantine, before we took the oath, the sergeant major brought our uniforms: overcoats, forage caps, army shirts, skirts, and, instead of underwear, two long-sleeved men's shirts of unbleached calico, stockings instead of footwraps, and heavy American boots, iron shod at the heels and toes. By my height and constitution I turned out to be the smallest in the company, five feet tall, shoe size five, and, naturally, military industry did not provide for such tiny sizes, and America certainly did not supply us with anything that small. I was given a pair of size ten boots. I put them on and took them off without unlacing them, and they were so heavy that I dragged my feet on the ground as I walked. When I marched on stone pavement, my iron-shod boots made sparks, and my gait resembled anything but a marching step. It's awful to remember the nightmare of my first march. I was ready to do great deeds, but I wasn't ready to wear size ten boots instead of five. They were so heavy and ugly! So ugly!

The commander saw me marching and called me out.

"Smirnova, what kind of step is that? Haven't you been taught? Why don't you pick up your feet? Put in three extra turns of duty . . ."

I answered: "Yes, sir, Comrade First Lieutenant, three extra turns of duty!" I turned to go and fell down. I fell out of my boots . . . My feet were all bloody blisters . . .

Then it became clear that I could no longer walk. The company shoemaker, Parshin, was ordered to make me a pair of size five boots out of an old tarpaulin . . .

Antonina Grigoryevna Bondareva
LIEUTENANT OF THE GUARDS, SENIOR PILOT

And there was so much that was funny . . .

Discipline, regulations, insignia—we didn't master all this wisdom at once. We were standing guard by the plane. And the regulations say that if anyone comes, we should stop him: "Halt, who goes there?" My friend saw the regimental commander and shouted, "Halt, who goes there? Excuse me, but I'm going to shoot!" Imagine? She shouted, "Excuse me, but I'm going to shoot!" Excuse me . . . Ha-ha-ha . . .

Klavdia Ivanovna Terekhova
AIR FORCE CAPTAIN

The girls arrived at school with long braids . . . With their hair done up . . . I also had braids around my head . . . But how could we wash it? Where to dry it? Suppose you've just washed it, and there's an alarm, you have to run. Our commander, Marina Raskova, told us all to cut off our braids. The girls cut them and wept. Lilya Litvyak, later a famous pilot, couldn't bring herself to part with her braid.

I went to Raskova.

"Comrade Commander, your orders have been carried out, only Litvyak refused."

Marina Raskova, despite her feminine gentleness, could be a very strict commander. She sent me away.

"What kind of party organizer are you if you can't get your people to carry out an order! About-face, march!"

Dresses, high-heeled shoes . . . How sorry we were to put them away. It was boots during the day, and in the evening at least a little time in shoes in front of the mirror. Raskova saw it and a few days later came the order: pack all the women's clothes and mail them home. So there! But as a result we finished studying a new plane in six months instead of two years, as it would have taken in peaceful times.

In the first days of training we lost two teams. There were four coffins. All three of our regiments sobbed out loud.

Raskova stepped forward.

"Friends, wipe your tears. These are our first losses. There will be many of them. Clench your hearts like a fist . . ."

Later, at the front, we buried without tears. We stopped crying.

We flew fighters. The altitude itself was a terrible strain on a woman's whole body. Sometimes your stomach was pressed right up against your spine. But our girls flew and shot down aces, and what aces! You know, when we walked by, men looked at us with astonishment: "They're women pilots." They admired us . . .

Vera Vladimirovna Shevaldysheva
FIRST LIEUTENANT, SURGEON

In the fall I was summoned to the recruiting office . . . The commander received me and asked: "Do you know how to parachute?" I confessed that I was afraid. He spent a long time persuading me to become a paratrooper: handsome uniform, chocolate every day. But

I'd been afraid of heights since childhood. "And what about antiair-craft artillery?" As if I knew anything about antiaircraft artillery? Then he suggests: "Let's send you to a partisan unit." "And how can I write to mama in Moscow from there?" He takes a red pencil and writes on my assignment: "Steppe Front . . ."*

On the train a young captain fell in love with me. He spent a whole night standing in our car. He had already been burned by the war, had been wounded several times. He looked at me, looked, and then said: "Verochka, only don't lower yourself, don't become coarse. You're so delicate now . . . I've already seen everything!" And more in the same vein, meaning it's hard to come out pure from the war. From hell.

A friend and I spent a month traveling to the 4th Guards Army of the 2nd Ukrainian Front. We finally arrived. The chief surgeon came out for a few moments, looked us over, and led us to the surgery room: "Here's your operating table . . ." Ambulances were driving up one after another, big cars, "Studebakers." The wounded were lying on the ground, on stretchers. We only asked: "Who should we take first?" "The silent ones . . ." An hour later I was standing at my table, operating. And so it went . . . You operate around the clock, then take a short nap, quickly rub your eyes, wash—and go back to your table. And every third man was dead. We had no time to help them all. Every third man . . .

At Zhmerinka station we came under a terrible bombardment. The train stopped, and we ran. Our political commissar had had his appendix removed the day before, and that day he, too, ran. We sat in the forest all night, and our train was blown to pieces. In the morning German planes began combing the forest. Where to hide? I couldn't burrow into the ground like a mole. I put my arms around a birch tree and stood there: "Oh, mama, my mama! . . . Can it be I'll perish? If I survive, I'll be the happiest person in the world." When I told people

---

* The Steppe Front was a new formation, formed by the Soviet army on territory near the Ukrainian border after the German defeat at Stalingrad in February 1943.

afterward how I held on to the birch tree, they all laughed. I was such an easy target. Standing up tall, a white birch . . . Hilarious!

I met Victory Day in Vienna. We went to the zoo, I wanted so much to go to the zoo. We could have gone to see a concentration camp. They took everybody there to see it. I didn't go . . . Now it surprises me that I didn't go . . . I wanted something joyful. Funny. To see something from a different life . . .

Svetlana Vasilyevna Katykhina
PRIVATE IN A FIELD BATH-AND-LAUNDRY UNIT

There were three of us: mama, papa, and myself . . . My father was the first to leave for the front. Mama wanted to go with my father, she was a nurse, but he was sent in one direction, she in another. I was only sixteen . . . They didn't want to take me. I kept going to the recruiting office, and after a year they took me.

We traveled by train for a long time. Soldiers were returning from the hospitals with us, and there were also some young fellows. They told us about the front, and we sat listening open-mouthed. They said there would be shooting, and we sat and waited: when would the shooting begin? So that when we came we could say we had already been under fire.

We arrived. But they didn't give us rifles, they sent us to the cauldrons and tubs. The girls were all my age, loved and pampered in their families. I was an only child. But there we had to carry firewood, stoke the stoves. Then we took the ashes and used them in cauldrons instead of soap, because there was always a shortage of soap. The linen was dirty, full of lice. Bloody . . . In winter it was heavy with blood . . .

Sofya Konstantinovna Dubnyakova
SERGEANT MAJOR, MEDICAL ASSISTANT

To this day I remember my first wounded man. His face . . . He had a compound fracture of the middle third of the thigh bone. Imagine it, the bone sticking out, a shrapnel wound, everything turned inside out. That bone . . . I knew theoretically what to do, but when I crawled over to him and saw it, I felt faint, nauseous. And suddenly I hear: "Drink some water, dear nurse . . ." It was the wounded man speaking. He pitied me. I remember that picture as if it were now. When he said it I came to my senses: "Ah," I thought, "you damned Turgenev young lady! A man is perishing and you, tender creature, feel nauseous . . ." I opened a first-aid kit, covered up the wound—and felt better, and was able to give the man proper aid.

Now I watch films about the war: a nurse on the front line, she's neat, clean, not in thick pants, but in a skirt, a pretty forage cap on top of her head . . . Well, it's not true! How could we have pulled a wounded man out, if we were like that . . . You're not going to go crawling about in a skirt with nothing but men around. And to tell the truth, they issued us skirts only at the end of the war, for dressing up. We also got some knitted cotton underwear instead of men's shirts. We were so happy we didn't know what to do. We unbuttoned our tunics to show it off . . .

Anna Ivanovna Belyai
NURSE

A bombardment . . . They bombed and bombed, bombed and bombed and bombed. Everybody rushed and ran somewhere . . . I'm running, too. I hear someone moan: "Help . . . Help . . ." But I keep running . . . A few minutes later, something dawns on me, I feel the first-aid bag on my shoulder. And also—shame. Where did the fear go! I run back: it was a wounded soldier moaning. I rush to bandage him. Then a second, a third . . .

The battle ended during the night. In the morning fresh snow fell. Under it the dead . . . Many had their arms raised up . . . toward the sky . . . You ask me: what is happiness? I answer . . . To suddenly find a living man among the dead . . .

Olga Vasilyevna Korzh

MEDICAL ASSISTANT IN A CAVALRY SQUADRON

I saw my first dead man . . . I stood over him and cried . . . Mourned for him . . . Then a wounded man called to me: "Bandage my leg!" His leg was torn off, hanging out of the trouser leg. I cut the trouser leg off: "Put my leg down! Put it beside me." I did. If they're conscious, they won't give up their arm or leg. They take it along. And if they're dying, they ask that it be buried with them.

During the war I used to think I'd never forget anything. But things get forgotten . . .

Such a young, attractive fellow. And he lies there dead. I thought all the killed got buried with military honors, but they took him and dragged him into the hazel bushes. Dug a grave . . . Without a coffin, without anything, they put him in the ground and simply covered him over. The sun was shining brightly—on him, too . . . A warm summer day . . . There was no tarpaulin, nothing, they laid him out in his army shirt and jodhpurs, as he was, and it was all new, he had obviously arrived recently. So they laid him out and buried him. The hole was very shallow, just enough to lay him in. And the wound was small, a mortal one—in the temple, but there was little blood, and the man lay as if alive, only very pale.

After the artillery fire the bombing began. They bombed that place. I don't know what was left of it . . .

And how did we bury people in an encirclement? Right there, next to the trench we ourselves were sitting in, we put them in the ground—that's all. There was just a little mound. Of course, if the Germans came right after, or some tanks, they would trample it down at once. There would be ordinary ground left, not a trace. We often buried in the woods under the trees . . . Under the oaks, the birches . . .

Even now I can't go to the forest. Especially where there are old oaks or birches . . . I can't sit there . . .

Vera Borisovna Sapgir
SERGEANT, ANTIAIRCRAFT GUNNER

I lost my voice at the front . . . My beautiful voice . . .

My voice returned when I came back home. The family got together in the evening, we drank: "So, Verka, sing for us." And I began to sing . . .

I left for the front a materialist. An atheist. I left as a good Soviet schoolgirl, who had been well taught. And there . . . There I began to pray . . . I always prayed before a battle, I read my prayers. The words were simple . . . My own words . . . They had one meaning, that I would return to mama and papa. I didn't know any real prayers and didn't read the Bible. No one saw me pray. I did it in secret. On the sly. Cautiously. Because . . . We were different then, people lived differently. You understand? We thought and understood differently . . . Because . . . I'll tell you a story . . . Once a believer turned up among the new arrivals, and the soldiers laughed at him when he prayed: "Well, did your God help you? If he exists, how does he put up with all this?" They were unbelievers, like the man who cried at the feet of the crucified Christ, "If He loves you, why doesn't He save you?" I read the Bible after the war . . . Now I read it all the time . . . And that soldier, he was no longer a young man, he didn't want to shoot. He refused: "I can't! I won't kill!" Everybody agreed to kill, but he didn't. At that time . . . A terrible time . . . Because . . . They court-martialed him and two days later they shot him . . . Bang! Bang!

A different time . . . Different people . . . How can I explain it? How? . . .

Fortunately I . . . I didn't see those people, the ones I killed . . . But . . . All the same . . . Now I realize that I killed them. I think about it . . . Because . . . Because I'm old now. I pray for my soul. I told my daughter that when I die she should take all my medals and decorations, not to a museum, but to a church. Give them to the priest . . . They come to me in my sleep . . . The dead . . . My dead . . . Though I never saw them, they come and look at me. I keep searching with my eyes, maybe someone was only wounded, badly wounded, but could still be saved. I don't know how to put it . . . But they're all dead . . .

Maria Selivestrovna Bozhok
NURSE

The most unbearable thing for me was the amputations . . . They often amputated so high up that they'd cut off the whole leg, and I could barely hold it, barely carry it to the basin. I remember they were very heavy. I would take it quietly, so that the wounded man wouldn't hear, and carry it like a baby . . . A small baby . . . Especially if it was a high amputation, way above the knee. I couldn't get used to it. Under anesthesia the wounded men would groan or curse. Well-rounded Russian curses. I was always bloody . . . Blood is dark red . . . Very dark . . .

I wrote nothing to mama about it. I wrote her that everything was fine, that I had warm clothes and boots. She sent three of us to the front, it was hard for her . . .

Maria Petrovna Smirnova (Kukharskaya)
MEDICAL ASSISTANT

I was born and grew up in Crimea, near Odessa. In 1941 I finished tenth grade in the Slobodka high school, Kordymsky district. When the war began, I listened to the radio for the first few days. I realized that we were retreating. I ran to the recruiting office. They sent me home. I went there twice more and was refused twice more. On July 28 the retreating units passed through our Slobodka, and I went to the front with them without any call-up.

When I first saw a wounded man, I fainted. Later I got over it. When I went under fire to a wounded soldier for the first time, I screamed so loud that it seemed I drowned out the noise of the battle. Then I got used to it . . . Ten days later I was wounded. I extracted the shrapnel myself, and bandaged myself.

December 25, 1942 . . . Our 333rd Division of the 56th Army occupied an elevation on the approach to Stalingrad. The enemy decided to take it back at all costs. A battle began. Tanks attacked us, but our artillery stopped them. The Germans rolled back, and a wounded lieutenant, the artillerist Kostia Khudov, was left in no-man's-land. The orderlies who tried to bring him back were killed. Two first-aid sheepdogs (this was the first time I saw them) crept toward him, but were also killed. And then I took off my flap-eared hat, stood up tall, and began to sing our favorite prewar song: "I saw you off to a great deed," first softly, then more and more loudly. Everything became hushed on both sides—ours and the Germans'. I went up to Kostia, bent down, put him on a sledge, and took him to our side. I walked and thought: "Only not in the back, better let them shoot me in the head." So, right now . . . right now . . . The last minutes of my life . . . Right now! Interesting: will I feel the pain or not? How frightening, mama dear! But not a single shot was fired . . .

We could never have enough uniforms: they'd give us a new one, and a couple of days later it was all bloody. My first wounded man was First Lieutenant Belov, my last was Sergei Petrovich Trofimov, sergeant of a mortar platoon. In 1970 he came to visit me, and I showed my daughters his wounded head, where he still had a big scar. Altogether I carried 481 wounded soldiers from under fire. One of the journalists counted them up: a whole infantry battalion . . . We hauled men two or three times our weight. When they're wounded they're still heavier. You carry him, his weapon, plus there's his overcoat, boots. So you hoist some 180 pounds on your back and carry it. Unload it . . . Go for the next one, and again it's 150 or 180 pounds . . . Five or six times in one attack. And you yourself weigh a hundred pounds—like a ballet dancer. It's hard to believe now . . . I myself find it hard to believe . . .

Vera Safronovna Davydova
FOOT SOLDIER

It was 1942 . . . we were going on a mission. We crossed the front line and stopped by some cemetery. We knew the Germans were three miles away from us. It was during the night, and they kept sending up flares. With parachutes. These flares burn for a long time and light up everything far around. The platoon commander brought me to the edge of the cemetery, showed me where the flares were fired from, where the bushes were that the Germans might appear from. I'm not afraid of dead people, even as a child I wasn't afraid of cemeteries, but I was twenty-two, I was standing guard for the first time . . . In those two hours my hair turned gray . . . It was my first gray hair, I discovered a whole streak in the morning. I stood and looked at those bushes, they rustled and moved, I thought the Germans were coming from them . . . And something else . . . Some monsters . . . And I was alone . . .

Is it a woman's job to stand guard by a cemetery at night? Men took it all more simply, they were already prepared for the thought that they had to stand guard, had to shoot . . . But for us in any case it was unexpected. Or to make a twenty-mile march. With combat gear. In hot weather. Horses dropped dead . . .

Lola Akhmetova
FOOT SOLDIER, RIFLEMAN

You ask what's the most frightening thing in war? You expect me . . . I know what you expect . . . You think I'll say the most frightening thing in war is death. To die.

Am I right? I know your kind . . . Your journalist's tricks . . . Ha-ha-ha . . . Why aren't you laughing? Eh?

But I'll say something else . . . For me the most terrible thing in war was—wearing men's underpants. That was frightening. And for me it was somehow . . . I can't find the . . . Well, first of all, it's very ugly . . . You're at war, you're preparing to die for the Motherland, and you're wearing men's underpants. Generally, you look ridiculous. Absurd. Men's underpants were long then. Wide. Made of sateen. There were ten girls in our dugout, all wearing men's underpants. Oh, my God! Winter and summer. For four years.

We crossed the Soviet border . . . As our commissar used to say at political sessions, we were finishing the beast off in his own den. Near the first Polish village we got a change of clothes: new uniforms and . . . And! And! And! For the first time they issued us women's underpants and brassieres. For the first time in the whole war. Ha-ha-ha . . . Well, of course . . . We saw normal women's underwear . . .

Why aren't you laughing? You're crying . . . Why?

Nina Vladimirovna Kovelenova

SERGEANT MAJOR, MEDICAL ASSISTANT
IN AN INFANTRY COMPANY

They wouldn't send me to the front . . . I was too young, just barely sixteen. But they did accept a woman we knew, a paramedic. She was very upset and wept, because she had a little son. I went to the recruiting office: "Take me instead of her . . ." Mama didn't want me to go: "Nina, no, how old are you? Maybe the war will be over soon." Mama is mama.

The soldiers used to save things for me, one a dry crust, another a piece of sugar. They looked out for me. I didn't know we had a Katyusha rocket launcher under cover behind us. It started shooting. It shoots, there's thunder all around, everything's on fire . . . And I was so shocked, I was so frightened by this thunder and fire, that I fell into a puddle and lost my forage cap. The soldiers laughed: "What's wrong, Ninochka? What's wrong, dear girl?"

Hand-to-hand combat . . . What do I remember? I remember crunching . . . Once hand-to-hand combat begins, there's immediately this crunching noise: the breaking of cartilage, of human bones. Animal cries . . . When there was an attack, I'd walk along with the fighters, well, just slightly behind, virtually next to them. It all happened before my eyes . . . Men stabbing each other. Finishing each other off. Breaking bones. Sticking a bayonet in the mouth, in the eye . . . In the heart, in the stomach . . . And this . . . How to describe it? I'm too weak . . . Too weak to describe it . . . In short, women don't know such men, they don't see such men at home. Neither women nor children. It's frightful to think of . . .

After the war I went home to Tula. I used to scream during the night. Mama and my sister sat with me at night. I'd wake up from my own screaming . . .

Nina Alexeevna Semyonova
PRIVATE, RADIO OPERATOR

We came to Stalingrad. There was deadly combat going on there. It was the most deadly place . . . The water and the earth were red . . . We had to cross from one bank of the Volga to the other. Nobody wanted to listen to us: "What? Girls? Who the hell needs you here? We need riflemen and machine gunners, not radio operators." And there were lots of us, eighty in all. Toward evening the older girls were taken, but another girl and I were left behind. We were small. Hadn't grown up yet. They wanted to leave us in the reserve, but I set up such a howl . . .

In my first battle the officers kept pushing me off the breastwork, because I stuck my head up to see everything. There was some sort of curiosity, childish curiosity . . . Naïveté! The commander shouts: "Private Semyonova! Private Semyonova, you're out of your mind! Fuck it all . . . You'll be killed!" I couldn't understand that: how could I be killed, if I'd only just arrived at the front? I didn't know yet how ordinary and indiscriminate death is. You can't plead or argue with it.

Old trucks kept bringing people's militias. Old men and young boys. They were given two grenades and sent into the battle without a rifle. They were supposed to find themselves a rifle in battle. After the battle there was nobody to bandage . . . They had all been killed . . .

Ekaterina Mikhailovna Rabchaeva
PRIVATE, MEDICAL ASSISTANT

I went through the whole war from beginning to end . . .

When I was hauling my first wounded man, my legs nearly gave way under me. I was hauling him and whispering: "Only let him not die . . . Only let him not die . . ." I was bandaging him and weeping, saying something gentle to him. And the commander passed by. He yelled at me, even used some dirty language . . .

Why did he yell at you?

I shouldn't have pitied him, shouldn't have wept like that. I'd just wear myself out, and there were many wounded.

We drove along, dead soldiers lay there, cropped heads, green as potatoes from the sun . . . They were scattered like potatoes . . . As they ran, so they lay on the plowed field . . . Like potatoes . . .

Natalya Ivanovna Sergeeva
PRIVATE, NURSE-AIDE

I can't tell you where it was . . . In what place . . . Once there were two hundred wounded men in a shed, and I was alone. The wounded were brought straight from the battlefield, lots of them. It was in some village . . . Well, I don't remember, so many years have gone by . . . I remember I didn't sleep or sit down for four days. Each of them cried out: "Nurse . . . dear nurse . . . help me, dear girl!" I ran from one to another, and once I stumbled and collapsed, and instantly fell asleep. I was awakened by shouting. Our commander, a young lieutenant, also wounded, raised himself a little on his healthy side and shouted: "Quiet! I order you to be quiet!" He realized that I was exhausted, and everybody was in pain and calling to me: "Nurse . . . dear nurse . . ." I leaped up and ran—I don't know where, why. And then, for the first time since I got to the front, I wept . . .

And so . . . You never know your own heart. In winter some captive German soldiers were led past our unit. They walked along all frozen, with torn blankets on their heads, holes burnt in their overcoats. It was so cold that birds dropped in flight. The birds froze. A soldier was marching in that column . . . A young boy . . . There were tears frozen on his face . . . And I was taking bread to the mess in a wheelbarrow. He couldn't take his eyes off that wheelbarrow; he didn't see me, only the wheelbarrow. Bread . . . Bread . . . I broke a piece off a loaf and gave it to him. He took it . . . Took it and didn't believe it . . . He didn't believe it!

I was happy . . . I was happy that I wasn't able to hate. I was astonished at myself then . . .

"I ALONE CAME BACK
TO MAMA . . ."

———

I'm on my way to Moscow . . . What I know about Nina Yakovlevna Vishnevskaya at the moment takes up only a few lines in my notebook: at seventeen she left for the front, went through the war as a medical assistant in the 1st Battalion of the 32nd Tank Brigade of the 5th Army. Took part in the famous tank engagement near Prokhorovka, a confrontation between a total, on both sides—Soviet and German—of 1,200 tanks and self-propelled guns. It was one of the biggest tank battles in world history.

Her address was furnished to me by the schoolboys of Borisovo, who had gathered a lot of material for their museum about the 32nd Tank Brigade, which had liberated their town. Ordinarily the medical assistants in tank units were men, but here was a girl. I prepared to go at once . . .

I had already begun to think about how to choose among dozens of addresses. At first I took notes from everybody I met. They learned about me through the grapevine; they phoned each other. They invited me to their reunions, or simply to one of their homes for tea and cakes. I began to receive letters from all over the country; my address was also passed around. They wrote, "You're one of us, you're a frontline girl, too." I soon realized that it was impossible to write it all down; some other principle of search and selection was needed. What would it be? Having sorted the available addresses, I came up with a formula: to try to record women of various military professions. We all see life through our occupations, through our place in life or the events we participate in. It could be supposed that a nurse saw one war, a baker another, a paratrooper a third, a pilot a fourth, the commander of a submachine-gun platoon a fifth . . . Each of these women had her own radius of visibility, so to speak. One had an operating table: "I saw so many cut-off arms and legs . . . It was even hard to believe that somewhere whole men existed. It seemed they were all either wounded or dead . . ." (A. Demchenko, sergeant major, nurse). Another had the pots and pans of a field kitchen: "Sometimes after a battle there was no one left to eat . . . I'd cook a whole pot of soup, a pot of kasha, and there'd be no one to give it to . . ." (I. Zinina, private, cook); a third a pilot's cockpit: "Our camp was in the forest. I came back from a mission and decided to go to the forest; it was already summer, the strawberries were ripe. I walked down the path and saw a dead German lying there . . . Already black . . . I was so frightened. I'd been in the war for a year and had never seen dead people. Up there it's a different matter . . . When you fly you have one thought: to find your target, bomb it, and come back. We didn't see dead people. We didn't have this fear . . ." (A. Bondareva, lieutenant of the guards, senior pilot). And for a partisan fighter, war to this day is associated with the smell of a burning campfire: "We did everything on the campfire: baked bread and cooked food; we put jackets and felt boots near the remaining coals to dry. During the night we warmed ourselves . . ." (E. Vysotskaya).

But I wasn't left alone with my thoughts for long. The attendant brought tea. The people in my compartment began to introduce themselves noisily and cheerfully. On the table the traditional bottle of Moskovskaya appeared, some homemade snacks, and—as usual with us—a heart-to-heart conversation began. About our family secrets and politics, about love and hate, about leaders and neighbors.

I understood long ago that we are a people of roads and conversations . . .

I also told them who I was going to and why. Two of my fellow travelers fought—one went as far as Berlin as commander of a sapper battalion, the other spent three years as a partisan in the Belorussian forests. We began talking about the war at once.

Later I noted down our conversation as it was preserved in my memory:

—We're a vanishing tribe. Mammoths! We belong to the generation that believed there is something more in a life than human life. There is the Motherland and the great Idea. Well, and also Stalin. Why lie? You can't leave a word out of a song, as they say.

—There's that, of course . . . We had a brave girl in our unit . . . She used to go to the railroad to plant explosives. Before the war her whole family had been arrested: the father, the mother, and two older brothers. She had lived with her aunt, her mother's sister. She sought out the partisans from the first days of the war. We could see in our unit that she was asking for trouble . . . She wanted to prove . . . Everybody got decorated, but she not once. They wouldn't give her a medal, because her parents were enemies of the people. Just before our army came, her leg was blown off. I visited her in the hospital . . . She wept . . . "But now," she said, "everybody will trust me." She was a beautiful girl . . .

—When some fool from the personnel department sent me two girls who were commanders of sapper platoons, I sent them back at once. They were terribly upset. They wanted to go to the front line and make mining passages.

—*Why did you send them back?*

—For many reasons. First, I had enough good sergeants who could do what these girls had been sent for. Second, I thought there was no need for a woman to go to the front line. To that hellfire. There were enough men. I also knew that I'd have to dig them a separate dugout, to surround their commanders' activities with a heap of different girly things. A lot of bother.

—*So, in your opinion, women are out of place in war?*

—We know from history that Russian women in all times didn't only send their husbands, brothers, sons to the war, and grieve and wait for them. Princess Yaroslavna already climbed onto the rampart and poured melted pitch on the heads of the enemy.* But we men had a sense of guilt about girls making war, and it has stayed with me . . . I remember, we were retreating. It was autumn, it rained around the

* Princess Yaroslavna is the wife of Prince Igor Svyatoslavich of Novgorod in the twelfth-century Old Slavic poem *The Lay of Igor's Campaign*.

clock, day and night. There was a dead girl lying by the road . . . She had a long braid, and she was all covered with mud . . .

—There's that, of course . . . When I heard that our nurses, being surrounded, shot at the enemy, defending the wounded soldiers, because they were helpless as children, I could understand that. But now picture this: two women crawl into no-man's-land with a sniper rifle to do some killing. Well, yes . . . I can't help feeling that that was a kind of "hunting," after all . . . I myself shot people . . . But I'm a man . . .

—*But they defended their native land. They saved the Fatherland* . . .

—There's that, of course . . . I'd go on a scouting mission with such a woman, but I wouldn't marry her . . . No . . . We're used to thinking of women as mothers and brides. The beautiful lady, finally.* My younger brother told me how he and some other boys shot stones from slingshots at captive Germans when they were led through our town. Our mother saw it and boxed his ear. And these Germans were greenhorns, the last scraps Hitler had recruited. My brother was seven years old, but he remembered mother looking at them and weeping: "May your mothers be struck blind: how could they let you go to war!" War is a man's business. What, don't you have enough men to write about?

—N-no . . . I'm a witness. No! Let's remember the catastrophe of the first months of the war: our air force was destroyed on the ground, our tanks burned like matchboxes. The rifles were old. Millions of soldiers and officers were captured. Several million! In six weeks Hitler was already near Moscow . . . University professors signed up to serve in the militia. Old professors! And girls were eager to get to the front voluntarily—a coward won't volunteer to go and fight. Those were brave, extraordinary girls. There are statistics: the losses at the front line among medical personnel were in second place after the

---

* In 1904 the Russian symbolist Alexander Blok (1880–1921) published a collection of poems entitled *Verses About the Beautiful Lady,* expressing his spiritual-erotic vision of the eternal feminine.

losses in the riflemen's battalions. In the infantry. What is it, for in-stance, to haul a wounded man from a battlefield? I'm going to tell you.

We mounted an attack, and the Germans started to mow us down with submachine-gun fire. And our battalion was no more. Every-body fell. They weren't all killed, many were wounded. The Germans didn't let up. Quite unexpectedly a girl leaped out of the trench, then a second, a third . . . They started bandaging and carrying the wounded men away. Even the Germans went dumb with astonishment for a moment. By ten o'clock in the evening all the girls had been badly wounded, but each of them had saved as many as two or three men. They were meagerly decorated; at the beginning of the war decora-tions weren't just thrown around. A wounded man had to be saved along with his personal weapons. The first question in the medical unit was: where are the weapons? We didn't have enough of them then. Rifles, submachine guns, machine guns—they had to carry all that as well. In 1941 Order No. 281 was issued concerning decorations for saving soldiers' lives: for saving fifteen badly wounded men, car-ried from a battlefield along with their personal weapons—the medal "For Distinguished Service"; for saving twenty-five men—the Order of the Red Star; for saving forty—the Order of the Red Banner; for saving eighty—the Order of Lenin. And I just told you what it meant to save at least one wounded man ⸪ . . Under fire . . .

—There's that, of course . . . I also remember . . . Well, yes . . . We sent our scouts to a village where a German garrison was stationed. Two of them went . . . Then one more . . . Nobody came back. The commander summoned one of our girls: "You go, Liusya." We dressed her as a cowherd, led her to the road . . . What could we do? There was no other solution. A man would be killed, but a woman could get through. Right . . . But to see a rifle in a woman's hands . . .

—*Did the girl come back?*

—I forget her last name . . . I just remember her first name—Liusya. She was killed . . . The peasants told us afterward . . .

——

There was a long *silence. Then we gave a toast to those who had been killed. The conversation took another turn: we talked about Stalin, how before the war he had destroyed the best commanders, the military elite. About the brutal collectivization and about 1937.* The camps and exiles. That without 1937 there would have been no 1941. There would have been no retreat all the way to Moscow. But after the war that was forgotten. The Victory overshadowed everything.*

"Was there love during the war?" I asked.

——I met many pretty girls at the front, but we didn't look at them as women. Though, in my view, they were wonderful girls. But they were our friends, who dragged us off the battlefield. Who saved us, took care of us. I was hauled off wounded twice. How could I have bad feelings about them? But could you marry your brother? We called them little sisters.

——And after the war?

——The war ended, and they all turned out to be terribly defenseless . . . Take my wife——an intelligent woman, but she has bad feelings about girls who were in the war. She thinks they went to the war to find husbands, that they all had love affairs there. Though, in fact, since we're having a sincere conversation, they were mostly honest girls. Pure. But after the war . . . After all the dirt, and lice, and death . . . We wanted something beautiful. Bright. Beautiful women . . . I had a friend, at the front there was a wonderful girl, as I now understand, who loved him. A nurse. But he didn't marry her; he was demobilized and found another, prettier one. And he's unhappy with his wife. Now he remembers the other one, his wartime love; she would have been a good companion to him. But after the front he left her. Because for four

* 1937 was the height of Stalin's purges and the Moscow show trials; in June of that year there was also a secret trial of Red Army commanders, followed by their execution, and later in the year there was a massive purge of Red Army officers.

years he had seen her only in old boots and a man's padded jacket . . . We wanted to forget the war. And we forgot our girls, too . . .

—There's that, of course . . . We were all young. We wanted to live . . .

None of us slept that night. We talked till morning.

. . . I made my way straight from the subway to a quiet Moscow courtyard. With a sandbox and children's seesaw. I walked and recalled the astonished voice on the phone: "You've come? And straight to me? You're not going to verify anything in the Veterans' Council? They have all my data, they've checked me." I was taken aback. I used to think that the sufferings a person goes through made him free; he belonged only to himself. He was protected by his own memory. Now I discovered: no, not always. Often this knowledge and even super-knowledge (there's no such thing in ordinary life) exist separately, as some sort of an emergency reserve or the specks of gold in layers of ore. You need to spend a long time removing the empty rock, rummaging together in the alluvial trifles, and in the end—a flash! A gift!

Then what are we in reality—what are we made of, what material? How durable is it—that I want to understand. That is why I'm here . . .

The door is opened by a short, plump woman. She offers me one hand in a manly greeting; the other is held by her little grandson. From his coolness and accustomed curiosity, I understand that there are frequent visitors to this house. They are expected here.

The big room is uncluttered; there is almost no furniture. Books on a home-made shelf—mostly war memoirs, many enlarged military photographs; a tank helmet hangs on an elk horn; on a polished table there is a row of little tanks with gift labels: "From the soldiers of N. Unit," "From the students of tank school" . . . Beside me on the sofa "sit" three dolls—in military uniforms. Even the curtains and the wallpaper in the room are of khaki color.

I realize that here the war hasn't ended and never will.

Nina Yakovlevna Vishnevskaya

SERGEANT MAJOR, MEDICAL ASSISTANT OF A TANK BATTALION

Where shall I begin? I've even prepared a text for you. Well, all right, I'll speak from the heart . . . This is how it was . . . I'll tell you as I would a friend . . .

I'll begin by saying that girls were accepted reluctantly into the tank forces. One could even say they weren't accepted at all. How did I get there? We lived in the town of Konakovo, in the Kalinin region. I had just passed my exams to go from junior high to high school. None of us understood then what war was; for us it was some sort of game, something from a book. We had been brought up on the romanticism of the revolution, on ideals. We believed the newspapers: the war would soon end in our victory. At any moment . . .

Our family lived in a big communal apartment. There were many families in it, and every day somebody left for the war: Uncle Petya, Uncle Vasya. We saw them off, and we, the children, were mostly overcome by curiosity. We went all the way to the train with them . . . Music played, women wept, but none of that frightened us; on the contrary, it amused us. The brass band always played the march "The Slav Girl's Farewell." We, too, wanted to get on the train and leave. To that music. The war as we pictured it was somewhere far away. I, for instance, liked uniform buttons, the way they shone. I was already taking courses to become a medical volunteer, but that was also like some sort of child's game. Then our school was closed, and we were mobilized to build defensive constructions. We were housed in a shed, in an open field. We were even proud that we had been sent to do something connected to the war. We were assigned to a battalion of weaklings. We worked from eight in the morning till eight in the evening, twelve hours a day. We dug antitank trenches. We were all girls and boys of fifteen or sixteen . . . And so once, as we were working, we heard voices, some shouting "Air raid!" and some "Germans!" The adults ran to hide, but we were interested in seeing German planes, in seeing what Germans were. They flew over us, but we couldn't see anything. We were even upset. After a while they turned and flew lower. We all saw black crosses. There was no fear; again there was only curiosity. And suddenly they opened machine-gun fire and started rattling away, and before our eyes our own boys and girls, with whom we had been studying and working, began to fall. We were petrified; we simply couldn't understand what was happening. We stood and watched . . . As if rooted to the spot . . . The adults ran up to us and threw us to the ground, and still there was no fear in us . . .

Soon the Germans came very close to our town; they were some seven miles away, we could hear the cannon fire. All of us girls ran to the recruiting office: we, too, had to go and defend the town, to be together. Nobody had any doubts. But they didn't take all of us; they took only the strong, sturdy girls, and above all those who were already eighteen. Good Komsomol girls. Some captain chose girls for a tank unit. He didn't even listen to me, of course, because I was seventeen, and I was only five foot three inches tall.

"An infantry soldier gets wounded," he explained. "He will fall to the ground. You can crawl to him, bandage him on the spot, or drag him to cover. It's not the same with a tank soldier . . . If he gets wounded inside the tank, he has to be pulled out of it through the hatch. How are you going to do that? Tank soldiers are all big and sturdy, you know. You have to climb up on the tank, it's being shelled, there are bullets, shells flying. And do you know how it is when a tank catches fire?"

"But I'm a Komsomol girl like all the others, aren't I?" I began to cry.

"Of course you're also a Komsomol girl. But a very small one."

And my girlfriends, the ones I studied with at school and at the medical courses—big, strong girls—were taken. I was offended that they were going and I was left behind.

I said nothing to my parents, of course. I went to see the girls off, and they took pity on me: they hid me in the back under a tarpaulin. We traveled in an open truck, all wearing different colored kerchiefs—black, blue, red . . . And I had mama's blouse tied on my head instead of a kerchief. As if I was going not to the war, but to an amateur concert. Quite a sight! Like a movie . . . I can't think of it now without smiling . . . Shura Kisseleva even took her guitar along. We rode for a while; the trenches were already in sight. The soldiers saw us and shouted, "Actors are coming! Actors are coming!"

We drove up to the headquarters. The captain ordered us to fall in. We all fell in; I was the last. The girls with their things, and me just so. Since I had left unexpectedly, I had nothing with me. Shura gave me her guitar: "So you won't be empty-handed."

The superior officer came out, and the captain reported to him: "Comrade Lieutenant Colonel! Twelve girls have arrived to serve under your command."

The man looked us over. "There are thirteen in all, not twelve."

The captain insisted, "No, twelve, Comrade Lieutenant Colonel." He was so sure there were twelve of us. Then he turned, looked, and asked me straight out, "Where did you come from?"

I answered, "I've come to fight, Comrade Captain."

"Step forward!"

"I've come with a friend . . ."

"You go to a dance with a friend. Here it's war . . . Come closer."

As I was, with my mother's blouse on my head, I went up to them. I showed my certificate as a medical volunteer. I began to beg: "Don't doubt, sirs, I'm strong. I worked as a nurse . . . I gave blood . . . Please, let me . . ."

They looked over all my papers, and the lieutenant colonel ordered, "To be sent home! In the first vehicle going that way!"

And till the vehicle came, they assigned me temporarily to a medical platoon. I sat and made cotton swabs. The moment I saw some vehicle approaching headquarters, I'd run into the forest. I'd sit there for an hour or two, the vehicle would leave, I'd come back out. And I

did that for three days, until our battalion went into combat. The
1st Tank Battalion of the 32nd Tank Brigade . . . Everybody went to
fight, and I was preparing dugouts for the wounded. Half an hour
hadn't gone by before they started bringing the wounded . . . and the
dead . . . One of our girls was killed in that battle. And they all forgot
that I was to be sent home. They got used to me. The superiors no
longer mentioned it . . .

Now what? Now I had to get into military dress. We were all given
kit bags to put our things in. They were brand-new. I cut off the
straps, ripped out the bottom, and put it on. It looked like a military
skirt . . . Somewhere I found an army shirt that wasn't too ragged, put
on a belt, and decided to show myself off to the girls. I had just started
turning around before them, when the sergeant major came into our
dugout, followed by the commander of the unit.

The sergeant major: "Ten-hut!"

The lieutenant colonel entered, and the sergeant said to him,
"Comrade Lieutenant Colonel, permission to speak, sir! There has
been an incident with the girls. I issued them kit bags to keep their
things in, and they got into them themselves."

At this point the commander of the unit recognized me. "Ah, it's
you, the 'stowaway'! Well, then, sergeant, we must put the girls in
uniforms."

What did they issue us? Tank soldiers have canvas trousers with
thick pads on the knees, but we got thin cotton overalls. The ground
there was half mixed with metal, stones were sticking up everywhere—so again we went around ragged, because we didn't sit in the
tank, but crawled outside on the ground. Tanks often burned. A tank
soldier, if he survives, is all covered with burns. We, too, used to get
burned, because to pull them out of burning tanks we had to go into
the fire. It's very hard to get a man through the hatch, especially a tur-
ret gunner. A dead man is heavier than a living one. Much heavier. I
learned all that quickly . . .

We were untrained, didn't understand who was which rank, and the sergeant major kept teaching us that we were now real soldiers, had to salute anyone of higher rank, and go about trim, with buttoned overcoats.

The soldiers, seeing we were such young girls, liked to make fun of us. Once I was sent from the medical platoon to get some tea. I came to the cook. He looked at me.

"What have you come for?"

I say, "T-tea . . ."

"The tea isn't ready yet."

"Why not?"

"The cooks are washing in the cauldrons. Once they're done washing, we'll make tea . . ."

I believed him. I took it quite seriously, picked up my buckets, and went back. I met the doctor.

"Why are you coming back empty-handed? Where's the tea?"

"The cooks are washing in the cauldrons," I answered. "The tea isn't ready yet."

He clutched his head. "Which cooks are washing in the cauldrons?"

He went back with me, gave that cook a good going-over, and they poured me two buckets of tea.

I was carrying this tea, and I met the head of the political section and the commander of the brigade. I remembered at once how they taught us that we had to salute everybody, because we were rank-and-file soldiers. And here there are two of them. How am I to greet them both? I tried to decide as I went. When I came up to them, I set the buckets down, put both hands to my visor, and saluted the two of them. They had been walking along without noticing me, but when I did that they froze in astonishment.

"Who taught you to salute that way?"

"The sergeant major. He said we were to salute everybody. And there were two of you coming at once . . ."

For us girls, everything in the army was difficult. It was very hard for us to sort out the different insignia. When we came to the army, there were still diamonds, cubes, stripes, so just try figuring out what his rank is. They say, "Take this letter to the captain." And how can I tell he's a captain? The word itself slips out of your mind on the way. I go.

"Sir, the other sir told me to give you this . . ."

"What other sir?"

"The one who always wears a soldier's shirt. Without a tunic."

What we remembered was not whether this or that officer was a lieutenant or a captain, but whether he was handsome or not, redheaded, tall . . . "Ah, him, the tall one!" Of course, when I saw singed overalls, burned hands, burned faces . . . I . . . It's astonishing . . . I lost the ability to cry . . . The gift of tears, the woman's gift . . . When tank soldiers jumped out of burning vehicles, everything on them was burning. Smoking. They often had broken arms or legs. Those were very badly wounded. A man would lie there and ask, "If I die, write to my mother, write to my wife . . ." And I wasn't able. I didn't know how to tell someone about death . . .

When the tank soldiers picked me up with my legs crippled and brought me to a Ukrainian village—it was in the Kirovograd region— the woman who owned the cottage that housed the medical platoon kept repeating, "What a young lad!"

The tank soldiers laughed. "What do you mean 'lad,' granny, she's a girl!"

She sat down beside me and looked me over. "What do you mean 'girl'? That's not a girl. It's a young lad . . ."

My hair was cut short, I was wearing overalls, a tank helmet—a lad. She yielded me her warm place over the stove and even slaughtered a young pig, so I'd recover more quickly. And she kept pitying me. "Don't they have enough men, that they recruit such children? . . . Little girls? . . ."

From her words, her tears . . . I lost all courage for a while, I felt so sorry for myself, and for mama. What am I doing here among men? I'm a girl. What if I come home with no legs? I had all kinds of thoughts . . . Yes, I did . . . I don't conceal it . . .

At the age of eighteen, at the Kursk Bulge, I was awarded the medal "For Distinguished Service" and the Order of the Red Star; at nineteen, the Order of the Patriotic War, second degree. When fresh reinforcements arrived, all of them young boys, they were surprised, of course. They were also eighteen or nineteen, and sometimes they asked me mockingly, "What did you get your medals for?" or "Have you been in combat?" Or they would taunt me: "Can a bullet pierce the armor of a tank?"

One of them I later bandaged on the battlefield, under fire, and I even remember his last name—Shchegolevatykh. He had a broken leg. I was putting a splint on it, and he asked my forgiveness.

"Forgive me, dear nurse, for offending you that time. To be honest, I liked you."

What did we know about love then? If there was anything, it was a schooltime love, and schooltime love is still childish. I remember we once fell into an encirclement . . . We dug into the ground with our own hands, we had nothing else. No shovels . . . Nothing . . . We were pressed on all sides. We had already decided: that night we would either break through or die. We thought most likely we would die . . . I don't know if I should tell about this or not. I don't know . . .

We camouflaged ourselves. We sat there. We waited for night so as to try and break through somehow. And Lieutenant Misha T.— he was replacing our wounded battalion commander, he was about twenty—began to recall how he loved to dance, to play the guitar. Then he asked, "Have you tried it?"

"What? Tried what?" I was terribly hungry.

"Not what, but who . . . I mean baba!"*

Before the war there was a pastry called "baba."

"No-o-o . . ."

And I never had. We might die and not even know what love is like . . . We'd be killed that night . . .

* "Baba" is both a pastry and a familiar spoken Russian word for "woman."

"Oh, come on, you fool!" Then I finally understood what he meant.

We went to die for life, without knowing what life was. We had only read about it in books. I liked movies about love . . .

Medical assistants in tank units died quickly. There was no room provided for us in a tank; you had to hang on to the armor plating, and the only thought was to avoid having your legs drawn into the caterpillar tread. And we had to watch for burning tanks . . . To jump down and run or crawl there . . . We were five girlfriends at the front: Liuba Yasinskaya, Shura Kiseleva, Tonya Bobkova, Zina Latysh, and me. The tank soldiers called us the Konakovo girls. And all the girls were killed . . .

Before the battle in which Liuba Yasinskaya was killed, she and I sat in the evening hugging each other. We talked. It was 1943. Our division was approaching the Dnieper. She suddenly said to me, "You know, I'll be killed in this battle. I have some sort of premonition. I went to the sergeant major, asked to be issued new underwear, and he turned stingy: 'You got some just recently.' Let's go in the morning and ask together."

I tried to calm her down: "We've been fighting for two years; by now bullets are afraid of us." But in the morning she persuaded me to go to the sergeant major anyway, and we got him to give us new sets of underwear. So there she was in this new undershirt. Snow white, with laces . . . It was all soaked in blood . . . This white and red together, with crimson blood—I remember it to this day. That was how she had imagined it.

The four of us carried her together on a tarpaulin, she'd become so heavy. We lost many in that battle. We dug a big common grave. We put them all in it, without coffins, as usual, and Liuba on top. I still couldn't grasp that she was no longer with us, that I would never see her again. I wanted to take at least something from her to remember her by. She had a ring on her finger, gold or something cheap—I don't know. I took it. The boys held me back: don't you dare, it's bad luck.

But when we were taking leave of her, and each one threw a handful of earth into the grave, I threw some, too, and the ring fell off with it into the grave . . . to Liuba. Then I remembered that she loved that ring very much . . .

Her father went through the whole war and came back alive. Her brother, too. The men of her family came back . . . But Liuba was killed . . .

Shura Kiseleva . . . She was the prettiest of us. Like an actress. She got burned up. She hid the badly wounded among the hayricks, shelling began, the hay caught fire. Shura could have saved herself, but she would have had to abandon the wounded . . . She burned up with them . . .

I found out the details of Tonya Bobkova's death only recently. She shielded the man she loved from a mine fragment. The fragments take a fraction of a second to reach you . . . How did she have time? She saved Lieutenant Petya Boichevsky, she loved him. And he survived.

Thirty years later Petya Boichevsky came from Krasnodar. Found me. And told me all about it. He and I went to Borisov and found the clearing where Tonya was killed. He took some earth from her grave . . . Carried it and kissed it . . .

There were five of us girls from Konakovo . . . But I alone came back to mama.

Unexpectedly for me, Nina Yakovlevna bursts into poetry:

> A brave girl leaps onto the armor plating,
> And she defends her Motherland.
> She's not afraid of bullets or shells—
> Her heart is all aflame.
> Remember, friend, her modest beauty,
> When her body's borne away . . .

She confesses that she composed it at the front. I already know that many of them wrote verses at the front. Even now they are carefully copied out and kept in family archives—artless and touching. Hence their war albums—and they show me albums in every home—often resemble girls' diaries. Only there it's about love, and here it's about death.

I have a close-knit family. A good family. Children, grandchildren . . . But I live in the war, I'm there all the time . . . Ten years ago I tracked down our friend Vanya Pozdnyakov. We thought he had been killed, but it turned out he was alive. His tank—he was a commander—was destroyed by two German tanks at Prokhorovka, and they set fire to it. The crew were all killed, only Vanya was left—without eyes, burned all over. We sent him to the hospital, but we didn't think he would live. There wasn't a living spot on him. All his skin . . . all . . . It came off in big pieces . . . Peeled off. I found his address thirty years later . . . half a lifetime . . . I remember going up the stairs, my legs giving way under me: was it him or wasn't it? He opened the door himself, touched my face with his hands, recognized me: "Ninka, is it you? Is it you?" Imagine, after so many years he recognized me.

His mother is a little old woman, he lives with her; she sat with us at the table and cried. I was surprised.

"Why are you crying? You should rejoice that companions at arms have met again."

She replied, "My three sons went to the war. Two were killed; Vanya alone came home alive."

Vanya lost both eyes. She's been leading him by the hand ever since.

I asked him, "Vanya, the last thing you saw was that field at Prokhorovka, the tank battle . . . What do you remember of that day?"

And do you know what he answered?

"I regret only one thing: that I gave the command for the crew to leave the burning vehicle too early. The boys died anyway. But we could have destroyed one more German tank . . ."

That's what he regrets . . . To this day . . .

He and I were happy during the war . . . No word had been spoken between us yet. Nothing. But I remember . . .

Why was I left alive? What for? I think . . . As I understand, it's in order to tell about it . . .

My meeting with Nina Yakovlevna had a sequel, but in writing. Having transcribed her account from the tape recorder and chosen what astonished and impressed me most, I sent her a copy, as I had promised. Several weeks later a weighty registered package came from Moscow. I opened it: newspaper clippings, articles, official reports about military and patriotic work conducted by the war veteran Nina Yakovlevna Vishnevskaya in Moscow schools. The material I had sent was also returned; very little was left of it—a lot had been crossed out: the amusing lines about the cooks who washed in the cauldrons, and even the harmless: "Sir, the other sir told me to give you this . . ." had been removed. And in the margins of the story about Lieutenant Misha T. stood three indignant question marks and a note: "I am a heroine for my son. A deity! What is he going to think of me after this?"

More than once afterward I met with these two truths that live in the same human being: one's own truth driven underground, and the common one, filled with the spirit of the time. The smell of newspapers. The first was rarely able to resist the massive onslaught of the second. If, for instance, besides the storyteller, there was some family member or friend in the apartment, or a neighbor (especially a man), she would be less candid and confiding than if it was just the two of us. It would be a conversation for the public. For an audience. That would make it impossible to break through to her personal impressions; I would immediately discover strong inner defenses. Self-control. Constant correction. And a pattern even emerged: the more listeners, the more passionless and sterile the account. To make it suit the stereotype. The dreadful would look grand, and the incomprehensible and obscure in a human being would be instantly explained. I would find myself in a desert of the past, filled with nothing but monuments.

Great deeds. Proud and impervious. So it was with Nina Yakovlevna: one war she remembered for me—"like a daughter, so you'll understand what we mere girls had to live through." The other was meant for a big audience—"the way other people tell and they write in the newspapers—about heroes and great deeds, so as to educate the youth with lofty examples." I was struck each time by this mistrust of what is simple and human, by the wish to replace life with an ideal. Ordinary warmth with a cold luster.

And I couldn't forget how we drank tea the family way, in the kitchen. And how we both wept.

"TWO WARS LIVE IN
OUR HOUSE . . ."

———

A gray cinder-block house on Kakhovskaya Street in Minsk. Half of our city has been built over with these nondescript high-rises, which turn gloomier by the year. But all the same this one is special. "Two wars are living here in our one apartment," I will hear, when the door is opened. Sergeant Major First Class Olga Vasilyevna Podvyshenskaya fought in a naval unit in the Baltic. Her husband, Saul Genrikhovich, was a sergeant in the infantry.

Everything is repeated . . . Again I spend a long time studying the family albums, carefully and lovingly designed and always put on display for guests. And for themselves as well. Each of these albums has a title: Our Family, The War, The Wedding, The Children, The Grandchildren. I like this respect for their own lives, the well-documented love for what has been lived through. For dear faces. It is quite rare that I meet with such a sense of home, with people studying their forebears, their line, though I've already visited hundreds of apartments, been with various families—cultivated and simple. Urban and rural. Frequent wars and revolutions have probably broken our habit of maintaining a connection with the past, of lovingly weaving the family web. Of looking far back. Of taking pride. We hasten to forget, to wipe away the traces, because preserved facts can become evidence, often at the cost of life. No one knows anything further back than their grandparents; no one looks for their roots. They made history, but live for the day. On short memory.

But here it is different . . .

"Is this really me?" Olga Vasilyevna laughs and sits down beside me on the sofa. She takes the photograph in which she is wearing a sailor suit with combat

decorations. "*Each time I look at these photos, I get surprised. Saul showed them to our six-year-old granddaughter. She asked me: 'Grandma, you were a boy first, right?' "*

"*Olga Vasilyevna, did you go to the front at once?*"

My war began with evacuation . . . I left my home, my youth. On the way, our train was strafed, bombed; the planes flew very, very low. I remember how a group of boys from a vocational school jumped out of the train; they were all wearing black uniform jackets. Such a target! They were all shot. The planes flew just above ground . . . It felt as if they shot them and counted them off . . . Can you imagine?

We worked at a factory; they fed us there, it wasn't bad. But my heart was burning . . . I wrote letters to the recruitment office. One—a second—a third . . . In June of 1942 I was called up. We were transported to besieged Leningrad across Lake Ladoga on open barges under fire. Of my first day in Leningrad I remember the white night and a detachment of sailors marching in black uniforms. The atmosphere was tense, no one in the streets, only searchlights and sailors marching along wearing cartridge belts, like during the Civil War. Can you imagine? Something from a movie . . .

The city was completely encircled. The front was very close. Tram No. 3 took you to the Kirov factory, and the front began right there. When the weather was clear, there was artillery shelling. They pounded us with direct fire. Pounded, pounded, pounded . . . The big ships moored by the pier were camouflaged, of course, but even so the possibility of a hit was not excluded. We became smoke-screeners. A special unit of smoke camouflage was organized, commanded by a former commander of the division of torpedo boats, Captain Lieutenant Alexander Bogdanov. The girls mostly had secondary technical education or else one or two years of university. Our task was to protect the ships by covering them with smoke. When the shelling began, the sailors would say: "The girls better hurry up and hang the smoke. It feels safer." We went there in vehicles with a special mixture, while everybody was hiding in bomb shelters. In a way, we called the shelling down on ourselves. The Germans shelled this smoke screen . . .

We ate "siege" food, you know, but somehow we bore with it . . . Well, first of all, a matter of youth, that's important, and, second, we had the Leningraders for comparison. We were at least somehow provided for, there was some food, though minimal, but they collapsed from weakness. They died walking. Several children came to us, and we fed them a little from our meager rations. They weren't children, they were some sort of little old people. Mummies. They told us their siege menu, if I can call it that: soup made from leather belts or new leather shoes, aspic made from woodworker's glue, pancakes made from mustard . . . All the cats and dogs in the city had been eaten. The sparrows and magpies had disappeared. Even mice and rats were caught and eaten . . . They fried them somehow . . . Then the children stopped coming, and we waited a long time for them. They probably died. So I think . . . In winter, when Leningrad remained without heating, we were sent to break up the houses in one of the areas where wooden buildings still stood. The most painful moment was when you came up to the house . . . There stood a fine house, but the owners had either died or left, but most often had died. You could tell by the dishes left on the table, by the belongings. For maybe half an hour nobody could raise a crowbar. Can you imagine? We all stood and waited for something. Only when the commander came up and drove in his crowbar could we start knocking it down.

We did logging; we lugged boxes of ammunition. I remember I was dragging one box and fell flat on my face: it was heavier than I was. That was one thing. A second was how hard it was for us as women. Later on I became commander of a section. The section was all young boys. We spent the whole day on a motorboat. The boat was small, and there was no head on it. The boys could do the necessary overboard, and that was that. But what about me? A couple of times I held myself back so long that I just jumped overboard and swam around. They shouted: "Sergeant Major overboard!" And they pulled me out. That's such an elementary trifle . . . But was it such a trifle? I later had to be treated . . . Can you imagine? And the weight of the weapons? Also too heavy for a woman. They began by giving us rifles, and the rifles were taller than we were. Girls walked along, and the bayonets stuck two feet above their heads.

It was easier for men to adjust to it all. To that ascetic life . . . To those relationships . . . But we missed, we missed terribly our homes, our mothers, our comforts. There was a Muscovite among us, Natasha Zhilina; she received a medal "For Courage," and as a bonus she got leave to go home for a few days. When she came back we sniffed her. We literally lined up and sniffed her. We said she smelled like home. We missed home so much . . . We were so overjoyed at the mere sight of an envelope with a letter . . . In papa's handwriting . . . If there happened to be a moment of leisure, we embroidered something, some sort of handkerchiefs. They issued us footwraps, and we made scarves out of them and tied them on our necks. We wanted to do some women's work. There wasn't enough women's work for us; it was simply unbearable. You looked for any pretext to pick up a needle, to mend something, to take back your natural image at least for a time. Of course there was joy and laughter, but all that was not like before the war. It was some peculiar state . . .

The tape recorder records the words, preserves the intonation. The pauses. The weeping and embarrassment. I realize that, when a person speaks, something more takes place than what remains on paper. I keep regretting that I cannot "record" eyes, hands. Their life during the conversation, their own life. Separate. Their "texts."

"We have two wars here . . . That's just it . . ." Saul Genrikhovich enters the conversation. "We begin to remember, and I have the feeling that she remembers her war and I mine. I, too, had something like what she told about the house, or how they lined up to smell the girl who came from home. But I don't remember it . . . It flitted past me . . . It seemed like a trifle at the time. Nonsense. But she didn't tell you about the sailor caps yet . . . Olya, how could you forget such a thing?"

"I didn't. It's the most . . . I'm always afraid to call this story up from my memory. Each time . . . It was like this—at dawn our boats put out to sea. Several dozen of them . . . Soon we heard the battle begin. We waited . . . Listening . . . The battle lasted several hours, and there was a moment when it came very close to the city. But it died down somewhere nearby. Before evening I went to the shore: there were sailor caps floating down the Morskoy Canal. One after another. Sailor caps and big red stains on the waves . . . Splinters of wood . . . Our boys had been thrown into the water somewhere. As long as I stood there, these sailor caps kept floating by. I began to count them, but then I stopped. I couldn't leave and I couldn't look. The Morskoy Canal became a common grave . . ."

"Saul, where's my handkerchief? I just had it in my hands . . . Well, where is it?"

"I memorized many of her stories and 'tagged' them, as they now say, for the grandchildren. Often I tell them not about my war, but about hers. I noticed it's more interesting for them," Saul Genrikhovich continues. "I have more specific military knowledge, but she has more feelings. And feelings are always more intense, they're always stronger than facts. We also had girls in the infantry. As soon as one of them appeared among us, we pulled ourselves together. You can't imagine . . . You can't!" He catches himself. "I also picked up that little word from her. But you can't imagine how good it is to hear a woman's laughter at war! A woman's voice.

"Was there love in the war? There was! The women we met there are excellent wives. Faithful companions. Those who married in the war are the happiest people, the happiest couples. We, too, fell in love with each other at the front. Amid fire and death. That makes for a strong bond. There were other things, I won't deny it, because it was a long war and there were many of us in it. But I mostly remember what was bright. Noble.

"I became better in the war . . . Unquestionably! I became better as a human being, because in war there is a lot of suffering. I saw a lot of suffering and I suffered a lot myself. There what's not most important in life is immediately swept aside, it's superfluous. There you understand that . . . But the war took its revenge on us. But . . . We're afraid to admit it to ourselves . . . It caught up with us . . . Not all our daughters' personal lives worked out well. And here's why: their mothers, who were at the front, raised them the way they themselves were raised at the front. And the fathers, too. According to the same moral code. At the front, as I've already said, you see at once how a person is, what he's worth. You can't hide there. Their girls couldn't imagine that life could be different than in their homes. They had not been warned about the world's cruel underside. And these girls, getting married, easily fell into the hands of swindlers, who deceived them, because it was all too easy to deceive them. This happened with many children of our friends from the front. And with our daughter, too . . ."

"For some reason we didn't tell our children about the war. We were probably afraid and took pity on them. Were we right?" Olga Vasilyevna ponders. "I didn't wear my ribbons. There was an occasion when I tore them off and never pinned them on again. After the war I worked as a director of a bread-baking factory. I came to a meeting and my superior, also a woman, saw my ribbons and said in front of everybody: 'Why have you pinned them on like a man?' She herself had the Order of Labor, and she always wore it, but for some reason she disliked my military decorations. When we were alone in the office, I explained it all to her in sailor fashion. She was embarrassed, but I did lose the wish to wear the decorations. I still don't pin them on. Though I'm proud of them.

"It was only decades later that the well-known journalist Vera Tkachenko wrote about us in the central newspaper *Pravda,* about the fact that women were also in the war. And that there are frontline women who have remained single, have not arranged their lives, and still have nowhere to live. And that we were in debt to these saintly women. And then little by little people began to pay more attention to these frontline women. They were forty or fifty years old, and they lived in dormitories. Finally they began to give them individual apartments. My friend . . . I won't mention her name, she might suddenly get offended . . . An army paramedic . . . Wounded three times. When the war ended, she studied in medical school. She had no family; they had all been killed. She lived in great want, had to scrub floors at night for a living. She didn't want to tell anybody that she was an invalid and was entitled to benefits. She tore up all her certificates. I asked her: 'Why did you tear them up?' She wept: 'And who would have married me?' 'Well, so,' I said, 'you did the right thing.' And she wept still louder: 'Those papers would be very useful to me now. I'm very ill . . . ' Can you imagine? She wept.

"To celebrate the thirty-fifth anniversary of the Victory a hundred sailors were invited to Sevastopol, the city of Russian naval glory— veterans of the Great Patriotic War from all the fleets, and among them three women. My friend and I were two of them. And the admiral of the fleet bowed to each of us, thanked us before everybody, and kissed our hands. How can I forget it?!"

"And would you like to forget the war?"

"Forget? Forget . . ." Olga Vasilyevna repeats my question.

"We're unable to forget it. It's not in our power." Saul Genrikhovich breaks the prolonged pause. "Remember, Olya, on Victory Day, we met an old, old mother, who had a little old poster hanging on her neck: 'Looking for Kulnev, Tomas Vladimirovich, reported missing in 1942 in besieged Leningrad.' You could tell by her face that she was well over eighty. How many years has she been looking for him? And she'll go on looking till her last hour. We're the same."

"And I'd like to forget. I want to . . ." Olga Vasilyevna utters slowly, almost in a whisper. "I want to live at least one day without the war. Without our memory of it . . . At least one day . . ."

I remember the two of them together, as in the wartime pictures, one of which they gave me. They're young in them, much younger than I am now. At once everything acquires a different meaning. It comes closer. I look at these young photos and already hear differently what I had just heard and recorded. The time between us disappears.

"TELEPHONES DON'T
SHOOT . . ."

———

They all meet me and talk to me differently . . .

Some start telling their story at once, while still on the phone: "I remember . . . I keep it all in my memory as if it was yesterday . . ." Others put off the meeting and the conversation for a long time: "I have to prepare myself . . . I don't want to wind up in that hell again . . ." Valentina Pavlovna Chudaeva is one of those who was fearful for a long time, reluctant to let me into her troubled world. For several months I called her every now and then, but one day we talked on the phone for two hours and finally decided to meet. At once—the very next day.

And so—here I am . . .

"We'll eat pies. I've been fussing about since morning . . ." the hostess greets me cheerfully on the threshold. "We can talk later. And weep our fill . . . I've lived with my grief for a long time . . . But first of all—the pies. With bird cherry. Like we make in Siberia. Come in.

"Forgive me for addressing you informally. It's a frontline habit: 'Hey girls! Come on, girls!' We're all like that, you know by now . . . You've heard . . . We haven't acquired any crystal, as you see. All that my husband and I have squirreled away fits into a tin candy box: a couple of orders and medals. They're in the cupboard, I'll show you later." She takes me inside. "The furniture's old, too, you see. We'd be sorry to get rid of it. When things live in the house for a long time, they acquire a soul. I believe that."

She introduces me to her friend Alexandra Fyodorovna Zenchenko, a Komsomol worker in besieged Leningrad.

I sit down at the set table . . . Well, so, if it's pies, let it be pies, the more so if they're Siberian, with bird cherry, which I had never tried before.

Three women. Hot pies. But the conversation immediately turns to the war.

"Only don't interrupt her with questions," Alexandra Fyodorovna warns me. "If she stops, she starts crying . . . And after the tears, she'll say nothing . . . So don't interrupt . . ."

Valentina Pavlovna Chudaeva

SERGEANT, COMMANDER OF ANTIAIRCRAFT ARTILLERY

I'm from Siberia . . . What prompted me, a girl from far-off Siberia, to go to the front? From the end of the world, as they call it. Concerning the end of the world, a French journalist asked me that question at a meeting. He looked at me so intently in the museum, I even became embarrassed. What does he want? Why does he stare like that? Then he came up and asked through the interpreter to have an interview with Mrs. Chudaeva. I, of course, became very nervous. I thought: Well, what does he want? Hadn't he listened to me at the museum? But he was evidently not interested in that. The first thing I heard from him was a compliment: "You look so young today . . . How could you have gone through the war?" I answered him: "That proves, as you see, that we were very young when we went to the front." But he was wondering about something else: how did I get to the front from Siberia—it was the end of the world! "No," I figured out, "evidently you're wondering why I, a schoolgirl, would go to the front, if there was no general mobilization." He nodded his head "Yes." "Very well," I said, "I'll answer that question." And I told him my whole life, as I'm going to tell it to you. He wept . . . The Frenchman wept . . . In the end he confessed, "Don't be offended, Mrs. Chudaeva. For the French, World War I caused a greater shock than World War II. We remember it; there are graves and monuments everywhere. But we know little about you. Today many people, especially the young, think it was only America that defeated Hitler. Little is known about the price the Soviet people paid for the victory—twenty million human lives in four years. And about your sufferings. Immeasurable. I thank you—you have shaken my heart."

. . . I don't remember my mother. She died young. My father was a representative of the Novosibirsk local party committee. In 1925 they sent him to his native village to get bread. There was great want in the country, and the kulaks hid the bread and let it rot. I was nine months old then. My mother wanted to go to the village with my father, and he took her along. She took me and my sister, because she had no one to leave us with. Papa once worked as a farmhand for that kulak, whom he threatened at the evening meeting: "We know where you hide the bread. If you don't hand it over yourself, we'll come and take it by force. We'll take it in the name of the revolutionary cause."

The meeting ended, and the family all gathered together. Papa had five brothers. Afterward none of them came back from the Great Patriotic War, and neither did my father. So they all sat down at the festive table—traditional Siberian dumplings. The benches stood along the windows . . . My mother sat between windows, one shoulder by a window, the other by my father, and my father sat where there was no window. It was April . . . At that time in Siberia you can still have frosts. Mother must have been cold. I understood that later, when I grew up. She stood up, threw father's leather jacket over her shoulders, and began to nurse me. At that moment a rifle shot rang out. They were aiming at my father, at his leather coat . . . Mother only managed to say "Pa . . ." and dropped me onto the hot dumplings . . . She was twenty-four years old . . .

Later my grandfather was chairman of the village council in that village. He was poisoned with strychnine; they put it in his water. I've kept a photograph of my grandfather's funeral. There is a cloth draped over his coffin with the inscription "Died at the hands of the class enemy."

My father was a hero of the Civil War, commander of an armored train, which fought against the rebellion of a Czechoslovakian corps. In 1931 he was awarded the Order of the Red Banner. At the time very few people were given that order, especially in Siberia. It was a great honor, and was greatly respected. My father was wounded nineteen times; there wasn't an unhurt place on his body. My mother told— not me, of course, but our relatives—that the White Czechs sentenced my father to twenty years of hard labor. She requested a meeting with him; at the time she was in the last month of pregnancy with Tasya, my older sister. There was such a long corridor in that prison, and they didn't let her walk down it to my father, they said, "Crawl, Bolshevik scum!" And she, just days before giving birth, crawled to my father along this long cement corridor. That's how they had their meeting. She didn't recognize my father; his hair was all gray. A gray-haired old man. He was thirty.

Could I sit there indifferently when the enemy again came to my land, if I had grown up in such a family, with such a father? I was of his blood . . . his dear blood. He had lived through so much . . . He was denounced in 1937; they wanted to slander him. To make him out as an enemy of the people. Well, there were those horrible Stalin purges . . . Yezhovshchina* . . . As Comrade Stalin said, when you chop wood, the chips fly. A new class struggle was proclaimed, so the country never stopped living in fear. In submission. But my father managed to be received by Kalinin,† and his good name was restored. Everybody knew my father.

My relatives told me about these things afterward . . .

And now it's 1941 . . . My last school bell just rang. We all had our plans, our dreams, we were young girls. After the commencement ball, we went for a boat ride down the river Ob to an island. So cheerful, happy . . . As yet unkissed, as they say. I'd never even had a boyfriend. We met the dawn on the island and went back . . . The whole city is seething; people are weeping. All around they repeat, "War!

---

* Nikolai Yezhov (1895–1940) was head of the NKVD and directed the Great Purge of 1936 to 1938, which was called "Yezhovshchina" ("Yezhov's thing") after him.

† Mikhail Kalinin (1875–1946), an early Bolshevik and close ally of Stalin's, became chairman of the All-Russian Central Executive Committee in 1919, a position he held until his retirement in 1946.

War!" Radios are turned on everywhere. We couldn't fathom it. What war? We were so happy, we had made such grandiose plans: who was going to study where, to become what. And suddenly—war! The grown-ups wept, but we weren't afraid; we assured each other that within a month we'd "beat the fascists' brains out." We sang prewar songs. Our army would certainly crush the enemy on their own territory . . . There wasn't a shadow of doubt . . . Not a shred . . .

We began to understand it all when death notices started to come back. I simply got sick: "So it was all lies?" The Germans were already preparing to parade on Red Square . . .

My father was not taken to the front. But he stubbornly haunted the recruiting office. Later my father went. And that with his health, his gray hair, his lungs: he had chronic tuberculosis. Just doctored a bit. And at what age? But he went. He joined the Steel Division, or Stalin Division, as it was called.* There were many Siberians in it. We also thought that without us the war wasn't right, that we, too, had to fight. Give us weapons at once! Our whole class ran to the recruiting office. On October 10 I left for the front. My stepmother cried a lot: "Valya, don't go . . . What are you doing? You're so small, so thin, what kind of fighter are you?" I had been rachitic for a long time, a very long time. It happened after my mother was killed. I didn't walk till I was five . . . Where did all this strength come from!?

We rode in freight cars for two months. Two thousand girls, a whole train. A Siberian train. What did we see as we approached the front? I remember one moment . . . I'll never forget it: a broken-down train station and sailors hopping about the platform on their hands. They had no legs or crutches. They walked on their hands . . . The platform was full of them . . . They also smoked . . . They saw us and laughed. Joked. My heart went thump-thump . . . Thump-thump . . . What are we getting into? Where are we going? We sang to cheer ourselves up, sang a lot.

There were commanders with us. They instructed us, encouraged

---

*   Stalin took his name from the Russian word сталь, "steel."

us. We studied communications. We arrived in Ukraine, and there we were shelled for the first time. Just when we were in the bathhouse for decontamination. When we came to wash, there was a man on duty there, in charge of the bathhouse. We felt shy with him there; well, we were girls, quite young ones. But once the shelling began, we all clung to him for safety. We got dressed any old way, I wrapped my head with a towel, I had a red towel, and we ran outside. A first lieutenant, also young, shouted, "Run to the shelter, girl! Drop that towel! It breaks cover . . ."

I ran away from him: "I'm not breaking any cover! Mama told me not to go out with a wet head."

He found me after the shelling: "Why didn't you obey me? I'm your commander."

I didn't believe him. "That's all I need, you as my commander . . ."

I argued with him like a kid. We were the same age.

We were issued big, thick overcoats. We were like wheat sheaves in them; we didn't walk, we waddled. At first there were no boots for us. What they had were men's sizes. Then they issued us other boots: the foot part was red, and the upper was black tarpaulin. We strutted around in them! We were all skinny; the men's army shirts hung loose on us. Those who could sew tailored them somehow. But we were girls; that wasn't enough for us! So the first lieutenant started taking measurements. We laughed and cried. The battalion commander came: "Well, has the first lieutenant issued you all your women's things?" The lieutenant says, "Measurements taken. They'll get everything."

And I became a radio operator in an antiaircraft unit. On duty at the command point, in communications. And maybe I would have stayed on as a radio operator for the rest of the war, if I hadn't received a notice that my father had been killed. My beloved papa was no more. The closest person I had. The only one. I started begging, "I want revenge. I want to pay them back for my father's death." I wanted to kill . . . I wanted to shoot . . . They tried to tell me that the telephone was very important in the artillery. But telephones don't shoot . . . I submitted a request to the commander of the regiment. He refused. Then, without thinking twice, I addressed myself to the commander of the division. Colonel Krasnykh came to us, lined us all up, and asked, "Where is the girl who wants to be a gun commander?" I stepped forward: thin, skinny neck, and on that neck a submachine gun hanging, a heavy submachine gun, seventy-one cartridges . . . I was obviously such a pathetic sight that he even smiled. Second question: "What do you want?" I said, "I want to shoot." I don't know what he thought. He said nothing for a long time. Not a word. Then turned sharply and left. "Well," I thought, "that's it, he'll refuse." The commander came running: "The colonel has given his permission . . ."

Do you understand that? Can it be understood now? I want you to understand my feelings . . . You can't shoot unless you hate. It's a war, not a hunt. I remember at political classes they read us the article "Kill Him!" by Ilya Ehrenburg.* As many times as you meet a German, so many times you kill him. A famous article, everybody read it then, learned it by heart. It made a strong impression on me. I carried it in my bag all through the war, that article and papa's death notice . . . Shoot! Shoot! I had to take revenge . . .

I completed a short-term course, very short-term—three months of studies. I learned to shoot. And I became an artillery commander. They sent me to the 1357th Antiaircraft Regiment. At first I kept bleeding from the nose and ears, my stomach was completely upset . . . My throat was so dry I was nauseous . . . At night it wasn't too bad, but in daytime it was very frightening. It seemed the plane was flying straight at you, precisely at your gun. About to ram you! Another moment and it would reduce you to nothing. It's all over! That wasn't for a young girl . . . Not for her ears, not for her eyes . . . First we had the eighty-five millimeters. They proved good around Moscow. Then they were sent against tanks, and we were given thirty-seven millime-

---

* Ilya Ehrenburg (1891–1967) was a prolific Soviet writer and journalist. His article "Kill Him!" (the actual title was simply "Kill!"), published in 1942, was widely read.

ters. That was at the Rzhevsk front . . .* There were such battles there . . . In spring the ice began to break up on the Volga . . . and what did we see? We saw a red-and-black ice block floating along, and on it two or three Germans and one Russian soldier . . . They had perished like that, clutching each other. They were frozen into this ice block, and the ice block was all bloody. All our Mother Volga was bloody . . .

She suddenly stopped. "I need to catch my breath . . . Or else I'll start sobbing, and our meeting will be ruined . . ." She turned to the window to get control of herself. A moment later she was already smiling. "Honestly, I don't like to cry. As a child I learned not to cry . . ."

"And listening to Valya, I remembered besieged Leningrad." *Alexandra Fyodorovna, who had been silent till then, entered the conversation.* "Especially one incident that astounded us all. They told us about an old woman who opened her window every day and threw water out with a dipper, and each time she managed to throw it further and further. First we thought: well, she's probably crazy, all sorts of things happened during the siege, and we went to her to find out what was the matter. Listen to what she said to us: 'If the fascists come to Leningrad, and set foot on my street, I'll scald them with boiling water. I'm old, there's nothing else I can do, so I'll scald them with boiling water.' And she practiced . . . Every day . . . The siege had just begun, there was still hot water . . . She was a very cultivated woman. I even remember her face.

"She chose a way of fighting for which she was still strong enough. Imagine that moment. The enemy was already close to the city, combat went on at the Narva Gates, the Kirov Factory was being shelled . . . Each person thought of doing something to defend the city. To die was too easy; you had to do something. To act. Thousands of people thought the same . . ."

"I want to find the words . . . How can I express it all?" *Valentina Pavlovna asked either us or herself.*

---

* The Rzhevsk front, around the town of Rzhev to the west of Moscow, was the scene of a series of battles from October 1941 to March 1943. The front came to be known as the "Rzhev meat grinder" owing to the immense loss of both military and civilian lives.

―――

I came back from the front crippled. I had been wounded in the back by shrapnel. The wound wasn't big, but I had been thrown way off into a snowdrift. And for several days I hadn't dried my felt boots. Maybe there wasn't enough firewood, or it wasn't my turn to dry them at night. Our stove was small, and there were many of us. Before they found me, my feet got badly frostbitten. I was obviously covered with snow, but I could breathe, and an opening formed itself in the snow . . . A sort of pipe . . . The first-aid dogs found me. They dug into the snow and took my ear-flapped hat. My death passport was in it; we all had these passports: which family members to inform, and where. They dug me out, put me on a tarpaulin, my jacket was soaked with blood . . . But nobody paid attention to my feet . . .

I spent six months in the hospital. They wanted to amputate my leg, amputate it above the knee, because gangrene was setting in. And here I turned a little fainthearted, I didn't want to go on living as a cripple. What should I live for? Who needs me? No father, no mother. A burden in life. Who needs a stump like me? I'll strangle myself . . . And I asked the nurse-aide for a big towel instead of a small one . . . They all teased me in the hospital: "And here's granny . . . Old granny's lying here." Because when the head of the hospital saw me for the first time, he asked: "Well, and how old are you?" I said quickly, "Nineteen . . . I'll be nineteen soon . . ." He laughed: "Oh! That's old, old. A ripe old age." So the nurse-aide Aunt Masha also teased me that way. She said to me, "I'll give you the towel, because they're preparing you for surgery. But I'll keep an eye on you. I don't like your look, girl. Have you got something naughty in mind?" I said nothing . . . But I saw it was true: they were preparing me for surgery. And I didn't know what surgery was, I had never once been under the knife, not like now, when my body's a geographical map, but I could guess. I hid the big towel under my pillow and waited till everybody left or fell asleep. We had iron beds. I thought I'd tie the towel to the bed and strangle myself. If I had strength enough. But Aunt Masha didn't leave my side all night. She saved my young life. She didn't sleep . . . She saved foolish me . . .

My ward doctor, a young lieutenant, went after the head doctor and asked, "Let me try. Let me try . . ." And the head doctor: "What are you going to try? One of her toes is already black. The girl's nineteen. She'll die because of you and me." It turned out that my ward doctor was against the surgery. He suggested another treatment, new at the time. To inject oxygen under the skin with a special needle. Oxygen nourishes . . . Well, I don't quite know how it works, I'm not a medic . . . And he, this young lieutenant, persuaded the head doctor. They didn't cut off my leg. They started using that treatment. And after two months I began to walk. With crutches, of course; my legs were like rags, no support at all. I saw them, but I didn't feel them. Then I learned to walk without the crutches. They congratulated me: you've been born for the second time. After the hospital I was supposed to rest. Rest how? Where? I had no one. I went back to my unit, to my gun. There I joined the Party. At the age of nineteen . . .

I met Victory Day in East Prussia. For two days it was quiet, there was no shooting, then in the middle of the night a sudden signal: "Alert!" We all jumped up. And there came a shout: "Victory! Capitulation!" Capitulation was all right, but victory—that really got to us. "The war's over! The war's over!" We all started firing whatever we had: submachine guns, pistols . . . We fired our gun . . . One wiped his tears, another danced: "I'm alive, I'm alive!" A third fell to the ground and embraced it, embraced the sand, the stones. Such joy . . . And I was standing there and I slowly realized: the war's over, and my papa will never come home. The war was over . . . The commander threatened later, "Well, there won't be any demobilization till the ammunition's paid for. What have you done? How many shells have you fired?" We felt as if there would always be peace on earth, that no one would ever want war, that all the bombs should be destroyed. Who needed them? We were tired of hatred. Tired of shooting.

How I wanted to go home! Even if papa wasn't there, and mama wasn't there. Home is something greater than the people who live in it, and greater than the house itself. It's something . . . a human being should have a home . . . But I bow down to my stepmother . . . She met me like a mother. I've called her mama ever since. She waited for me, waited so much. Although the hospital director had written that my leg had been amputated, that I'd be brought to her a cripple. He wanted to prepare her. He promised that I could stay with her for a while, and afterward I'd be taken away . . . But she wanted me to come home . . .

She waited for me . . . I resembled my father very much . . .

We left for the front at the age of eighteen or twenty and came back at twenty or twenty-four. First there was joy, but then fear: what were we going to do in civilian life? There was a fear of peaceful life . . . My girlfriends had managed to finish various institutes, but what about us? Unfit for anything, without any professions. All we knew was war, all we could do was war. I wanted to get rid of the war as quickly as possible. I hastily remade my uniform coat into a regular coat; I changed the buttons. Sold the tarpaulin boots at a market and bought a pair of shoes. When I put on a dress for the first time, I flooded myself with tears. I didn't recognize myself in the mirror. We had spent four years in trousers. There was no one I could tell that I had been wounded, that I had a concussion. Try telling it, and who will give you a job then, who will marry you? We were silent as fish. We never acknowledged to anybody that we had been at the front. We just kept in touch among ourselves, wrote letters. It was later that they began to honor us, thirty years later . . . to invite us to meetings . . . But back then we hid, we didn't even wear our medals. Men wore them, but not women. Men were victors, heroes, wooers, the war was theirs, but we were looked at with quite different eyes. Quite different . . . I'll tell you, they robbed us of the victory. They quietly exchanged it for ordinary women's happiness. Men didn't share the victory with us. It was painful . . . Incomprehensible . . . Because at the front men treated us marvelously well; they always protected us. I've never encountered such an attitude toward women in peaceful life. When we retreated, we'd lie down to rest on the bare ground, they stayed in their army shirts and gave us their overcoats: "The girls . . . The girls need to be covered . . ." They'd find a piece of cotton wool or a bandage somewhere: "Take it, you might need it . . ." They'd share a last little rusk. We saw and knew nothing but kindness and warmth during the war. And after the war? I'm silent . . . Silent . . . What keeps us from remembering? The unbearableness of the memories . . .

My husband and I arrived in Minsk. We had nothing, not even a sheet, or a mug, or a fork . . . Two overcoats, two army shirts. We found a good map, mounted on cotton fabric. We soaked it . . . it was a big map . . . This cotton was our first sheet. Later, when our daughter was born, we cut it up for diapers. This map . . . I still remember, it was a political map of the world . . . And our daughter slept in a suitcase . . . The plywood suitcase my husband brought from the front served as a cradle. Besides love there was nothing in the house. I'll say that . . . Once my husband came: "Let's go, I saw a discarded old sofa" . . . And we went to get the sofa—at night, so that nobody would see us. How we rejoiced over that sofa!

All the same we were happy. I now had so many girlfriends! It was a hard time, but we were never downcast. We'd get food with our coupons and call each other: "Come, I got some sugar. We'll have tea . . ." We had nothing over our heads, nothing under us, no rugs, no crystal, nothing . . . And we were happy. Happy because we were still alive. We talked, we laughed. We walked in the streets . . . I admired things all the time, though there was nothing to admire—broken stones all around, even the trees were crippled. But we were warmed by the feeling of love. People somehow needed people; we all needed each other very much then. It was later that we separated, each on his own, in his own home, his own family, but then we were still together. Shoulder to shoulder, like in a trench at the front . . .

Now I'm often invited to meetings at the war museum . . . Asked to lead excursions. Yes, now. Forty years later! Forty! Recently I appeared before some young Italians. They asked me questions: What kind of doctor treated me? What were my illnesses? For some reason they wanted to know whether I consulted a psychiatrist. And what sort of dreams did I have? Did I dream about the war? A Russian woman who fought with weapons was a riddle to them. Who is this woman who not only saved people and bandaged wounds, but herself shot guns and blew things up . . . Killed men . . . They were also interested in whether I was married. They were sure that I wasn't. That I was single. And I laughed, "Everybody brought trophies home from war, and I brought my husband . . . I have a daughter. Now my grandchildren are growing up . . ." I haven't told you about love . . . I won't be able to, my heart isn't strong enough. Some other time . . . There was love! There was! Can a human being live without love? Survive without love? Our battalion commander fell in love with me at the front . . . During the whole war he protected me, wouldn't let anyone go near me, but once he was demobilized he sought me out in the hospital. Then he declared himself . . . Well, about love later . . . You come, be sure to come. You'll be my second daughter . . . Of course, I dreamed of having many children, I love children. But I have only one daughter . . . My dear daughter . . . I had no health, no strength. And I couldn't study—I was often sick. My feet, always my feet . . . They're my weak point . . . Before I retired I worked as a technician in the Polytechnical Institute. Everybody liked me, professors and students. Because there was a lot of love in me, a lot of joy. That's how I understood life, that's how I wanted to live after the war. God didn't make us for shooting, He made us for love. What do you think?

Two years ago our chief of staff, Ivan Mikhailovich Grinko, visited me. He retired long ago. He sat at this same table. I also baked pies. He talked with my husband, reminisced . . . Mentioned our girls. And I burst into tears: "Honor, you say, respect. But those girls are almost all single. Unmarried. They live in communal apartments. Who pitied them? Defended them? Where did you all disappear to after the war? Traitors!!" In short, I ruined their festive mood . . .

The chief of staff was sitting where you are now. "Show me," he pounded his fist on the table, "show me who offended you. Just show him to me!" He asked my forgiveness. "I can't say anything to you,

Valya, I can only weep." But there's no need to pity us. We're proud. Let them rewrite history ten times. With Stalin or without Stalin. But this remains—we were victorious! And our sufferings. What we lived through. This isn't junk and ashes. This is our life.

Not a word more . . .

Before I leave she hands me a packet of pies. "They're Siberian. Special. You can't buy them in any store." I also get a long list of addresses and phone numbers. "They'll all be glad to see you. They're waiting. I'll explain to you: it's terrible to remember, but it's far more terrible not to remember."

Now I understand why they speak all the same . . .

"THEY AWARDED US
LITTLE MEDALS . . ."

———

Every morning I open my mailbox . . .

My personal mail resembles more and more the mail of a recruiting office or a museum. "Greetings from the women pilots of the Marina Raskova Air Regiment." "I am writing to you on behalf of the women partisans of the Zhelezniak Brigade." "The women of the Minsk Underground congratulate you . . . We wish you success in the work you are beginning . . ." "The privates of the Women's Field Bath-and-Laundry Detachment address you . . ." In all the time of my search I have had only a few desperate refusals: "No, it's like a terrible dream . . . I can't! I won't!" or "I don't want to remember! I don't want to! It took me so long to forget . . ."

I remember yet another letter, with no return address: "My husband, a chevalier of the Order of Glory, got ten years in the labor camps after the war . . . That is how the Motherland met her heroes. The victors! He had written in a letter to his university friend that he had difficulty being proud of our victory—our own and other people's land was covered with heaps of Russian corpses. Drowned in blood. He was immediately arrested . . . His epaulettes were torn off . . .

"He came back from Kazakhstan after Stalin's death . . . Sick. We have no children. I don't need to remember the war, I've been at war all my life . . ."

Not everyone ventures to write down their memories, and not everyone succeeds in entrusting to paper their feelings and thoughts. "Tears hamper me . . ." (A. Burakova, sergeant, radio operator). And so the correspondence, against my expectations, provides only addresses and new names.

V. Gromova
MEDICAL ASSISTANT

I have enough metal in me . . . I carry a fragment from a wound I received near Vitebsk in my lung, within an inch of my heart. A second fragment in the right lung. Two in the region of the stomach . . .

Here is my address . . . Come. I cannot write more, I don't see anything for my tears . . .

V. Voronova
TELEPHONE OPERATOR

I have no big decorations, only medals. I don't know whether you would be interested in my life, but I would like to tell it to somebody . . .

Alexandra Leontievna Boiko
FIRST LIEUTENANT, TANKMAN

My husband and I lived in the Far North, in Magadan. My husband worked as a driver, I as a ticket collector. As soon as the war began, we both asked to be sent to the front. We were told to work where we were needed. Then we sent a telegram addressed to Comrade Stalin, saying that we were contributing fifty thousand rubles (a lot of money at the time, it was all we had) to the construction of a tank, and we both wanted to go to the front. We received an expression of gratitude from the government. And in 1943 my husband and I were sent to the Chelyabinsk tank training school, which we finished as externs.

In that school they also assigned us a tank. We were both senior driver mechanics, and a tank needs only one. The superiors decided to appoint me commander of an IS-122 tank, and my husband a senior driver mechanic. We went through the whole war as far as Germany. Both wounded. Have decorations.

There were quite a few girl tankmen of medium-sized tanks, but I was the only one who worked on a heavy tank. I sometimes think it would be good if some writer wrote about my life. I do not know how to do it myself . . .

I. A. Levitsky

COMMANDER OF THE 5TH SECTION OF THE 784TH ANTIAIRCRAFT ARTILLERY REGIMENT

1942 . . . I was made commander of a section. The regimental commissar warned me, "Bear in mind, Captain, you are taking charge not of an ordinary section, but a 'girls' section. It is half made up of girls, and they require a special approach, special attention and care." I knew, of course, that girls served in the army, but I could not picture it very well to myself. We career officers were apprehensive of "the weaker sex" being involved in military affairs, which from time immemorial had been considered men's work. Well, nurses, let's say— that was a usual thing. They had already proved themselves in World War I, then in the Civil War. But what would girls do in the antiaircraft artillery, where they would have to carry very heavy shells? How to place them in a battery where there is only one dugout, and there are men in the crew? They have to sit for hours at the controls, and they are metal, and the seats are also metal, and that's not good for girls. Where, finally, would they wash and dry their hair? A mass of questions arose, it was such an unusual thing . . .

I started going around the batteries, taking a closer look. I confess, I felt a little out of sorts. A girl is standing guard with a rifle, a girl is on the watchtower with binoculars—and here I've come from the front, from the front line. And they were so different—bashful, timorous, mincing, or resolute, fired up. Not all of them knew how to submit to military discipline; women's nature resists army rules. She would forget what she had been ordered to do, or else she would receive a letter from home and spend the whole morning weeping. You punish them, and another time you cancel the punishment—out of pity. I kept thinking, "These people will be the end of me!" But soon I had to abandon all my doubts. The girls became real soldiers. We walked a hard path together. Do come. We'll have a long talk . . .

The most diverse addresses—Moscow, Kiev, the town of Apsheronsk in the Krasnodar region, Vitebsk, Volgograd, Yalutorovsk, Suzdal, Galich, Smolensk . . . How can I include them all? The country is enormous. And here chance comes to my aid. An unexpected prompting. One day the mail brings me an invitation from the veterans of the 65th Army of General P. I. Batov: "We usually gather on May 16 and 17 in Moscow on Red Square. A tradition, and a ritual. Everyone who is still strong enough turns up. They come from Murmansk and Karaganda, from Alma-Ata and Omsk. From everywhere. From all over our boundless Motherland . . . In short, we'll be waiting . . ."*

. . . The Hotel Moscow. The month of May—the month of the Victory. Everywhere people embrace, weep, take pictures. I can't tell the flowers pressed to people's breasts from the medals and decorations pinned to them. I enter this stream, and it bears me up and carries me, draws me in irresistibly, and soon I find myself in an almost unfamiliar world. On an unfamiliar island. Among people I recognize or don't recognize, but I know one thing—I love them all. Usually they are lost among us and invisible, because they are already departing, there are fewer and fewer of them, and more of us, but once a year they gather together, in order to go back if only for a moment to their time. And their time is their memories.

On the seventh floor, room 52, Hospital No. 5257 has gathered. At the head of the table—Alexandra Ivanovna Zaitseva, military doctor, captain. She is glad to see me and happily introduces me to everybody as if she and I had known

---

* General Pavel Ivanovich Batov (1897–1985), a much-decorated general of the Red Army, commanded the 65th Army from 1942 to the end of the war, on the Don front, at Kursk, and later in Belorussia.

each other for a long time. Yet I had knocked on this door completely by chance.
At random.

I write down: Galina Ivanovna Sazonova, surgeon; Elizaveta Mikhailovna
Aizenstein, doctor; Valentina Vasilyevna Lukina, surgery nurse; Anna Ig-
natyevna Gorelik, senior surgery nurse; Nadezhda Fyodorovna Potuzhnaya,
Klavdia Prokhorovna Borodulina, Elena Pavlovna Yakovleva, Angelina
Nikolaevna Timofeeva, Sofya Kamaldinovna Motrenko, Tamara Dmitrievna
Morozova, Sofya Filimonovna Semeniuk, Larissa Tikhonovna Deikun,
nurses.

OF DOLLS AND RIFLES

—Ehh, girls, how vile it was, this war . . . When you look at it with
our eyes. Simple women's eyes . . . As frightful as can be. That's why
they don't ask us . . .

—Do you remember, girls, we were riding in the freight cars . . . And
the soldiers laughed at how we held our rifles. We didn't hold them
the way you hold a weapon, but like this . . . Now I can't even show
it . . . The way you hold a doll . . .

—People wept, shouted . . . I hear the word "War!" And I think,
"What war, if we have an exam tomorrow at the institute? An exam—
it's so important. What kind of war can there be?"

A week later the bombings began; we were already saving people.
Three courses in medical school meant something at such a time. But
in the first days I saw so much blood that I began to be afraid of it.
There's a half-doctor for you, there's "honors" in practical courses.
But people behaved exceptionally well. And that was encouraging.

I told you, girls . . . The bombing was over, and I see the ground in front of me stirring. I run there and begin to dig. With my hands I felt a face, hair . . . It was a woman . . . I dug her out and began to weep over her. But she, when she opened her eyes, didn't ask what happened to her, she started worrying, "Where's my purse?"

"What do you want with your purse now? You'll find it."

"My papers are in it."

Her thoughts were not about how she was, whether she was hurt, but where her party card and military ID were. I immediately started looking for her purse. Found it. She laid it on her breast and closed her eyes. Soon the ambulance came, and we put her in. I checked once more whether the purse was there.

In the evening I came home, told my mother about it, and said I had decided to go to the front . . .

—Our troops were retreating . . . We all came out to the road . . . An elderly soldier walks by, stops at our house and bows very low before my mother. "Forgive me, mother . . . Try to save your girl! Aie, save your girl!" I was sixteen then, I had a very long braid . . . And black eyelashes—like this!

—I remember how we went to the front . . . A truckload of girls, a big covered truck. It was night, dark, and the branches brushed against the canvas, and we were so tense, it seemed like it was bullets, that we were under fire . . . The war brought about a change in words and sounds . . . The war . . . Ah, it's always right next to us now! You say "mama" and it's quite a different word; you say "home" and it's also quite different. Something was added to them. More love was added, more fear. Something else . . .

But from the first day I was convinced that they wouldn't defeat us. Our country is so big. Endless . . .

———

—Mama's girl . . . I had never left our town, never slept in anyone else's house, and I wound up as a junior doctor in a mortar battery. What it did to me! The mortars would begin to shoot—and I would go deaf at once. It was as if I was burned all over. I'd sit down and whisper, "Mama, dear mama . . . Dear mama . . ." We were stationed in the forest. I'd get up in the morning—it was quiet, dewdrops hanging. Can this be war? When it's so beautiful and so good . . .

They told us to wear uniforms, and I was five feet tall. I put the trousers on and the girls pulled them all the way up to my shoulders. So I wore my own clothes and tried to hide from the superiors. They put me in the guardhouse for violating army discipline . . .

—I would never have believed . . . I didn't know I could sleep while I walked. You march in a column and you sleep. You bump into the one marching ahead of you, wake up for a second, and fall asleep again. A soldier's sleep is sweet everywhere. Once, in the dark, instead of going straight I swerved to the side and walked into a field. I walked and slept, until I fell into some kind of ditch. Then I woke up and ran to overtake the others.

Soldiers sit during a halt—they have one hand-rolled cigarette for the three of them. One smokes, the other two sleep. Even snore . . .

—I'll never forget it: they brought a wounded man, took him off the stretcher . . . Someone felt his pulse, "No, he's dead." We stepped aside. And then the wounded man breathed. I knelt in front of him and heard him breathing. I sobbed and shouted, "Doctor! Doctor!" They roused the doctor, shook him, and he fell like a sheaf of wheat, he was so fast asleep. They couldn't rouse him even with sal ammoniac. He hadn't slept for three days before then.

And how heavy the wounded are in winter . . . The army shirts get stiff from blood and melted snow, the tarpaulin boots from blood and ice—impossible to cut. They're all cold, like the dead.

You look out the window—winter, indescribably beautiful. Magic white firs. You forget everything for a moment . . . Then again . . .

—It was a ski battalion . . . All tenth-graders . . . They were mowed down by machine guns . . . One of them was brought in; he was crying. And we're the same age, but already older from experience. You embrace him, "Dear child." And he: "If you'd been there, you wouldn't say 'child' . . . " He was dying and screaming all night long: "Mama! Mama!" There were two fellows there from Kursk; we called them "the Kursk nightingales." You come to wake him up, he's sound asleep, his lips wet with spittle. They were like little children . . .

—We stood at the operating table around the clock . . . You stand there, and your arms drop by themselves. Once my head sank down right onto the man I was operating on. Sleep! Sleep! Sleep! Our feet were swollen; they wouldn't get into the tarpaulin boots. Our eyes were so tired it was hard to close them . . .

My war has three smells: blood, chloroform, and iodine . . .

—Ohh! And the wounds . . . Big, deep, jagged . . . You could lose your mind . . . Fragments of bullets, grenades, shells in the head, in the guts—all over the body. Along with metal we take out uniform buttons, pieces of overcoats and shirts, leather straps. I remember one, his whole chest was turned inside out, you could see his heart . . . Still beating, but he was dying . . . I'm bandaging him for the last time and can barely hold back my tears. I must finish quickly, I think, and go to some corner and cry my fill. He says, "Thank you, dear nurse . . ." and he hands me some small metal object. I look: it's a crossed saber and rifle. "Why are you giving it to me?" I ask. "Mama said this talis-man would save me. But I don't need it anymore. Maybe you're luck-ier than me?" He said it and turned to the wall.

By evening we had blood in our hair, it had soaked through the gown to our bodies, was on our caps and masks. Black, sticky, mixed with everything there is in a man. With urine, with excrement . . .

Another time one of them would call me, "Nurse, my leg hurts." But there was no leg . . . Most of all I was afraid of carrying the dead. The wind lifts the sheet, and he looks at you. If his eyes were open, I couldn't carry him, I had to close them . . .

—A wounded man was brought . . . He lay all bandaged on the stretcher; the wound was to the head, you could see almost nothing of him. Just a little. But I obviously reminded him of someone, and he addressed me, "Larissa . . . Larissa . . . Larochka . . ." Apparently a girl he loved. And that is my name, but I knew I'd never met this man before. Yet he was calling me. I went to him, didn't know what to think, kept looking at him. "You've come? You've come?" I took his hands, bent down . . . "I knew you'd come . . ." He whispered some-thing, but I didn't understand what he whispered. Even now I can't talk about it calmly; when I remember it, tears come to my eyes. "When I was leaving for the front," he said, "I didn't have time to kiss you. Kiss me . . ."

So I bent down and kissed him. A tear welled up, ran off into the bandages, and vanished. And that was all. He died . . .

OF DEATH AND ASTONISHMENT
IN THE FACE OF DEATH

—People didn't want to die . . . We responded to every moan, every cry. One wounded man, when he felt he was dying, seized me by the shoulder, embraced me, and wouldn't let go. It seemed to him that if someone was next to him, if the nurse was there, life wouldn't leave him. He asked, "Just five more minutes of life. Just two more minutes . . ." Some died inaudibly, quietly; others cried out, "I don't want to die!" Men cursed: "Fuck it all . . ." One man started to sing . . . A Moldavian song . . . A man is dying, but he still doesn't think, doesn't believe he's dying. But you see this yellow, yellow color coming from under the hairline, you see the shadow moving first over the face, then down under the clothes . . . He lies dead, and on his face there's some sort of astonishment, as if he's lying there thinking, "How is it I'm dead? Can it be I'm dead?"

As long as he can hear . . . Till the last moment you tell him, no, no, how could you die? You kiss him, embrace him. There now, there now. He's already dead, eyes fixed on the ceiling, but I still whisper something . . . soothing him . . . The names are erased, gone from my memory, but the faces are still there . . .

—They bring the wounded . . . They're crying . . . Crying not from pain, but from impotence. It was their first day at the front; some of them hadn't fired a single shot. They weren't given any rifles, because in the first year of the war weapons cost their weight in gold. And the Germans had tanks, mortars, airplanes. Their comrades fell, they picked up their rifles. Grenades. They went into combat barehanded . . . Like into a fistfight . . .

And ran straight into tanks . . .

———

—When they were dying . . . The way they looked around . . . The way they . . .

—My first wounded man . . . A bullet had hit him in the throat. He lived for several more days, but he couldn't speak . . .

When an arm or a leg is amputated, there is no blood. There is clean white flesh; the blood comes later. To this day I can't cut up a chicken, if it's clean white flesh. It makes my mouth taste very salty . . .

—The Germans didn't take women soldiers prisoner . . . They shot them at once. Or led them before their lined-up soldiers and showed them off: look, they're not women, they're monsters. We always kept two bullets for ourselves, two—in case one misfired.

One of our nurses was captured . . . A day later we took back that village. There were dead horses lying about, motorcycles, armored vehicles. We found her: eyes put out, breasts cut off. They had impaled her on a stake . . . It was freezing cold, and she was white as could be, and her hair was all gray . . . She was nineteen years old.

In her knapsack we found letters from home and a green rubber bird. A child's toy . . .

—We retreat . . . They shell us. During the first year we kept retreating. The fascist planes flew very low, hunting down each person. It always seemed it was you he was after. I'm running . . . I see and hear that the plane is aiming at me. I see the pilot, his face, and he sees that we're young girls . . . It's a hospital train . . . He rattles away along the wagons, and even smiles. He's having fun . . . Such an insolent, terrible smile . . . A handsome face . . .

I can't stand it . . . I shout . . . I run into a cornfield—he's there; I turn toward the forest—he presses me to the ground. I reach the underbrush . . . I ran into the forest and hid in some old leaves. My nose bled from fear, I didn't know whether I was alive or not. I was alive . . . Since then I've been very afraid of planes. It's still far away, but I'm already afraid; I don't think of anything anymore, except that it's flying, where can I hide, where can I huddle, so as not to see and hear. To this day I can't stand the sound of planes. I never fly . . .

—Ehh, girls . . .

—Before the war I wanted to get married . . . to my music teacher. It was a crazy story. I was seriously in love . . . So was he . . . Mama didn't allow it: "You're too young!"

Soon the war began. I asked to be sent to the front. I wanted to leave home, to become an adult. At home they wept as they got me ready for the road. Warm socks, underwear . . .

I saw my first dead man on the first day . . . A stray fragment happened to fly into the schoolyard where our hospital was and mortally wounded our paramedic. And I thought: my mother decided I was too young to marry, but I'm not too young for the war . . . My beloved mama . . .

—We've just arrived . . . We set up the hospital, fill it with the wounded, and then the order: evacuate. We put some of the wounded in trucks, not all. There aren't enough trucks. They hurry us: "Leave them . . . Go without them . . ." You're getting ready to go, they look at you. Follow you with their eyes. There's everything in their look: humility, hurt . . . They ask, "Brothers! Dear sisters! Don't leave us to the Germans. Finish us off." So sad! So sad! Whoever can walk leaves with us. Those who can't—lie there. And you have no strength left to help any of them, you're afraid to raise your eyes . . . I was young, I cried all the time . . .

When we began to advance we didn't leave a single one of our wounded. We even picked up the German wounded. And for a while I worked with them. I got used to it, I bandaged them, it was all right. Then I'd remember 1941, when we had to leave our wounded, and what they did to them . . . How they treated them . . . We saw . . . It seemed I'd never be able to go near them . . . The next day I'd go and bandage them . . .

—We saved lives . . . But many were sorry they were medics and could only bandage, and hadn't taken up arms. Didn't shoot. I remember . . . I remember that feeling. I remember that the smell of blood on the snow was especially strong . . . The dead . . . They lay in the fields. Birds tore their eyes out, pecked their faces, their hands. Aie, an impossible life . . .

—Toward the end of the war . . . I was afraid to write letters home. I won't write, I thought, because what if I'm suddenly killed, and mama will weep that the war was over, and I died just before the Victory. Nobody talked about it, but everybody thought about it. We already sensed that we'd soon be victorious. The spring had already begun.

I suddenly saw that the sky was blue . . .

—What do I remember . . . What's imprinted in my memory? The silence, the extraordinary silence in the wards of the badly wounded . . . The worst . . . They didn't talk among themselves. Didn't call anyone. Many were unconscious. Most often they just lay there silently. Thinking. Looking off somewhere to the side and thinking. You call out to him and he doesn't hear.

What were they thinking about?

OF HORSES AND BIRDS

—We rode and rode . . .

There were two trains standing next to each other at the station . . . One with the wounded, and the other with horses. And then a bombardment began. The trains caught fire . . . We started to open the doors, to save the wounded, so that they could get away, but they all rushed to save the burning horses. When wounded people scream, it's terrible, but there's nothing more terrible than the neighing of wounded horses. They're not guilty of anything, they don't answer for human deeds. And nobody ran to the forest, everybody rushed to save the horses. All those who could. All of them!

I want to say . . . I want to say that the fascist planes flew just over the ground. Low, very low. Later I thought: the German pilots saw it all, can it be that they weren't ashamed? What were they thinking?

—I remember one time . . . We came to a village, and there were some dead partisans lying near a forest. What they had done to them I can't tell you, my heart won't bear it. They had been cut up into pieces . . . They were trussed like pigs. They lay there . . . and horses were grazing not far away. They must have been the partisans' horses; they even had saddles. Either they had escaped from the Germans and then came back, or the Germans hadn't managed to take them away—I don't know. They didn't go far. There was a lot of grass. I thought: how could those people do such things in front of horses? In front of animals? The horses had watched them . . .

—The field and forest were burning . . . The meadow was smoky. I saw burned cows and dogs . . . An unusual smell. Unfamiliar. I saw . . .

Burned barrels of tomatoes, of cabbage. Birds were burned. Horses . . .
Many . . . Many completely charred ones lay on the road. We also had
to get used to that smell . . .

I realized then that anything can burn . . . Even blood burns . . .

—During a bombardment, a goat latched on to us. She lay down with
us. Simply lay down nearby and screamed. When the bombing ceased,
she went with us and kept clinging to people—well, she's alive, she's
also afraid. We came to a village and said to some woman, "Take her
out of pity." We wanted to save her . . .

—Two wounded men lay in my ward . . . A German and our badly
burned tank driver. I come to look at them: "How do you feel?"

"I'm all right," our tank driver replies, "but he's in a bad way."

"This fascist . . ."

"No, I don't know, but he's in a bad way."

They were no longer enemies, but people, simply two wounded
men lying next to each other. Something human arose between them.
I observed more than once how quickly it happened . . .

—How is it . . . How . . . Remember . . . Birds are flying in late
fall . . . Long, long flocks. Our artillery and the Germans' are firing,
and they're flying. How to call out to them? How to warn them:
"Not here! There's shooting here!" How?! The birds are falling, falling to the ground . . .

—They brought us some SS officers to be bandaged. A nurse comes to
me: "How are we to bandage them?"

"Normally. They're wounded . . ."

And we bandaged them normally. Two of them later escaped. They were caught, and to keep them from escaping again, I cut the buttons off their long drawers . . .

—When they told me . . . These were the words: "The war is over!" I just sat on the sterilized table. The doctor and I had agreed that when they said "The war is over!" we'd sit on the sterilized table. Do something unbelievable like that. I never let anyone come near that table, not even within gunshot of it. I had gloves, I wore a mask, I had a sterilized smock on, and I handed over all necessary things: swabs, instruments . . . And now I just sat on that table . . .

What did we dream of? First, of course, of being victorious; second, of staying alive. One said, "Once the war is over, I'll give birth to a whole slew of children." Another: "I'll enroll in the university." Yet another: "I'll spend all my time at the hairdresser's. I'll dress up in pretty clothes and pamper myself." Or: "I'll buy nice perfume. Buy a scarf and a brooch."

And now that time had come. Everybody suddenly grew quiet . . .

—We took back a village . . . We looked for where to draw some water. We entered a courtyard where we noticed a well sweep. A carved wooden well . . . A shot man was lying in the yard . . . Next to him sat his dog. He saw us and began to whimper. It took us a while to realize he was calling us. He led us to the cottage . . . We followed him. On the threshold lay the man's wife and three children . . .

The dog sat next to them and wept. Really wept. Like a human being . . .

—We entered our villages . . . There were only stoves standing—that was all. Nothing but stoves! In Ukraine we came to villages where there was nothing, just watermelons growing. People ate nothing but these watermelons; it was all they had. They came to meet us and brought watermelons . . . Instead of flowers . . .

I returned home. In a dugout—my mother, three children, and a little dog, all eating boiled goosefoot. They boiled the goosefoot, ate it themselves, and gave it to the dog. And the dog ate it . . . Before the war we had so many nightingales, but for two years after the war nobody heard them. The earth was all overturned, the so-called ancestors' dung had been dug under. Plowed in. The nightingales appeared only in the third year. Where had they been? Nobody knows. They came back after three years.

People put up houses, then the nightingales came back . . .

—Whenever I see wild flowers, I remember the war. We didn't pick flowers then. And if we made bouquets, it was only when we buried someone . . . When we bid farewell . . .

—Ehh, girls, how vile it was . . . This war . . . Let's drink to the memory of our friends . . .

"IT WASN'T ME . . ."

———

What do you remember most?

You remember most the quiet, often perplexed human voice. The woman feels astonished at herself, at what happened to her. The past disappeared, it blinded her with its scorching whirl and vanished, but the human being remained. Remained in the midst of ordinary life. Everything around is ordinary except her memory. And I also become a witness. A witness to what people remember and how they remember, to what they want to talk about and what they try to forget or remove to the furthest corner of memory. Curtain off. How they desperately seek for words, yet wish to reconstruct what is gone in the hope that from a distance they may be able to find its full meaning. To see and understand what they hadn't seen and understood then. There. They study themselves, meet themselves anew. Most often it is already two persons—this one and that one, the young one and the old one. The one in the war and the one after the war. Long after the war. The feeling that I am hearing two voices at the same time never leaves me . . .

At that time, in Moscow, on Victory Day, I met Olga Yakovlevna Omelchenko. All the women were wearing spring dresses, bright scarves, but she wore an army uniform and an army beret. Tall, strong. She did not talk and did not weep. She was silent all the time, but this was some sort of special silence, which implied more than could be said, more than words. It was as if she talked to herself all the time. She no longer needed anybody.

We became acquainted, and afterward I came to see her in Polotsk.

Before me yet another page of the war opened, before which any fantasy will fall silent . . .

Olga Yakovlevna Omelchenko

MEDICAL ASSISTANT IN AN INFANTRY COMPANY

Mama's talisman . . . Mama wanted me to be evacuated together with her. She knew that I was eager for the front, and she tied me to the cart on which our things were being transported. But I quietly untied myself and left with a piece of that rope still on my arm . . .

Everybody was on the move . . . Fleeing. Where was I to go? How to reach the front? On the road I met a group of girls. One of them said to me, "My mother lives nearby, let's go to my place." We came at night, we knocked. Her mother opened the door, looked at us, and we were dirty, ragged. "Stay there in the doorway," she ordered. We stood there. She brought enormous cauldrons, took all our clothes off. We washed our hair with ashes (there was no soap anymore), climbed on the stove,* and I fell fast asleep. In the morning this girl's mother cooked cabbage soup, baked some bread from bran and potatoes. How tasty that bread seemed to us and how sweet the cabbage soup! And so we stayed four days, and she fed us up. She gave us a little at a time, otherwise she was afraid we'd eat too much and die. On the fifth day she said, "Go." And before that a neighbor came. We were sitting on the stove. The mother put her finger to her lips, so that we'd be quiet. She hadn't told her neighbors that her daughter had come back; she told everybody that her daughter was at the front. This was her only daughter, but she didn't feel sorry for her. She couldn't forgive the disgrace of her coming back. Of not fighting.

During the night she woke us up, gave us small bundles of food, embraced each of us, and said, "Go . . ."

---

* Russian tile stoves are elaborate structures that include "shelves" for sleeping.

She didn't even try to keep her daughter home?

No, she kissed her and said, "Your father's fighting, you go and fight, too."

Back on the road this girl told me that she was a nurse, her unit had fallen into an encirclement . . .

For a long time I wandered from place to place and finally wound up in the city of Tambov and found a job in a hospital. The hospital was good; after going hungry for a long time I ate well, I became plump. And then when I turned sixteen, they told me that, like all the nurses and doctors, I could give blood. I started giving blood every month. The hospital constantly needed hundreds of liters, there was never enough. I gave a pint of blood twice a month. I was given a donor's ration: two pounds of sugar, two pounds of farina, two pounds of sausage, to restore my strength. I was friends with a floor attendant, Aunt Niura. She had seven children, and her husband had been killed at the start of the war. The oldest boy, who was eleven, went to the grocery store and lost their ration cards, so I gave them my donor's ration. One day the doctor said to me, "Let's attach your address, in case somebody suddenly turns up who has had a transfusion of your blood." We wrote out my address and stuck the label to the vial.

And a while later, two months, not more, I finished my shift and went to sleep. They came and roused me. "Get up! Get up, your brother has come."

"What brother? I don't have a brother."

Our dormitory was on the top floor. I went down, looked: there stood a handsome young lieutenant. I asked, "Who wants to see Omelchenko?"

He said, "I do." And he showed me the label the doctor and I had written. "Here . . . I'm your blood brother."

He brought me two apples, a bag of candy—it was impossible then to buy candy anywhere. My God! How tasty those candies were! I went to the head of the hospital: "My brother has come . . ." They gave me a leave. He said, "Let's go to the theater." It was the first time in my life I went to the theater, and with a young fellow, at that. A handsome young fellow. An officer!

He left several days later. He had orders to go to the Voronezh front. When he came to say goodbye, I opened the window and waved to him. I couldn't get a leave: just then a lot of wounded arrived.

I had never received letters from anybody; I had no idea what it was—to receive a letter. And suddenly they handed me a little triangle. I opened it, and there was written, "Your friend, commander of a machine-gun platoon . . . died a hero's death . . ." It was my blood brother. He was from an orphanage, and probably mine was the only address he had. My address . . . When he was leaving he kept asking me to stay in this hospital, so that after the war he could easily find me. "It's easy to lose each other during the war," he said. And a month later I received this letter, that he had been killed . . . And I was so frightened. I was struck to the heart . . . I decided to do all I could to go to the front and avenge my blood; I knew that my blood had been spilled somewhere there . . .

But it wasn't so easy to go to the front. I applied three times to the head of the hospital, and the fourth time I came to him and said, "If you don't let me go to the front, I'll run away."

"Very well. I'll give you an order, since you're so stubborn."

The most terrible thing, of course, is the first battle. It's because you don't know anything yet . . . The sky throbs, the ground throbs, your heart seems about to burst, your skin feels ready to split. I never thought the ground could crackle. Everything crackled, everything rumbled. Heaved . . . The ground heaved . . . It was more than I could take . . . How was I to live through all that . . . I thought I couldn't endure it. I was so terribly frightened, and then I decided: so as not to turn coward, I took my Komsomol card, dipped it in the blood of a wounded soldier, put it in my pocket over my heart, and buttoned it. And by doing that I made myself an oath that I had to endure, and above all not to turn coward, because if I did it in my first battle, I wouldn't be able to take a step afterward. I'd be removed from the front line and sent to the medical battalion. And I only wanted to be at the front line; I wanted sometime to see at least one fascist face-to-face . . . Personally . . . And we advanced, we walked through the grass, and the grass was waist high. Nothing had been sown there for several years. It was very hard to walk. This was at the Kursk Bulge . . .

After the battle the chief of staff summoned me. It was some sort of ruined hut, with nothing inside. There was one chair, and he was standing. He sat me in the chair.

"I look at you and think: what made you come to this hellfire? You'll be killed like a fly. It's war! A meat grinder! Let me at least transfer you to a medical unit. It's all very well if they kill you, but what if you're left without eyes, without arms? Have you thought of that?"

I reply, "I have, Comrade Colonel. And I ask you one thing: don't transfer me from the company."

"All right, go!" he shouted at me. I even got scared. And he turned to the window.

Heavy combat. Hand-to-hand . . . That is a horror . . . Not for a human being . . . They beat, they stab with a bayonet, they strangle each other. They break each other's bones. There's howling, shouting. Moaning. And that crunching . . . That crunching! Impossible to forget it . . . the crunching of bones . . . You hear a skull crack. Split open . . . Even for war it's a nightmare; there's nothing human in it. I won't believe anyone who says that war isn't terrifying. Now the Germans rise up and advance; they always march with their sleeves rolled up to the elbows. Another five or ten minutes and they attack. You begin to shake. To shiver. But that's before the first shot . . . And then . . . Once you hear the command, you no longer remember anything; you rise up with everybody and run. And you no longer think about being afraid. But the next day you can't sleep, you're afraid. You remember everything, all the details, and it dawns on you that you could have been killed, and you're insanely frightened. Right after an attack it's better not to look at faces; they're some sort of totally different faces, not like people usually have. They themselves cannot raise their eyes to each other. They don't even look at the trees. You go up to someone and he says, "Go a-way! A-way . . ." I can't express what it is. Everybody seems slightly abnormal, and there's even a glimpse of something bestial. Better not to see it. To this day I can't believe I stayed alive. Alive . . . Wounded and shell-shocked, but whole. I can't believe it . . .

I close my eyes and see it all again in front of me . . .

A shell hit the ammunition depot, and it caught fire. The soldier who was standing guard next to it got scorched. Turned into a black piece of meat . . . He kept jumping around . . . And everybody watched from the trench, and nobody budged, they were all at a loss. I grabbed a sheet, ran over, covered the soldier with it, and lay down on him. Pressed him to the ground. The cold ground . . . Like that . . . He thrashed about till his heart burst, then grew still . . .

I was all covered with blood . . . One of the older soldiers came up and embraced me. I heard him say, "The war will end, and if she's still alive, there'll be nothing human left of her anyway, it's all over." Meaning that I was in the midst of such horror, and living through it, at such a young age. I was shaking as if in a fit; they took me under the arms to the dugout. My legs wouldn't hold me up . . . I was shaking as if an electric current was running through me . . . I can't describe how it felt . . .

Then the battle began again . . . At the Sevsk the Germans attacked us seven or eight times a day. So that day I also carried the wounded with their weapons. When I crawled to the last one, his arm was completely smashed. Hanging by little pieces . . . by the sinews. He was all bloody . . . His arm had to be urgently amputated and bandaged, otherwise it was impossible to bandage him. But I had no knife or scissors. My kit was loose on my shoulder, and things had fallen out. What was I to do? I bit his flesh off with my teeth. I bit it off and bandaged him . . . I was bandaging, and the wounded man said, "Make it quick, nurse, I'll go and fight some more . . ." In delirium . . .

A few days later, when the tanks came against us, two men turned coward. They fled . . . The whole line wavered . . . Many of our comrades were killed. The wounded that I had dragged to a shell hole were taken prisoner. An ambulance was supposed to come for them . . . But when those two turned coward, panic set in. The wounded were abandoned. Later on we came to the place where they lay, some with their eyes put out, some with their guts ripped open . . . After I saw it my face turned black overnight. I was the one who had gathered them in one place . . . I . . . It frightened me so much . . .

In the morning the whole battalion lined up, those cowards were brought out and placed before us. The order that they be shot was read. Seven men were needed to carry out the sentence . . . Three men stepped forward; the rest stood there. I took a submachine gun and stepped forward. Once I stepped forward . . . a young girl . . . everybody followed me . . . Those two could not be forgiven. Because of them such brave boys were killed!

And we carried out the sentence . . . I lowered the submachine gun, and became frightened. I went up to them . . . they lay there . . . One had a living smile on his face . . .

I don't know, would I have forgiven them now? I can't tell . . . I don't want to lie. There are moments when I want to weep. But I can't . . .

I forgot everything in the war. My former life. Everything . . . And I forgot love . . .

The commander of the scout company fell in love with me. He sent me little notes through his soldiers. I came to see him once. "No," I said. "I love a man who was killed long ago." He moved very close to me, looked straight into my eyes, turned, and went away. There was shooting, but he walked on and didn't even duck his head . . .

Later—this was already in Ukraine—we liberated a big village. I thought: "I'll take a stroll, look around." The weather was clear, the cottages white. And outside the village—graves, freshly dug earth . . . The graves of those who fought for this village. I didn't know why, but I was drawn there. On each grave there was a photograph and a last name on a plank . . . Suddenly I saw a familiar face . . . The commander of the scout company who was in love with me. And his last name . . . And I felt so uneasy. Such great fear . . . as if he saw me, as if he was alive . . . And just then his men came to the grave, from his company. They all knew me; they had delivered his notes to me. Not one of them looked at me, as if I wasn't there. Invisible. Later, too, whenever I met them, it seemed to me . . . so I think . . . They wanted me to die, too. It was hard for them to see that I was . . . alive . . . I sensed it . . . As if I was guilty before them . . . And before him . . .

I came back from the war and fell gravely ill. For a long time I went from one hospital to another, until I happened upon an old professor. He began to treat me . . . He treated me more with words than with medications; he explained my illness to me. He said that if I had left for the front at eighteen or nineteen, my body would have been stronger, but since I had just turned sixteen—it was a very early age—I had been badly traumatized. "Of course, medications are one thing," he explained. "They may treat you, but if you want to restore your health, if you want to live, my only advice is: you should get married and have as many children as possible. Only that can save you. With every child your body will be reborn."

How old were you?

When the war ended, I was going on twenty. Of course I didn't even think of getting married.

Why?

I felt very tired, much older than my peers, even simply old. My friends went to dances, had fun, and I couldn't, I looked at life with old eyes. From another world . . . An old woman! Young fellows courted me. Mere boys. But they didn't see my soul, what was inside me. Here I've told you about one day . . . The fighting at Sevsk. Just one day . . . After which I had blood flow out of my ears during the night. In the morning I woke up as if after a grave illness. A bloody pillow . . .

And in the hospital? In the surgery room we had a big tub behind a screen where they put the amputated arms, legs . . . Once a captain came from the front and brought his wounded friend. I don't know how he got behind there, but he saw that tub and . . . fainted.

I can go on and on remembering. I can't stop . . . But what is the most important thing?

I remember the sounds of the war. Everything around booms and clangs, crackles from fire . . . In war your soul ages. After the war I was never young . . . That's the most important thing. To my mind . . .

Did you get married?

I got married. I gave birth to five sons and raised them. Five boys. God didn't give me girls. What surprises me most is that after such great fear and horror I could give birth to beautiful children. And I turned out to be a good mother and a good grandmother.

I recall it all now and it seems that it wasn't me, but some other girl . . .

I was on my way home, bringing four cassettes (two days of conversations) with "yet another war," having various feelings: shock and fear, perplexity and admiration. Curiosity and bewilderment, and tenderness. At home I retold some episodes to my friends. Unexpectedly for me, the reactions were all similar: "Too frightening. How could she stand it? And not go out of her mind?" Or: "We're used to reading about a different war. In that war there are clear distinctions: us and them, good and evil. But here?" But I noticed they all had tears in their eyes, and they all fell to thinking. Probably about the same things as I. There have been thousands of wars on earth (I read recently that they've counted up more than three thousand—big and small), but war remains, as it has always been, one of the chief human mysteries. Nothing has changed. I am trying to bring that great history down to human scale, in order to understand something. To find the words. Yet in this seemingly small and easily observable territory— the space of one human soul—everything is still less comprehensible, less predictable than in history. Because before me are living tears, living feelings. A living human face, which the shadows of pain and fear pass over as we talk. Occasionally a subversive hunch even creeps in of the barely perceptible beauty of human suffering. Then I get frightened of my own self . . .

There is only one path—to love this human being. To understand through love.

"I REMEMBER THOSE EYES
EVEN NOW . . ."

———

The search continues . . . But this time I don't have far to go . . .

The street I live on in Minsk is named after the Hero of the Soviet Union Vasily Zakharovich Korzh—participant in the Civil War, hero of battles in Spain, commander of a partisan brigade during the Great Patriotic War. Every Belorussian has read a book about him, at least in school, or seen a movie. He is a Belorussian legend. Having written his name hundreds of times on envelopes or telegram forms, I had never thought about him as a real man. The myth has long replaced the once-living person. Has become his double. But this time I walked down the familiar street with a new feeling: a half-hour trolleybus ride to the other end of the city, and I'll see his daughters—they both fought at the front—and his wife. Before my eyes the legend will come alive and turn into a human life, descend to earth. The great will become small. However much I love to look at the sky or the sea, still I'm more fascinated by a grain of sand under a microscope. The world in a single drop. The great and incredible life I discover in it. How can I call the small small and the great great, when both are so boundless? I've long ceased to distinguish between them. For me one human being is so much. There is everything in him—you can get lost.

I find the address I need—again a massive and unwieldy multistoried building. Here is entrance 3; in the elevator I press the button for the seventh floor . . .

The door is opened by the younger sister—Zinaida Vasilyevna. The same wide dark eyebrows and the stubbornly open gaze as her father's in the photographs.

"We're all here . . . My sister Olya came from Moscow this morning. She lives there. Teaches at Patrice Lumumba University. And our mama is here. So, thanks to you, we've all gotten together."

Both sisters, Olga Vasilyevna and Zinaida Vasilyevna Korzh, had been medical assistants in cavalry squadrons. They sat next to each other and looked at their mother, Feodosia Alexeevna.

It was she who began:

"Everything was burning . . . They told us to evacuate . . . We rode for a long time. We reached the Stalingrad region. Women with children moved to the rear, and men moved up. Combine drivers, tractor drivers, everybody went. Whole truckloads. One man, I remember, stood up and shouted, 'Mothers, sisters!! Go to the rear, harvest bread, so we can defeat the enemy!' And they all took their hats off and looked at us. And all we had time to bring with us were our children. We held them. Some in our arms, some by the hand. He begged, 'Mothers, sisters! Go to the rear, harvest bread . . .' "

During the whole time of our conversation she did not utter another word. Her daughters would quietly stroke her hand every once in a while to calm her down.

Zinaida Vasilyevna

We lived in Pinsk. I was fourteen and a half, Olya was sixteen, our brother Lenya thirteen. Just during those days we sent Olya to a children's sanatorium, and father wanted to go with us to the country. To his family . . . But in fact he didn't spend that night at home. He worked in the regional party committee, was summoned during the night, and came home only in the morning. He stopped in the kitchen, grabbed something to eat, and said, "Children, war has begun. Don't go anywhere. Wait for me."

We left by night. Father had a most precious souvenir from Spain—a hunting rifle, richly ornamented, with a cartridge belt. It was a reward for courage. He tossed the rifle to my brother. "You're the eldest now, you're a man, you must look after mama and your little sisters . . ."

We kept that rifle all through the war. Whatever nice things we had, we sold or exchanged for bread, but we kept the rifle. We couldn't part with it. It was our memory of father. He also threw a big sheepskin coat into the car with us. It was the warmest thing he had.

At the station we got onto a train, but before we reached Gomel, we came under heavy shelling. The command: "Off the train, into the bushes, lie flat!" When the shelling was over . . . First silence, then shouting . . . everybody ran . . . Mama and my brother managed to jump back onto the train, but I stayed. I was very frightened . . . Very! I had never been alone before. And here I was—alone. It seems I even lost speech for a time . . . I went dumb . . . Somebody asked me something, and I was silent . . . Then I attached myself to some woman and helped her to bandage the wounded—she was a doctor. They addressed her as "Comrade Captain." And I rode on with her medical unit. They were nice to me, fed me, but soon it occurred to them: "How old are you?"

I realized that if I told the truth they would send me to some children's home. I figured it out at once. But I no longer wanted to lose these strong people. I wanted to fight the way they did. It had been instilled in us—and my father had said—that we'd fight on foreign territory, that it was all temporary, that the war would soon end in victory. All that without me? Those were the childish thoughts I had. I told them I was sixteen, and they let me stay. Soon they sent me to training courses. I studied for about four months at these courses. I studied and at the same time took care of the wounded. Got used to the war . . . Of course we had to get used to it . . . I didn't study at the school, but right there, in the medical battalion. We were retreating and taking the wounded with us.

We didn't follow the roads; the roads were being bombed, shelled.

We moved across the swamps, along the waysides. We moved in a scattered way. Various units. Where they became concentrated, it meant they were giving battle. And so we went on, and on, and on. Went across the fields. What a harvest! We walked and trampled down the rye. And the harvest that year was unprecedented, the grain stood very tall. Green grass, bright sun, and dead men lying there, blood . . . Dead men and animals. Blackened trees . . . Destroyed train stations . . . Charred people hanging from black train cars . . . We went on like that as far as Rostov. I was wounded there during a bombardment. I regained consciousness on a train and heard an elderly soldier, a Ukrainian, barking at a young one, "Your wife didn't cry so bad giving birth as you're crying now." When he saw me open my eyes, he said, "But you cry away, dear, cry away. It'll make things easier. Go ahead." I remembered mama and wept . . .

After the hospital I was given a leave, and I tried to find my mama. And she was looking for me, and my sister Olya was looking for us both. Oh, miracle! We all found each other through some acquaintances in Moscow. We all wrote to their address, and so found each other. A miracle! Mama was living near Stalingrad in a kolkhoz. I went there.

It was the end of 1941 . . .

How did they live? My brother worked on a tractor; he was still quite young, thirteen years old. First he was a trailer hand, and when all the tractor drivers were taken to the front, he became a driver. He worked day and night. Mama followed the tractor or sat next to him. She was afraid he would get sleepy and fall off. The two of them slept on someone's floor . . . They didn't undress, because there was nothing to cover themselves with. That was their life . . . Soon Olya came; they gave her a job as an accountant. She wrote to the recruiting office asking to be sent to the front, and kept being refused. And we decided—I was already a seasoned warrior—that we'd go to Stalingrad together and find some unit there. We set mama at ease, by deceiving her that we were going to Kuban, the rich parts, where father had acquaintances . . .

I had an old uniform overcoat, an army shirt, two pairs of trousers. I gave one pair to Olya; she had nothing at all. We also had one pair of boots for the two of us. Mama knitted something like socks or slippers for us, out of sheep's wool, something warm. We walked forty miles on foot all the way to Stalingrad. One of us wore the boots, the other mama's slippers. Then we'd change. We walked through freezing cold. It was February; we were frozen, hungry. What did mama make for us for the road? She made a sort of aspic from boiled bones and several flatcakes. And we were so hungry . . . If we fell asleep and dreamed, it was only about food. Loaves of bread flew over me in my sleep.

We made it to Stalingrad, and there nobody wanted us. Nobody wanted to listen to us. Then we decided to go to Kuban, where mama had sent us, to the address papa had given. We got on some freight train. I put on the overcoat and sat, and Olya hid under the seats. Then we'd change places: I'd get under the seats and Olya would sit. They didn't touch the military. And we had no money at all . . .

We got to Kuban . . . a sort of miracle . . . Found the acquaintances. And there we were told that a volunteer Cossack corps was being formed. This was the 4th Cossack Cavalry Corps; later on it became a Guards corps. It was formed entirely of volunteers. There were people of all ages: seasoned Cossacks that Budenny and Voroshilov had once led to the attack,* and young ones as well. They took us. To this day I don't know why. Maybe because we asked so many times. And there was nothing else they could do with us. We were enlisted in the same squadron. Each of us was issued a uniform and a horse. Your horse had to be fed, watered, fully taken care of. Luckily when I was little we had a horse, and I got used to it and loved it. So when they gave me a horse, I mounted it—and wasn't scared at all. I didn't manage it right away, but I wasn't afraid. My horse was small,

* For Budenny, see note, p. 30. Kliment Voroshilov (1881–1969) was a prominent military figure, one of the first five Marshals of the Soviet Union, and a member of the Central Committee of the Communist Party from 1921 to 1961. He played a major role in Stalin's Great Purge.

tail down to the ground, but it was quick, obedient, and I somehow learned to ride it quickly. Even showed off . . . Later I rode Hungarian and Romanian horses. And I came to love horses so much, and to know them so well, that even now I can't pass by a horse with indifference. I hug them. We slept under their feet. The horse would move its leg carefully, and would never step on a human being. It would never step on a dead man, and if a living man was only wounded, it would never go away and abandon him. Very intelligent animals. For a cavalryman, a horse is a friend. A faithful friend.

The first baptism in combat . . . It was when our corps took part in repelling tanks at the Cossack village of Kushchevskaya. After the battle of Kushchevskaya—it was the famous cavalry attack of the Kuban Cossacks—the corps was raised to the rank of a Guards corps. It was a dreadful battle . . . And for Olya and me—the most dreadful, because we were still very afraid. Though I had already fought and knew how it was . . . But still . . . When the cavalrymen went it was like an avalanche—capes flying, sabers bared, horses snorting, and a horse when it races is so strong . . . This whole avalanche went against the tanks, the artillery—it was like in an otherworldly dream. Unreal . . . And there were lots of fascists, lots more than us. They walked with their submachine guns at the ready, walked beside the tanks—and they couldn't hold out against it, you see, they couldn't hold out against that avalanche. They abandoned their submachine guns . . . Abandoned their cannons and fled . . . That was a picture . . .

Olga Vasilyevna

I was bandaging the wounded . . . There was a fascist lying there. I thought he was dead and paid no attention to him, but he was only wounded . . . And he wanted to kill me . . . I felt it, as if somebody nudged me, and turned around to him. I managed to knock the submachine gun away with my foot. I didn't kill him, but I didn't bandage him either, I left. He was wounded in the stomach . . .

Zinaida Vasilyevna

I was leading a wounded man and suddenly saw two Germans coming from behind a tankette. The tankette had been hit, but they must have had time to get out. A split second! If I hadn't managed to give them a burst, they would have shot me and the wounded man. It happened so unexpectedly. After the battle I went to them; they lay with their eyes open. I remember those eyes even now . . . One was such a handsome young German. It was a pity, even though he was a fascist, all the same . . . That feeling didn't leave me for a long time. You see, I didn't want to kill. There was such hatred in my soul: why had they come to our land? But when you yourself kill, it's frightening . . . There's no other word . . . Very frightening. When you yourself . . .

The battle was over. The Cossack hundreds were breaking camp, and Olya wasn't there. I was the last one to leave, I rode at the end, I kept looking back. It was evening. Olya wasn't there . . . I got word that she stayed to pick up the wounded. There was nothing I could do, I just waited for her. I'd lag behind my hundred, wait a little, then catch up with everybody. I wept: Can it be I lost my sister in the first battle? Where is she? What's happened to her? Maybe she's dying somewhere, calling me . . .

Olya . . . Olya, too, was all in tears . . . She found me at night . . . All the Cossacks wept when they saw us meet. We hung on each other's necks, unable to let go. And then we realized that it was impossible, it was unbearable for us to fight together. Better to separate. Our hearts wouldn't be able to stand it if one of us was killed before the other's eyes. We decided that I should ask to be transferred to another squadron. But how to part? How?

Afterward we fought separately, first in different squadrons, later even in different divisions. We would just send greetings, if the chance came along, to find out whether the other was alive . . . Death watched our every step. Lay in wait . . . I remember it was near Ararat . . . We were camped in the sands. Ararat had been taken by the Germans. It was Christmas, and the Germans were celebrating. A squadron was chosen and a forty-millimeter battery. We set out at around five and kept moving all night. At dawn we met with our scouts, who had set out earlier.

The village lay at the foot of a hill . . . As if in a bowl . . . The Germans never thought we could get through such sand, and they set up very little defense. We passed through their rear very quietly. We descended the hill, captured the sentries, and burst into this village, flew into it. The Germans came running out completely naked, only with submachine guns in their hands. There were Christmas trees standing around . . . they were all drunk . . . And in every yard there were no less than two or three tanks. Tankettes stood there, armored vehicles . . . All their machinery. We destroyed it on the spot, and there was such shooting, such noise, such panic . . . Everybody rushed about . . . The situation was such that each one was afraid of hitting his own men. Everything was on fire . . . The Christmas trees, too, were on fire . . .

I had eight wounded men . . . I helped them up the hill . . . But we committed one blunder: we didn't cut the enemy's communications. And the German artillery blanketed us with both mortar and long-range fire. I quickly put my wounded on an ambulance wagon, and they drove off . . . And before my eyes a shell landed on the wagon, and it was blown to pieces. When I looked, there was only one man left alive there. And the Germans were already going up the hill . . . The wounded man begged, "Leave me, nurse . . . Leave me, nurse . . . I'm dying . . ." His stomach was ripped open . . . His guts . . . All that . . . He gathered them himself and stuffed them back in . . .

I thought my horse was bloody because of this wounded man, but then I looked: he was also wounded in the side. I used up a whole individual kit on him. I had several pieces of sugar left; I gave him the sugar. There was shooting on all sides now; you couldn't tell where the Germans were and where ours. You go ten yards and run into wounded men . . . I thought: I've got to find a wagon and pick them all up. So I rode on, and I saw the slope, and at the foot of it three roads: this way and that way and also straight. I was at a loss . . . Which way to go? I had been holding the bridle firmly; the horse went wherever I pointed him. Well, so here, I don't know, some instinct told me, or I'd heard somewhere, that horses sense the road, so before that fork I let go of the bridle, and the horse went in a completely different direction from where I was going to go. He went on and on . . .

I sit there with no strength left; I no longer care where he goes. What will be will be. So he goes on and on, and then more and more briskly, he wags his head, I've picked up the bridle again, I'm holding it. I bend down and put my hand to his wound. He goes more and more cheerfully, then: whinny-whinny-whinny . . . As if he's heard somebody. I was worried it might be the Germans. I decided to set the horse free first, but then I saw a fresh trail: hoof prints, the wheels of a machine-gun cart; no less than fifty people had passed this way. Another two or three hundred meters and my horse ran smack into a wagon. There were wounded men in the wagon, and here I saw the remainder of our squadron.

Aid was already arriving, wagons, machine-gun carts . . . The order was to pick up everybody. Under bullets, under artillery fire, we picked them all up to a man—the wounded and the dead. I also rode in the cart. Everybody was there, even the man wounded in the stomach. We took them all. Only the dead horses were left behind. It was already morning; we rode on and saw—a whole herd lying there. Beautiful, strong horses . . . The wind stirred their manes . . .

One wall of the big room we're sitting in is all covered with enlarged prewar and wartime photos of the sisters. Here they are still schoolgirls—hats, flowers. The snapshot was taken two weeks before the start of the war. Ordinary childish faces, ready to laugh, slightly restrained by the importance of the moment and the wish to look adult. Now they are already in Cossack coats, cavalry capes. The picture was taken in 1942. A year's difference, but the face is not the same, the person is not the same. And this snapshot Zinaida Vasilyevna sent to her mother from the front: on her army shirt the first medal "For Courage." This one shows them both on Victory Day . . . I memorize the movement of the face: from soft, childish features to a confident woman's gaze, even a certain tough-ness, severity. It is hard to believe that this change took place in a few months, or years. Ordinary time performs this task much more slowly and imperceptibly. A human face is molded over a long time. The soul is slowly traced on it.

But the war quickly created its image of people. Painted its own portraits.

Olga Vasilyevna

We took a big village. Some three hundred houses. There was an abandoned German infirmary in the building of the local hospital. The first thing I saw was a big hole dug in the yard and some patients lying in it shot—before leaving, the Germans themselves shot their own wounded. They evidently decided that we would do it anyway. That we would do to their wounded what they did to ours. Only one ward was left, which they evidently didn't get to, didn't have time, or maybe they were abandoned because they all had no legs.

When we entered this ward they looked at us with hatred: they evidently thought we came to kill them. The interpreter said that we don't kill the wounded, we treat them. Then one of them even started to make demands: they'd had nothing to eat for three days, their ban-dages hadn't been changed for three days. I looked—in fact, it was horrible. They hadn't seen a doctor for a long time. The wounds were festering, the bandages were growing into the flesh.

Did you pity them?

I can't call what I felt then pity. After all, pity is compassion. That I didn't feel. It was something else . . . There was an incident with us . . . a soldier hit a prisoner . . . I found that intolerable, and I inter-vened, though I understood . . . It was a cry from his soul . . . He knew me, he was older, of course, he cursed. But he stopped hit-ting . . . He swore at me, "Have you forgotten, fuck it all! Have you forgotten how they, fuck it all . . ." I hadn't forgotten anything. I re-membered those boots . . . When they set up in front of their trenches a row of boots with cut-off legs in them. It was in winter, they stood there like stakes . . . Those boots . . . That was all we saw of our com-rades . . . What was left of them . . .

I remember some sailors coming to help us . . . Many of them were blown up by mines; we had stumbled into a big minefield. These sail-ors lay there for a long time. In the sun . . . The corpses puffed up, and because of their striped jerseys they looked like watermelons. Big wa-termelons on a big field. Giant ones.

I hadn't forgotten, I hadn't forgotten anything. But I couldn't hit a prisoner, if only because he was already defenseless. Everybody de-cided that for himself, and it was important.

Zinaida Vasilyevna

In battle near Budapest . . . It was winter . . . I was carrying a wounded sergeant, the commander of a machine-gun crew. I was wearing trou-sers and a warm jacket, a flap-eared cap on my head. I'm carrying him and I see this blackish snow . . . charred . . . I realize that it's a deep shell hole, which is what I need. I go down into the hole and there's someone alive—I sense he's alive, and I hear a metallic scraping . . . I turn and there's a wounded German officer, wounded in the legs, lying there and aiming his submachine gun at me . . . My hair had slipped from under my cap, and I also had a medical kit on my shoul-der with a red cross . . . When I turned, he saw my face, realized I was a girl, and went, "Ha-a-ah!" His nerves relaxed, and he threw aside his submachine gun. He no longer cared . . .

And so the three of us are in the same hole—our wounded man, me, and this German. The hole is small, our legs touch. I'm all cov-ered with their blood; our blood mingles. The German has such huge eyes, and he looks at me with those eyes. What am I going to do?

Cursed fascist! He threw the submachine gun aside at once, you see? That scene . . . Our wounded man doesn't understand what's going on, he clutches his pistol . . . reaches out and wants to strangle him . . . But the German just stares at me . . . I remember those eyes even now . . . I'm bandaging our man, and the other one's lying in blood, he's losing blood, one of his legs is completely smashed. A little longer and he'll die. I see that very well. And, before I finished bandaging our man, I tore up the German's clothes, twisted them into a tourniquet, bandaged him, and then went back to bandaging ours. The German says, "*Gut . . . Gut . . .*" He keeps repeating that word. Our wounded man, before he lost consciousness, shouted something at me . . . threatened . . . I caressed him, soothed him. When the ambulance came, I pulled them both out . . . and put them in. The German, too. You see?

Olga Vasilyevna

When men saw a woman at the front line, their faces became different; even the sound of a woman's voice transformed them. Once during the night I sat by a dugout and began to sing softly. I thought everybody was asleep and no one would hear me, but in the morning the commander said to me, "We didn't sleep. Such longing for a woman's voice . . ."

I was bandaging a tankman . . . The battle goes on, the pounding. He asked, "What's your name, girl?" He even paid me some compliment. It felt so strange to pronounce my name, Olya, amid this pounding, this horror . . . I always tried to look neat, trim. People often said to me, "Lord, how can she have been in battle, she's so clean." I was very afraid that if I was killed, I'd lie there looking unattractive. I saw many girls killed . . . In mud, in water . . . Well . . . How shall I . . . I didn't want to die like that. Sometimes I hid from shelling, not so much thinking they won't kill me this way, but just to hide my face. My hands. I think all our girls thought about it. And the men laughed at us, they thought it was funny. Meaning, it's not death they think about, but devil knows what, something stupid. Women's nonsense.

Zinaida Vasilyevna

Death can't be tamed . . . No . . . You can't get used to it . . . We were retreating from the Germans into the mountains. We had to leave five men badly wounded in the stomach. These wounds were deadly, another day or two and they would all die. We couldn't take them along, we had nothing to transport them in. They left me and another medical assistant, Oksanochka, with them in a shed, promising, "We'll come back in two days and take you." They came back in three days. We were with these wounded men for three days. They were fully conscious, robust men. They didn't want to die . . . And we had only some powders, nothing else . . . They asked to drink all the time, but they weren't allowed to drink. Some understood, but others cursed. There was all this foul language. One flung a mug at me, another a boot. Those were the most terrible days of my life. They were dying in front of our eyes, one after another, and we just looked on . . .

The first award . . . They awarded me the medal "For Valor." But I didn't go to collect it. I was offended. By God, it was funny! You see why? My friend was awarded the medal "For Military Services" and I got the medal "For Valor." She had only been in one battle, and I had already been at the battle of Kushchevskaya Station and several other operations. So I was offended: she got "Military Services" for one battle—a lot of service—and I only "For Valor," as if I had showed myself only once. The commander came and laughed when he found out what was the matter. He explained that "For Valor" was the biggest medal, almost an order.

Near Makeevka, in the Donbas region, I was wounded in the hip. A little fragment got in and sat there like a little stone. I felt blood, I folded an individual gauze pad and put it there. And I went on running around bandaging. I was embarrassed to tell anybody, a girl wounded, and where—in a buttock. In the behind . . . When you're sixteen, it's embarrassing to tell anybody. It's awkward to admit it. So I ran all over, bandaging, until I fainted from loss of blood. My boots were full of blood . . .

Our soldiers looked and evidently decided I had been killed. The orderlies would come and pick me up. The fighting moved on. A little longer, and I would have died. But some tankmen on reconnaissance came and saw a girl on the battlefield. I lay there without my cap, the cap had rolled off. They saw blood flowing from under me, meaning I was alive. They brought me to the medical battalion. From there to the hospital, first one, then another. Ahh . . . A quick end to my war . . . Six months later they transferred me to the reserves for reasons of health. I was eighteen . . . No longer in good health: wounded three times, plus a heavy concussion. But I was a young girl, and of course I concealed it. The wounds I talked about, but the concussion I concealed. Yet I did feel the aftereffects. I was hospitalized again. They gave me disability . . . And what did I do? I tore up those papers and threw them out; I didn't even go to get some money. For that I'd have had to go through all kinds of commissions, tell about myself: when I got the concussion, when I got wounded. Where.

In the hospital, the squadron commander and the sergeant major came to visit me. I liked the commander very much during the war, but at the time he didn't notice me. A handsome man, the uniform suited him very well. All men looked good in uniform. And what did women look like? In trousers, braids weren't allowed, we all had boys' haircuts. Only toward the end of the war did they allow us to have some sort of hairstyle, and not to cut it short. In the hospital my hair grew back. I could braid it, I looked better, and they . . . My God, it's so funny! They both fell in love with me . . . Just like that! We had gone through the whole war together, and there had been nothing of the sort, and now both of them, the squadron commander and the sergeant major, proposed to me. Love! Love . . . How we all wanted love! Happiness!

That was the end of 1945 . . .

After the war we wanted to forget it as soon as possible. In this our father helped me and my sister. He was a wise man. He took our medals, decorations, official acknowledgments, put it all away, and said, "There was a war, you fought. Now forget it. There was a war, but now a new life is beginning. Put on some nice shoes. You're both beautiful girls . . . You should study, you should get married."

Olya somehow couldn't get used to this different life all at once. She was proud. She didn't want to take off her soldier's overcoat. And I remember how father said to mother, "It's my fault that the girls went to war at such a young age. I hope it hasn't broken them . . . Otherwise they'll be at war all their lives."

They gave me some sort of special coupons for my decorations and medals, so that I could go to the military store and buy myself something. I bought a pair of rubber boots that were fashionable then, a coat, a dress, some ankle shoes. I decided to sell the overcoat. I went to the market . . . I came in a light-colored summer dress . . . With my hair pinned up . . . And what did I see there? Young fellows without arms, without legs . . . All fighting men . . . With orders, medals . . . Whoever has hands sells homemade spoons. Women's bras, underpants. Another . . . without arms, without legs . . . sits bathed in tears. Begs for small change . . . There were no wheelchairs then; they rolled around on homemade platforms, pushing them with their hands, if they had them. Some are drunk. Singing about an orphan, "Forgotten, abandoned." Such scenes. I left, I didn't sell my overcoat. And all the while I lived in Moscow, probably five years, I couldn't go to the market. I was afraid one of these cripples would recognize me and shout, "Why did you pull me out of the fire then? Why did you save me?" I remembered a young lieutenant . . . His legs . . . One was cut off by shrapnel, the other still hung on by something. I bandaged him . . . under the bombs . . . And he shouted at me, "Don't drag it out! Finish me off! Finish me . . . I order you . . ." You see? I was always afraid of meeting that lieutenant . . .

When I was in the hospital, there was a handsome young fellow. The tankman Misha . . . Nobody knew his last name, but everybody knew he was Misha . . . They amputated his legs and his right arm, all he had was the left one. They amputated high up by the hip, so he couldn't have prostheses. They rolled him around in a wheelchair. They made a high wheelchair specially for him and rolled him around, anyone who could. Many civilians came to the hospital to help with the care, especially of such badly wounded men as Misha. Women and schoolchildren. Even young children. This Misha was carried in their arms. And he didn't lose heart. He wanted so much to live! He was only nineteen, he hadn't lived at all yet. I don't remember whether he had any family, but he knew that he wouldn't be abandoned in his plight; he believed that he wouldn't be forgotten. Of course the war went all over our land, there was devastation everywhere. When we liberated villages, they were all burned down. All people had left was the land. Nothing but the land.

My sister and I did not become doctors, though that had been our dream before the war. We could have gone to medical school without exams; we had the right to do that as war veterans. But we had seen so much human suffering, so many deaths. We couldn't imagine seeing more of it again . . . Even thirty years later I talked my daughter out of studying medicine, though she wanted to very much. After decades . . . As soon as I close my eyes I see . . . Spring . . . We go around some field, just after a battle, looking for the wounded. The field is trampled all over. I come upon two dead men—a young soldier of ours and a young German. Lying in young wheat and looking into the sky . . . No signs of death on them yet. Just looking into the sky . . . I still remember those eyes . . .

Olga Vasilyevna

The last days of the war . . . I remember this . . . We were driving and suddenly there was music somewhere. A violin . . . For me the war ended that day . . . It was such a miracle: suddenly music. Different sounds . . . As if I woke up . . . We all imagined that after the war, after such oceans of tears, there would be a wonderful life. Beautiful. After the Victory . . . after that day . . . We imagined that all people would be very kind, would only love each other. They would all become brothers and sisters. How we waited for that day . . .

"WE DIDN'T SHOOT . . ."

There are many people in war . . . And many duties in war . . .

There is much work not only around death, but also around life. There is not only shooting and killing people, mining and demining, bombing and exploding, going into hand-to-hand combat—there is also laundering, cooking kasha, baking bread, cleaning cauldrons, tending horses, repairing machinery, planing and nailing down coffins, delivering mail, mending boots, supplying tobacco. Even during war life consists by more than half of banal things. And of trifles, too. It's unusual to think so, isn't it? "There are mountains of our ordinary women's work there," recalls nurse-aide Alexandra Iosifovna Mishutina. The army marched first, and behind it "the second front"—laundresses, cooks, auto mechanics, mailmen . . .

One of them wrote to me, "We're not heroes, we were backstage." What was there backstage?

OF NICE LITTLE SHOES AND
A CURSED WOODEN LEG

Tatyana Arkadyevna Smelyanskaya
MILITARY JOURNALIST

We walk through the mud. Horses sink into this mud or fall down dead. Big trucks stall . . . Soldiers drag artillery by themselves. Pull wagons with bread and linen. Boxes of tobacco. I see one box of tobacco tumble into the mud, followed by a well-rounded Russian curse . . . They cherish ammunition, they cherish tobacco . . .

My husband says to me, he repeats all the time, "Keep your eyes peeled! This is epic! Epic!"

Irina Nikolaevna Zinina
PRIVATE, COOK

Before the war I had a happy life . . . With papa and mama. My papa fought in the Finnish War. He came back with a finger missing on his right hand, and I asked him, "Papa, why is there war?"

War soon came, and I still wasn't quite grown up. We were evacuated from Minsk. They brought us to Saratov. There I worked on a kolkhoz. The chairman of the village council summoned me: "I think about you all the time, girl."

I was surprised. "What do you think, Uncle?"

"If it weren't for this cursed wooden leg! It's all this cursed wooden leg . . ."

I stood there; I didn't understand anything.

He said, "There's this letter, I have to send two people to the front, and I have nobody to send. I would've gone myself, except there's this cursed wooden leg. I can't send you, you're not local. But maybe you'll go? I've got two young girls here: you and Maria Utkina."

Maria was such a tall one, a fine girl, but not me. I was so-so.

"Will you go?"

"Will they give me footwraps there?"

We were all ragged, because we had no time to take anything with us!

"You're such a pretty one, they'll give you nice little shoes."

I agreed.

. . . They unloaded us from the train, and a fellow came to pick us up, sturdy, mustached, but nobody went with him. I don't know why, I didn't ask, I wasn't an activist and never pushed myself forward. We didn't like the fellow. Then a handsome officer came. A doll! He talked us into it, and we went. We arrived at the unit, and that mustached one was there, laughing. "So you snub-noses didn't want to come with me?"

The major invited us one by one and asked, "What can you do?"

One girl said, "Milk cows." Another: "At home I boiled potatoes and helped mama."

He calls me up: "And you?"

"I can do laundry."

"I see you're a good girl. Can you cook?"

"I can."

The whole day long I cooked food, and in the evening I had to do laundry for the soldiers. I stood guard. They shout, "Sentry! Sentry!"—and I can't respond. I don't even have strength enough to speak . . .

Svetlana Nikolaevna Liubich
MEDICAL VOLUNTEER

I went around on a hospital train . . . I remember I spent the whole first week crying: first, I missed mama, and also I wound up on the top shelf, where they put the luggage now. It was my "room."

How old were you when you went to the front?

I was in the eighth grade, but I didn't finish the school year. I ran away to the front. All the girls on the hospital train were my age.

What did your work consist of?

We took care of the wounded, gave them water, fed them, brought bedpans—all that was our job. I was on duty with an older girl. She tried to spare me at first: "If they ask for a bedpan, call me." There were badly wounded men: one without an arm, another without a leg. The first day I kept calling her, and then I remained alone, because she couldn't really stay with me day and night. So I stayed by myself. A wounded man called me, "Nurse, a bedpan."

I brought him a bedpan, and I saw he didn't take it. I looked: he had no arms. My brain was in a whirl; somehow I figured out what had to be done, but for several minutes I stood not knowing what to do. You understand me? I had to help him . . . And I didn't know what to do, I'd never seen it. They didn't even teach it in the courses . . .

Alexandra Semyonovna Masakovskaya
PRIVATE, COOK

I didn't shoot . . . I cooked kasha for the soldiers. They gave me a medal for that. I don't even remember about it: did I ever fight? I cooked kasha, soup for the soldiers. I carried cauldrons, pails. Very heavy . . . I remember our commander used to say, "I'd shoot all these pails . . . How are you going to give birth after the war?" And once he up and shot at all those pails. We had to find smaller ones in some village.

The soldiers would come back from the front line for some rest. The poor things were all filthy, exhausted, their hands and feet frostbitten. The Uzbeks and Tajiks were especially afraid of frost. In their parts it's always sunny, and here we had minus twenty to minus forty. The man couldn't get warm, I had to feed him, he couldn't bring the spoon to his mouth.

Maria Stepanovna Detko
PRIVATE, LAUNDRESS

I did laundry . . . I went all through the war with a tub. We did it by hand. Padded jackets, army shirts . . . They would deliver underwear, so worn out, infested with lice. White robes, you know, those camouflage ones. All bloody, not white, but red. Black from old blood. The first water is red or black—you can't launder in it . . . An army shirt without a sleeve, and with a big hole in the chest, trousers without a leg. You wash them with tears and rinse them with tears.

Heaps and heaps of these army shirts . . . Padded coats . . . My hands ache now as I remember it. In winter these coats were heavy, with frozen blood on them. I often see it in dreams now . . . A black heap of them . . .

Maria Nikolaevna Vasilevskaya
SERGEANT, RADIO OPERATOR

There were so many miracles during the war . . . I'll tell you . . .

Anya Kaburova is lying on the grass . . . Our radio operator. She's dying—a bullet hit her heart. Just then a wedge of cranes flew over us. Everybody raised their heads to the sky, and she opened her eyes. She looked: "What a pity, girls." Then paused and smiled: "Can it be, girls, that I'm going to die?" Just then our mailwoman, our Klava, comes running and shouting, "Don't die! Don't die! You've got a letter from home . . ." Anya doesn't close her eyes, she waits . . .

Our Klava sat next to her, opened the envelope. A letter from mama: "My dear, my beloved little daughter . . ." The doctor stands next to me, he says, "This is a miracle. A miracle! She lives contrary to all the laws of medicine . . ." They finished reading the letter . . . And only then did Anya close her eyes . . .

Vasilisa Yuzhnina
PRIVATE, HAIRDRESSER

My specialty . . . My specialty is men's haircuts . . .

A girl comes . . . I don't know how to cut her hair. She has luxuriant wavy hair. The commander enters the dugout. "Give her a man's haircut."

"But she's a woman."

"No, she's a soldier. She'll be a woman again after the war."

All the same . . . All the same, as soon as the girls' hair grew a little, I'd curl it during the night. We had cones instead of curlers . . . Dry pine cones . . . We could at least curl the forelock . . .

Anna Zakharovna Gorlach
PRIVATE, LAUNDRESS

I hadn't read many books . . . And I didn't know any fancy talk . . . We clothed the soldiers, laundered, ironed for them—that was our heroism. We rode on horseback, less often by train. Our horses were exhausted, you could say we got to Berlin on foot. And since we're remembering like this, we did everything that was necessary: helped to carry the wounded, delivered shells by hand at the Dnieper, because it was impossible to transport them. We carried them from several miles away. We made dugouts, built bridges . . .

We fell into an encirclement, I ran, shot, like everybody else. Whether I killed or not, I can't say. I ran and shot, like everybody else.

It seems I've remembered very little. But there was so much of everything! I'll remember . . . Come again . . .

Natalya Mukhametdinova
PRIVATE, BAKER

My story is a short one . . .

The sergeant major asks, "How old are you, girl?"

"Sixteen, why?"

"Because," he says, "we don't need minors."

"I'll do whatever you like. Even bake bread."

They took me . . .

Elena Vilenskaya
SERGEANT, CLERK

I was enlisted as a clerk . . . This is how they persuaded me to go work at headquarters . . . They told me: we know you worked as a photographer before the war, you'll be our photographer.

What I remember well was that I didn't want to take pictures of death. Of the dead. I took pictures when the soldiers were at rest—smoking, laughing—when awards were handed out. It's too bad I didn't have color film then, only black-and-white. Carrying the regimental banner . . . I could have taken a beautiful picture of that . . .

And today . . . Journalists come to me and ask, "Did you take pictures of the dead? The battlefield . . ." I began to look . . . I have few pictures of dead men . . . When someone was killed, the boys would ask me, "Have you got him alive?" We wanted to see him alive . . . Smiling . . .

Zoya Lukyanovna Verzhbitskaya
COMMANDER OF A UNIT IN A CONSTRUCTION BATTALION

We built . . . Built railroads, pontoon bridges, blinds. The front was close by. We dug the ground at night, so as not to be seen.

We cut down woods. My unit was mostly girls, all young. There were a few men, all from the reserves. How did we transport trees? We'd all pick one up and carry it. The whole unit carried one tree. We had bloody blisters . . . On our hands . . . on our shoulders . . .

Maria Semyonovna Kulakova
PRIVATE, BAKER

I finished teacher training . . . I got my diploma when the war was already going on. Because of the war they did not assign us to jobs but sent us home. I came home and a few days later was summoned to the recruiting office. Mama, of course, didn't want me to go. I was very young, only eighteen: "I'll send you to my brother and tell them you aren't home." I said, "I'm a Komsomol member." In the recruiting office they assembled us and said: Thus and so, we need women to bake bread at the front.

This work was very hard. We had eight cast-iron ovens. We came to a devastated village or town and set them up. Having set up the ovens, we needed firewood, twenty or thirty buckets of water, five sacks of flour. We were eighteen-year-olds, and we carried hundred and fifty pound sacks of flour. Two of us would pick one up and carry it. Or forty loaves of bread on a plank. I, for instance, couldn't lift it.

Day and night by the oven, day and night. We'd finish kneading one tub, there's the next one waiting. There's a bombardment and we're baking bread . . .

Elena Nikiforovna Ievskaya
PRIVATE, LOGISTICS

And I spent the whole four years of the war on wheels . . . Went around following the signposts: "Shchukin Supply Corps," "Kozhuro Supply Corps." We would get tobacco, cigarettes, flints at the warehouse—all these things a soldier can't do without at the front—and off we'd go. Sometimes in trucks, sometimes in wagons, and often on foot with one or two soldiers. We carried it on our backs. You couldn't go to the trenches with a horse, the Germans would hear the creaking. We carried it. All on our backs, my dear . . .

Maria Alexeevna Remneva
SECOND LIEUTENANT, POSTAL WORKER

At the beginning of the war . . . I was nineteen years old . . . I lived in the town of Murom, in the Vladimir region. In October 1941 we Komsomol members were sent to build the Murom-Gorki-Kulebaki highway. When we returned from the labor front we were mobilized.

I was sent to the school of communications in Gorki, to the courses for postal workers. On finishing the courses, I was appointed to the active army, to the 60th Infantry Division. I served as an officer in the regimental mail. With my own eyes I saw people weep, kiss envelopes, when they received a letter at the front line. Many of their relations had been killed or lived on territory occupied by the enemy. They couldn't write. So we used to write letters from an Unknown Sender: "Dear soldier, it is an Unknown Girl writing to you. How is the fight with the enemy going? When will you come home with the Victory?" We sat at night writing . . . I wrote hundreds of those letters during the war . . .

OF THE SPECIAL "K" SOAP
AND THE GUARDHOUSE

Valentina Kuzminichna
Bratchikova-Borshchevskaya

LIEUTENANT, POLITICAL COMMISSAR
OF A FIELD LAUNDRY UNIT

On May 1 I got married . . . And on June 22 the war began. The first German planes came flying. I worked in an orphanage for Spanish children who had been brought to Kiev. That was 1937 . . . The civil war in Spain . . . We didn't know what to do, but the Spanish children began to dig trenches in the yard. They already knew everything . . . They were sent to the rear, and I went to the Penza region. I was given an assignment to organize courses for nurses. By the end of 1941 I personally held the exams for these courses, because all the doctors had left for the front. I handed out the certificates and also asked to be sent to the front. They sent me to Stalingrad, to an army field hospital. I was the oldest of the girls. My friend Sonia Udrugova—I'm still friends with her—was sixteen then, she had just finished ninth grade, plus these medical courses. We'd been at the front for three days, and I see Sonia sitting in the woods and crying. I go up to her: "Sonechka, why are you crying?"

"Don't you understand? I haven't seen mama for three days."

When I remind her of this incident now, she laughs.

At the Kursk Bulge I was transferred from the hospital to the field laundry unit as a political commissar. The laundresses were all hired help. We used to go somewhere in carts: there were basins, tubs sticking out, samovars to heat up water, and on top of all that the girls sat in red, green, blue, gray skirts. Everybody laughed, "Hey, there goes the laundry army!" They called me the "laundry commissar." Later on my girls got better dressed, "gussied themselves up," as they say.

The work was very hard. No mention of any washing machines. By hand . . . It was all done by women's hands . . . We arrive, they give us some cottage, or a dugout. We wash the underwear, and before we dry it we soak it in the special "K" soap to prevent lice. We had insect powder, but it didn't work. We used "K" soap, very stinky, it smelled awful. We used to dry the underwear in the same space where we did the laundry, and we also slept there. They gave us up to an ounce of soap to wash one soldier's underwear. The underwear was black as earth. Many girls got ruptures from the work, from carrying heavy things, from strain. "K" soap caused eczema, nails came off, we thought they'd never grow back. But even so, after two or three days of rest the girls had to go back and launder.

The girls obeyed me . . .

Once we came to a place where a whole unit of pilots was staying. They saw us, and we were all wearing dirty old things, and these boys scornfully said, "Look at the laundresses . . ."

My girls were almost crying. "Commissar, see what they . . ."

"Never mind, we'll show them."

We made an arrangement. In the evening my girls put on the best things they had and went to a meadow. One of our girls played the accordion, and they all danced. They had agreed, though, not to dance with the pilots. The pilots came and invited them to dance, but they didn't; they danced with each other the whole evening. The boys finally pleaded, "One fool said something, and you took offense at all of us . . ."

The rule was not to put hired hands in the guardhouse, but what could you do, if there were a hundred girls there together? We had curfew at eleven, and that was it. They tried to run away—well, girls will be girls. I used to send them to the guardhouse. Once some superiors came from another unit, and I had two girls in the guardhouse.

"What's this? You have hired hands in the guardhouse?" they asked.

I said calmly, "Comrade Colonel, write a report to headquarters. That's your business. But I have to fight for discipline. And I have exemplary order here."

With that they left.

The discipline was strict. Once I met a captain. He passed by my house just as I came out. He even stopped.

"My God! You're coming out of there, but do you know who lives there?"

"Yes."

"The political commissar lives there. Do you know how nasty she is?"

I told him I had never heard that.

"My God! She's so mean she never smiles."

"Would you like to make her acquaintance?"

"My God, no!"

Well, at that point I confessed, "Let me introduce myself, I'm the commissar!"

"No, it can't be! The things they've told me about her . . ."

I took care of my girls. We had a beautiful girl named Valya. I was once summoned away for ten days to headquarters. I came back and they told me that all those days Valya had come home late, that she was with some captain. If she was, she was, it's a bygone thing. Two months went by, I found out that Valya was pregnant. I summoned her. "Valya, how could this happen? Where are you going to go? Your stepmother" (she had no mother, she had a stepmother) "lives in a dugout." She cried and said to me, "It's your fault, if you hadn't gone away, nothing would have happened." I was like a mother, like an older sister to them.

She had a light coat, it was already cold, so I gave her my overcoat. Off she went, my Valya . . .

March 8, 1945. We organized a party for Women's Day. Tea. Some sort of candies we managed to get. My girls came out of their house and suddenly saw two Germans coming from the woods, dragging their submachine guns . . . Wounded . . . My girls surrounded them. Well, as the commissar, I wrote in a report that "today, May 8, the laundry women captured two Germans."

The next day we had a meeting of the commanders. The head of the political section said first thing, "Well, comrades, I want to give you some good news: the war will soon be over. Yesterday the laundry women from the 21st Field Laundry Unit captured two Germans."

Everybody applauded.

While the war went on, we received no awards, but when it was over, they told me, "Present two people for awards." I was indignant. I took the floor and said that I was the political commissar of the laundry unit, that the work of the laundresses was very hard, that many of them had ruptures and eczema on their hands and so on, that the girls were all young and worked more than trucks, than tractors. They asked me, "Can you present award-worthy material by tomorrow? We'll give more awards." And the commander of the unit and I sat all night over the lists. Many girls received medals "For Valor," "For Military Services," and one laundress was awarded the Order of the Red Star. She was the best laundress, she never left the tub: everybody was exhausted, falling off their feet, and she went on laundering. She was an older woman, her whole family had been killed.

When I had to send the girls home, I wanted to give them something. They were all from Belorussia and Ukraine, where everything was devastated, destroyed. How could I let them go empty-handed? We were stationed in some German village, and there was a sewing workshop in it. I went to look: luckily, the sewing machines were there, untouched. And so we prepared a present for each girl who was leaving. I was so glad, so happy. That was all I could do for my girls.

They all wanted to go home, and they were afraid to go. No one knew what awaited them there . . .

Tamara Lukyanovna Torop
PRIVATE, CONSTRUCTION ENGINEER

My papa . . . My beloved papa was a Communist, a holy man. I never met a better man in my life. He educated me: "Well, who would I be without Soviet power? A poor man. I'd be a hired hand for some rich kulak. Soviet power gave me everything. I received an education, I became an engineer, I build bridges. I owe everything to our own power."

I loved Soviet power. I loved Stalin. And Voroshilov. All our leaders. So my papa taught me.

The war was going on, I was growing up. In the evenings papa and I sang "The Internationale" and "The Holy War." Papa accompanied on the accordion. When I turned eighteen, he went with me to the recruiting office . . .

I wrote a letter home from the army telling him that I had built and defended bridges. What joy that was for our family. Papa made us all fall in love with bridges; we loved them from childhood. When I saw a destroyed bridge—bombed or exploded—I felt about it as about a living being, not a strategic object. I wept . . . On my way I encountered hundreds of destroyed bridges, big and small; during the war they were the first thing to be destroyed. Target number one. Whenever we went past the ruins, I always thought: how many years will it take to rebuild it all? War kills time, precious human time. I remembered well that papa spent several years building each bridge. He sat up nights over the drafts, even on weekends. The thing I was most sorry for during the war was the time. Papa's time . . .

Papa's long gone, but I continue to love him. I don't believe it when people say that men like him were stupid and blind—believing in Stalin. Fearing Stalin. Believing in Lenin's ideas. Everyone thought the same way. Believe me, they were good and honest people, they believed not in Lenin or Stalin, but in the Communist idea. In socialism with a human face, as they would call it later. In happiness for everybody. For each one. Dreamers, idealists—yes; blind—no. I'll never agree with that. Not for anything! In the middle of the war Russia began to produce excellent tanks and planes, good weapons, but even so, without faith we would never have overcome such a formidable enemy as Hitler's army—powerful, disciplined, which subjugated the whole of Europe. We wouldn't have broken its back. Our main weapon was faith, not fear. I give you my honest Party-member's word (I joined the Party during the war and am a Communist to this day). I'm not ashamed of my Party card and have not renounced it. My faith has never changed since 1941 . . .

Elena Ivanovna Babina
MILITIA FIGHTER

The German troops were stopped at Voronezh . . . They were unable to take Voronezh for a long time. They kept bombing and bombing it. The planes flew over our village, Moskovka. I still hadn't seen the enemy, I had only seen their planes. But very soon I learned what war was . . .

Our hospital was informed that a train had been bombed near Voronezh. We came to the place and saw . . . What did we see? Nothing but ground meat . . . I can't even talk about it . . . Aie, aie! The first one to come to his senses was our head doctor. He shouted loudly, "Stretchers!" I was the youngest, I had just turned sixteen, and everybody kept an eye on me in case I fainted.

We walked along the rails, went inside the cars. There was no one to put on the stretchers: the cars were burning, there was no moaning or screaming. There were no whole people. I clutched my heart, my eyes were closing from fright. When we returned to the hospital, we all collapsed wherever: one put her head on a table, another on a chair—and we fell asleep like that.

I finished my shift and went home. I came all in tears, lay down, and as soon as I closed my eyes, I saw it all again . . . Mama came home from work, Uncle Mitya came.

I hear mama's voice: "I don't know what will become of Lena. Look what's happened to her face since she went to work in the hospital. She doesn't look herself, she's quiet, doesn't speak to anyone, and she cries out during the night. Where's her smile, where's her laughter? You know how cheerful she used to be. Now she never jokes."

I listened to my mother and my tears poured down.

. . . When Voronezh was liberated in 1943, I joined the defense militia. There were only girls in it. They were all from seventeen to twenty years old. Young, beautiful, I've never seen so many beautiful girls together. The first one I got to know was Marusya Prokhorova; she was friends with Tanya Fedorova. They were from the same village. Tanya was a serious girl, she liked neatness and order. And Marusya liked to sing and dance. She sang naughty couplets. Most of all she liked to put on makeup. She'd spend hours sitting in front of the mirror. Tanya scolded her: "Instead of painting your face, you'd do better to iron your uniform and tidy up your bed." We also had Pasha Litavrina, a very feisty girl. She was friends with Shura Batishcheva. This Shura was shy and modest, the quietest of us all. Liusya Likhacheva liked to have her hair curled. She'd put her hair in curlers and take her guitar. She went to bed with the guitar and woke up with the guitar. The oldest of us was Polina Neverova; her husband was killed at the front, and she was always sad.

We all wore military uniforms. When mama saw me in uniform for the first time, she turned pale. "Have you decided to join the army?"

I set her at ease. "No, mama. I told you I keep watch on the bridges."

Mama wept. "Soon the war will be over. And you'll take off the army coat at once."

I thought so, too.

Two days after learning that the war was over, we had a meeting in the reading room. The head of the militia, Comrade Naumov, took the floor. "My dear combatants," he said, "the war is over. But yesterday I received an order saying that militia combatants are needed for the Western Road."

Someone in the audience shouted, "But Bandera's men are there!"*

Naumov paused and then said, "Yes, girls, Bandera's men are there. They're fighting against the Red Army. But an order is an order, it has to be carried out. Whoever wants to go, please apply to the head of the militia. Only volunteers will go."

We returned to the barrack, and each lay down on her bed. It became very, very quiet. No one wanted to go far from their native places. And no one wanted to die after the war was over. The next day they gathered us again. I sat at the presiding table; the table was covered with a red cloth. And I thought that this was the last time I'd be sitting at this table.

The head of the militia made a speech: "I knew, Babina, that you'd be the first to volunteer. And you are all fine girls, no cowards. The war is over, you could go back home, but you go to defend your Motherland."

Two days later we were leaving. They put us on a freight train. There was hay on the floors, and it smelled of grass.

I had never heard of the town of Stryy before, but that was where we were stationed now. I didn't like the town—it was small and frightening. Every day music played and someone was buried: a policeman, or a Communist, or a Komsomol member. Again we saw death.

---

* Stepan Bandera (1909–1959) is a controversial Ukrainian political figure. A nationalist and leader of a movement for independence of Ukraine from the Soviet Union, he led forces against the advancing Red Army in 1944 with aid from Germany. In 1959 he was assassinated by the Soviet secret police.

I made friends with Galya Korobkina. She was killed there. And another girl . . . She too was stabbed in the night . . . There I completely stopped joking and smiling . . .

OF MELTED BEARINGS AND RUSSIAN CURSES

Antonina Mironovna Lenkova

CAR MECHANIC IN A FIELD-CAR AND TANK REPAIR SHOP

I'm all my father . . . His daughter . . .

My father, Miron Lenkov, made his way from a simple illiterate lad to commander of a platoon in the Civil War. He was a real Communist. When he died, mama and I stayed in Leningrad. What is best in me I owe to this city. My passion was books. I sobbed over the novels of Lidia Charskaya,* read and reread Turgenev. I loved poetry . . .

The summer of 1941 . . . At the end of June we went to the Don to visit my grandmother. The war overtook us on the road. On the steppes mounted messengers immediately appeared, racing at breakneck speed, delivering summonses from the recruiting office. Cossack women sang, drank, and sobbed as they saw the Cossacks off to war. I went to the village of Bokovskaya, to the regional recruiting office. They said curtly and severely, "We don't take children to the front. Are you a Komsomol member? Excellent. Help the collective farm."

We shoveled piles of grain to save it from rotting inside. Then we harvested vegetables. Calluses hardened on my hands, my lips were

---

* Lidia Charskaya (1875–1938) was an actress at the prestigious Alexandrinsky Theater in St. Petersburg and a prolific writer of popular fiction. Her work was officially banned in 1920.

cracked, my face was covered with a steppe tan. And if I was in any way different from the farm girls, it was only in that I knew many poems and could recite them by heart all the long way home from the fields.

The war was coming closer. On October 17, the Germans occupied Taganrog. People began to evacuate. My grandmother stayed, but she sent me and my sister off: "You're young. Save yourselves." We spent five days walking to the Oblivskaya station. We had to throw out our sandals, and we entered the village barefoot. The stationmaster warned us, "Don't wait for a passenger train, get onto the flatcars, we'll bring the locomotive at once and send you to Stalingrad." We were lucky—we got onto a flatcar with oats. We sank our bare feet into the grain, covered ourselves with a shawl . . . Clinging close to each other, we dozed off. We'd long been out of bread and out of honey, too. The last few days Cossack women gave us food. We were embarrassed, we had no money to pay them, but they insisted, "Eat, poor things. It's bad for everybody now, we must help each other." I made a vow never to forget this human kindness. Never! Not for anything! And I haven't.

From Stalingrad we went by steamboat and then again by train, and reached the Medveditskoe station at two o'clock in the morning. A human wave carried us out onto the platform. Having turned into a pair of icicles, we were unable to move. We stood, supporting each other so as not to fall down, not to break into smithereens, as a frog did once in front of my eyes, taken out of liquid oxygen and thrown on the floor. Fortunately, someone we had traveled with remembered us. A carriage filled with people came, and we were tied behind it. They gave us padded jackets. They said, "Walk, otherwise you'll freeze. You won't be able to get warm. You can't be driven . . ." At first we kept falling, but we walked, then even ran. Ten miles . . .

The Frank settlement, the "First of May" kolkhoz. The chairman was very glad when he learned that I was from Leningrad and had finished ninth grade. "That's good. You'll help me here. With the accounting."

For a moment I was even glad. But then behind the chairman's back I saw a poster saying, "Girls, to the steering wheel!"

"I'm not going to sit in an office," I answered the chairman. "If they teach me, I'll be able to drive a tractor."

The tractors stood buried in snow. We dug them out, took them apart, burning our hands against the frozen metal, leaving pieces of skin stuck to them. The rusted, tightly screwed bolts seemed welded. When we didn't succeed in unscrewing them counterclockwise, we tried to do it clockwise. As luck would have it . . . just at that moment . . . as if from under the earth, the foreman Ivan Ivanovich Nikitin appeared, the only real tractor driver and our instructor. He clutched his head and couldn't keep from using good Russian foul language. Ah, fuck it all! His curses sounded like groans. But all the same I wept for once . . .

I rode out to the field backward; most of the gears in the gearbox of my STZ were "toothless." The thinking was simple: within fifteen miles, one of the tractors would break down and its gearbox would replace mine. That is what happened. A young tractor driver, a girl like me, Sarochka Gozenbuck, didn't notice that there was no water left in the radiator, and she ruined her motor. Ah, fuck it all . . .

Before the war I hadn't even learned to ride a bicycle, but here was a tractor. We spent a long time heating the motors—with open flames, in violation of all the rules. I also found out what overwinding was. And how do you start the motor after such a procedure: you couldn't turn the handle all the way, and halfway wasn't enough . . . The lubricants and the fuel were rationed by the war norms. You answered with your head for every drop, as well as for melted bearings. Ah, fuck it all . . . For every drop . . .

That day . . . Before going to the field I opened the crankcase to check the oil. Some sort of whey came out. I shouted to the foreman that I had to fill up with motor oil. He came, rubbed a drop in his hands, sniffed it for some reason, and said, "No fear! You can work one more day." I objected, "No, you yourself said . . ." He flew off the handle: "I said it, so now it's on my head—there's no escaping you. City dolls! Much too educated. Ah, fuck it all . . ." Drive, devil take it . . . I drove off. It was hot, the tractor smoked, impossible to breathe, but it was all nonsense. What about the bearings? I thought there was a bit of knocking. I stopped—there was nothing. I stepped on the pedal—there's knocking! Then all of a sudden right under the seat: bam, bam, bam!

I cut the motor, ran to the access hatch, opened it: two bearings on the connecting rod were completely melted!

I sank on the ground, put my arms around the wheel and—for the second time during the war—burst into tears. It was my fault: I had seen what kind of oil I had! I got scared of his foul mouth. I should have answered him in kind, but no, I'm too genteel for that.

I turned at some sounds. Well, well! The chairman of the kolkhoz, the director of the machine-tractor station, the head of the political section and, of course, our foreman. Who caused it all!

And he stands there and can't move. He understands it all. Says nothing. Ah, fuck it all . . .

The director of the MTS asks, "How many?"

"Two," I reply.

By the law of wartime I should go on trial for that. For negligence and sabotage.

The head of the political section turns to the foreman. "Why don't you look after your girls? How can I put this baby on trial!"

So it got settled. With just talk. And the foreman never again used foul language in front of me. And I learned from it, too . . . Ah, fuck it all . . . I could make a scene . . .

Then happiness came: we found our mama. She came, and we were a family again. Mama suddenly said, "I think you should go back to school."

I didn't understand right away what she meant. "Go where?"

"Who else is going to finish high school for you?"

After all that I had lived through, it was strange to find myself at a school desk, solving problems, writing compositions, memorizing German verbs, instead of fighting the fascists! At a time when the enemy had reached the Volga!

I didn't have very long to wait: in four months I would turn seventeen. Not eighteen yet, but at least seventeen. Then nobody could force me to go home! Nobody!

In the regional committee everything went smoothly, but in the recruiting office I had to put up a fight. Because of my age, because of my eyesight. But the first helped the second . . . When they brought up the question of my age, I called the commissar a bureaucrat . . . And started a hunger strike . . . I sat next to him and didn't budge for two days, refusing the offered slice of bread and a mug of boiled water. I threatened to die of hunger, but first to write who was guilty of my death. I don't think this frightened him, but even so he sent me for a medical exam. All this was taking place in the same room. Next to him. When the doctor, having checked my vision, spread her arms, the commissar laughed and said that my hunger strike was unnecessary. He felt sorry for me. I answered that I could see nothing because of the hunger strike. Having gone to the window and closer to the ill-favored eye chart, I burst into tears. I wept . . . For a long time . . . until I learned the lower lines by heart. Then I wiped my tears and said that I was ready to be examined again. I passed.

On November 10, 1942, having stocked up on food for ten days, as we had been told to, we (some twenty-five young girls) got into the back of a shabby truck, and began to sing "The Order Is Given," replacing the words "for the Civil War" with "to defend our country."

From Kamyshino, where we took the oath, we marched on foot along the left bank of the Volga to Kapustin Yar. There an auxiliary regiment was stationed. And there, among the thousands of men, we somehow got lost. There were "buyers" coming from various units to recruit reinforcements. They tried to ignore us. Passed us over all the time . . .

On the way I became friends with Annushka Rakshenko and Asya Bassina. Neither of them had any specialization, and I considered my own to be unmilitary. And therefore, whatever specialization was called out, the three of us together took three steps forward, thinking that we could master any specialization quickly, on the spot. But we were bypassed.

But when we stepped forward at the command, "Drivers, tractor drivers, mechanics—three steps forward!" the "buyer"—he was a young first lieutenant—didn't succeed in passing us over. I took not three steps but five, and he stopped.

"Why do you select only men? I, too, am a tractor driver!"

He was surprised. "It can't be. Tell me the assignment number for tractor work."

"One, three, four, two."

"Have you melted any bearings?"

I confessed honestly that I had completely melted two connecting rod bearings.

"Very well. I'll take you. For your honesty." He nodded and went on.

My girlfriends were standing with me. Next to me. The first lieutenant pretended that that's how it should be. Ah, fuck it all . . .

The commander of the unit, reviewing the reinforcements, asked the first lieutenant a question, "Why did you bring these girls?"

The man was embarrassed and replied that he felt sorry for us: we might wind up in some place where we'd be killed like partridges.

The commander sighed.

"Very well. One to the kitchen, one to the stockroom, the most educated one to the headquarters as a clerk." He paused and added, "A pity, such beautiful girls."

The "most educated one" was me, but to work as a clerk! And what did our beauty have to do with it? Forgetting about military discipline, I went through the roof: "We're volunteers! We came to defend the Motherland. We'll only go to the combat units . . ."

For some reason the colonel yielded at once. "All right, let it be combat. These two—to the letuchki, to work on the machines, and the one with the glib tongue—to engine assembly."

This is how our service in the 44th Automobile–Armored Vehicle Field Shop began. We were a factory on wheels. On special trucks, called letuchki, machines were installed for milling, boring, polishing, turning. There was an electric generator, casting, vulcanization. Each machine was worked by two persons. Twelve hours of work without a moment of rest. The partner stayed while the other went to eat dinner, supper, breakfast. If one's turn came to go on assignment, the other worked twenty-four hours. We worked in snow, in mud. Under bombardment. And no one told us again that we were beautiful. But beautiful girls were pitied at the war, more pitied. That's true. It was a pity to bury them . . . A pity to send the death notice to their mamas . . . Ah, fuck it all . . .

I often have dreams nowadays . . . I know I have them, but I rarely remember them. But I'm left with the impression that I have been somewhere . . . And come back . . . In a dream, what took years in real life takes just a second. And sometimes I confuse dream and reality . . . I think it was in Zimovniki, I just lay down for a couple of hours, when the bombardment began. Eh, you! Fuck it all . . . Better to be killed than spoil the pleasure of a two-hour nap. There was a big explosion somewhere nearby. The house rocked. But I still went on sleeping . . .

Fear was absent in me, there was no such feeling. I give you my word. Only after the most violent raids, I had a throbbing in a tooth that had a cavity. And that not for long. I might still consider myself terribly brave, if, a few years after the war, owing to constant, unbearable, and totally incomprehensible pains in various parts of my body, I hadn't had to consult specialists. And a very experienced neuropathologist, having asked my age, said in amazement, "To have ruined your whole vegetative nervous system by the age of twenty-four! How are you going to live?"

I replied that I was going to live quite well. First of all, I was alive! I had dreamed so much of surviving! Yes, I had survived, but after just a few months of my civilian life, my joints got swollen, my right arm refused to work and was in terrible pain, my vision deteriorated, one of my kidneys turned out to have descended, my liver was not in the right place, and, as it turned out later, my vegetative nervous system was completely ruined. But all through the war I had dreamed that I would study. And the university became like a second Stalingrad for me. I finished it a year early, otherwise I would have run out of energy. Four years in the same overcoat—winter, spring, autumn—and an army shirt so faded it looked white . . . Ah, fuck it all . . .

"THEY NEEDED SOLDIERS . . .
BUT WE ALSO WANTED
TO BE BEAUTIFUL . . ."

———

Over several years I recorded hundreds of stories . . . Hundreds of cassettes and thousands of typed pages are arranged on my bookshelves. I listen and read attentively . . .

The world of war reveals itself to me from an unexpected side. Never before did I ask myself the questions: How could one, for instance, sleep for years in shallow trenches or on the bare ground by a bonfire, go around in heavy boots and overcoats, and finally—not laugh and dance? Not wear summer dresses? Forget about shoes and flowers . . . They were eighteen or twenty years old! I was used to thinking that there was no room for a woman's life in the war. It is impossible there, almost forbidden. But I was wrong . . . Very soon, already during my first meetings with them, I noticed: whatever the women talked about, even if it was death, they always remembered (yes!) about beauty. It was the indestructible part of their existence: "She was so beautiful lying in the coffin . . . Like a bride . . ." (A. Strotseva, infantry soldier) or: "They were going to award me a medal, and I had an old army shirt. I sewed myself a collar out of gauze. Anyway it was white . . . It seemed to me at that moment that I was so beautiful. There was no mirror, I couldn't see myself. Everything got smashed during a bombardment . . ." (N. Ermakova, radio operator). They told cheerfully and willingly about their naïve girlish ruses, little secrets, invisible signs of how in the "male" everyday life of war and the "male" business of war they still wanted to remain themselves. Not to betray their nature. Their astonishing memory (after all, forty years had gone by) preserved a great number of small details of war life. Details, nuances, colors, and sounds. In their world everyday life and essential life joined together, and the flow of essential life had a value of its own. They recalled the war as a time of life. Not so much of action as of life. I observed more than once how in their conversations the small overrode the great, even history. "It's a pity that I was beautiful only during the war . . . My best years were spent there. Burned up. Afterward I aged quickly . . ." (Anna Galai, submachine gunner).

At a distance of many years some events suddenly grew bigger, others diminished. The human, the intimate grew bigger, becoming for me and, most curiously, even for them, more interesting and close. The human overcame the inhuman, if only because it was human. "Don't be afraid of my tears. Don't pity me. Let it be painful for me, but I'm grateful to you that I've recalled myself when I was young . . ." (K. S. Tikhonovich, sergeant, antiaircraft gunner).

I also did not know this war. And did not even suspect it . . .

OF MEN'S BOOTS AND WOMEN'S HATS

Maria Nikolaevna Shchelokova

SERGEANT, COMMANDER OF A COMMUNICATIONS SECTION

We lived in the ground . . . like moles . . . But we did have some little trifles. In spring you would bring in a little sprig, set it up. Feel happy. Maybe tomorrow you won't be there—that's what we thought to ourselves. And you remember, remember . . . One girl received a woolen dress from home. We envied her, although wearing your own clothes wasn't allowed. The sergeant major—a man, that is— grumbled, "They'd do better to send you sheets. It's more useful." We had no sheets, no pillows. We slept on branches or on hay. But I had a pair of earrings stashed away; I'd put them on at night and sleep with them on . . .

When I got a concussion for the first time, I couldn't hear or speak. I said to myself, "If the voice doesn't come back, I'll throw myself under a train." I used to sing so well, and suddenly I had no voice. But my voice came back.

I was so happy, I put on my earrings. I arrived for duty and shouted with joy, "Comrade First Lieutenant, Sergeant Shchelokova reporting for duty . . ."

"And what's that?"

"What's what?"

"Get out of here!"

"What's the matter?"

"Pull the earrings off at once! What kind of soldier are you?"

This first lieutenant was very handsome. All our girls were a little in love with him. He used to tell us that in war soldiers were called for and only soldiers. They needed soldiers . . . But we also wanted to be beautiful . . . All through the war I was afraid that I'd be hit in the legs and get crippled. I had beautiful legs. What is it for a man? Even if he loses his legs, it's not so terrible. He's a hero anyway. He can marry! But if a woman is crippled, it's her destiny that's at stake. A woman's destiny . . .

Vera Vladimirovna Shevaldysheva
FIRST LIEUTENANT, SURGEON

I smiled all through the war . . . I figured that I had to smile as often as possible, because a woman should bring light. Before we left for the front, our old professor told us this: "You have to tell every wounded soldier that you love him. Your strongest medicine is love. Love protects, it gives the strength to survive." A wounded man lies there, he's in so much pain that he weeps, and you tell him, "There, my dearest.

There, my good one . . ." "Do you love me, nursie?" (They called all the young ones "nursie.") "Of course, I do. Only get well quickly." They could get offended, say bad things, but we never could. For one rude word they punished us with the guardhouse.

Hard . . . Of course it was hard . . . Even, say, climbing into a truck wearing a skirt, when there are only men around. Those were special ambulance trucks, very high ones. Climb to the very top! Just try it . . .

Nadezhda Vasilyevna Alexeeva

PRIVATE, TELEGRAPHER

They put us on a train . . . A freight train . . . We were twelve girls, the rest were all men. The train would go seven or ten miles and stop. Another seven or ten miles . . . Again a dead end. There was no water, no toilet . . . See?

Men would make a fire at a halt, shake out lice, get dry. And what were we to do? We would go to some nook and get undressed there. I wore a knitted sweater; lice sat on every sixteenth of an inch, on every stitch. I'd look and get sick. There are head lice, clothes lice, pubic lice . . . I had them all . . . What was I to do? I couldn't go and roast the lice together with the men. It was embarrassing. I threw the sweater out and stayed just in my dress. At some station an unknown woman gave me a jacket and some old shoes.

We rode for a long time, and then walked for a long time. It was freezing cold. I walked and kept looking in the mirror to see whether I was frostbitten. Toward evening I saw that my cheeks were frostbitten. I was so stupid . . . I'd heard that when the cheeks are frostbitten, they turn white. Mine were very red. I thought, let them stay frostbitten for good. But the next day they turned black . . .

Anastasia Petrovna Sheleg
JUNIOR SERGEANT, AEROSTAT OPERATOR

There were many pretty girls among us . . . We went to the bath-house, and there was a hairdresser's shop there. So, one after the other, we all dyed our eyebrows. The commander really gave it to us: "Have you come to fight or to a ball?" We spent the whole night crying and rubbing it off. In the morning he went around and repeated to each girl, "I need soldiers, not ladies. Ladies don't survive in war." A very strict commander. Before the war he had been a math teacher . . .

Stanislava Petrovna Volkova
SECOND LIEUTENANT, COMMANDER OF A SAPPER PLATOON

It seems to me as if I've lived two lives—a man's and a woman's . . .

When I came to training school, there was immediate military discipline. In class, at drill, in the barracks—everything was according to regulations. There were no allowances because we were girls. All we heard was, "Stop talking!" "Hey, you talkers!" In the evening we longed to sit and maybe do some embroidery . . . to recall something women do . . . It was strictly forbidden. We were all without a home, without domestic chores, and we felt out of sorts. We were given only one hour of rest: we could sit in the Lenin room, write letters, or stand at ease, talk. But without laughter or loudness—that wasn't allowed.

Could you sing songs?

No, we couldn't.

Why couldn't you?

It wasn't allowed. When you're on the march, you can sing, if the order is given. The order was, "Leader, strike up!"

So you couldn't just sing?

No, that was against regulations.

Was it hard to get used to?

I think I never really got used to it. You've just fallen asleep, and suddenly: "Reveille!" It was like the wind swept us off our beds. You begin to dress. A woman has more clothes than a man, you fuss with one thing, then another. Finally, belt in hand, you fly to the locker room. You grab your overcoat on the way and race to the armory room. There you put a cover on your shovel, hang it on your belt, attach a kit, buckle it anyhow. Grab a rifle, lock the bolt as you go, and literally roll down the stairs from the fourth floor. Once in line, you straighten yourself up. You're given a few minutes to do all that.

Now we're at the front . . . My boots are three sizes too big, deformed, engrained with dust. The woman I stay with brings me two eggs: "Take them for the road. You're so thin, you're about to snap in two." Quietly, so that she didn't see, I broke those two little eggs and cleaned my boots. I was hungry, of course, but the woman's instinct won out—I wanted to be pretty. You don't know how rough the overcoat is on the skin, how heavy it all is, these men's things: the belt and everything. I especially disliked the roughness of the overcoat on my neck, and also those boots. They changed your gait, changed everything . . .

I remember we were sad. We went around sad all the time . . .

Maria Nikolaevna Stepanova

MAJOR, HEAD OF COMMUNICATIONS
IN AN INFANTRY BATTALION

It was not so easy to make soldiers out of us . . . Not so simple . . .

We were issued uniforms. The sergeant major formed us up: "Align your toes."

We align them. The toes are even, but we're not, because our boots are size twelve or fourteen. He keeps at it. "The toes, the toes!"

Then, "Cadets, even up your chests!"

That, of course, we can't manage, and he yells at the top of his voice, "What have you got in your shirt pockets?"

We laugh.

"Stop laughing," shouts the sergeant major.

To drill us in the precise and correct way of saluting, he made us salute everything—from chairs to posters on the walls. Oh, he had a hard time with us.

In some town we marched up to the bathhouse. The men went to the men's half, we to the women's. The women shout, cover themselves: "Soldiers are coming!" They couldn't tell we were girls: we had boys' haircuts and wore army uniforms. Another time we went to the toilet, and the women brought a policeman. We asked him, "So where do we go?"

He then shouted at those women, "These are girls!"

"What kind of girls, these are soldiers . . ."

Bella Isaakovna Epstein
SERGEANT, SNIPER

All I remember is the road. The road . . . Advancing, retreating . . .

When we arrived at the 2nd Belorussian Front, they wanted to have us stay at division headquarters. Meaning: you're women, why go to the front line? "No," we said, "we're snipers, send us where we're supposed to go." Then they said, "We'll send you to a regiment where there's a good commander, he takes care of girls." There were all sorts of commanders. So we were told.

This colonel met us with these words: "Look out, girls, you've come to fight, so fight, but don't get up to anything else. There are men around, and no women. Devil knows how else I can explain the thing to you. It's war, girls . . ." He understood that we were still very young things. The first time planes flew over, I crouched down and covered my head with my hands, then I thought, And what about my poor hands? I wasn't ready for death yet.

I remember how in Germany . . . Ah, this is funny! In one German village we were billeted for the night in a castle. There were many rooms, whole big halls. Such halls! The wardrobes were filled with beautiful clothes. Each girl chose a dress for herself. There was a yellow one that I liked, and also a house robe. I can't tell you what a beautiful house robe it was—long, light . . . like a fluff of down! We had to go to bed, because we were terribly tired. We put these dresses on and went to bed, and fell asleep at once. I lay in that dress and the robe on top of it . . .

Another time, in an abandoned milliner's shop, the girls each chose a hat for herself and slept all night sitting, so as to wear a hat at least for a little while. In the morning we got up . . . looked once more in the mirror . . . Then took everything off, and put on our army shirts and trousers. We never took anything. On the road even a needle is heavy. A spoon tucked into the boot top, that's all . . .

Zinaida Prokofyevna Gomareva

TELEGRAPHER

Men . . . They're so . . . They didn't always understand us . . .

But our Colonel Ptitsyn we loved very much. We called him "Daddy." He wasn't like the others, he understood our woman's soul. We're near Moscow, it's the retreat, the most difficult time, and he says to us, "Girls, Moscow is close by. I'll bring you a hairdresser. Dye your eyebrows, eyelashes, curl your hair. That's not in the rules, but I want you to be pretty. This will be a long war . . . It won't end soon . . ."

And he brought us a hairdresser. We had our hair curled, put on makeup. We were so happy . . .

Sofya Konstantinovna Dubniakova
MEDICAL ASSISTANT

We raced over the ice of Lake Ladoga . . . advancing . . . Right away we came under heavy shelling. There was water all around; a wounded man goes straight to the bottom. I'm crawling around, bandaging. I crawl up to one, his legs are broken, he's losing consciousness, but he pushes me away and tries to get into his sidor—his kit bag, that is. He's looking for his reserve rations. To eat, at least, before he dies . . . When we started to advance over the ice, we got some food supplies. I want to bandage him, but he wants his kit bag and nothing else: men had a very hard time enduring hunger. It was worse than death for them . . .

And about myself I remember this . . . At first you're afraid of death . . . Amazement and curiosity live side by side in you. Then they both vanish—from fatigue. You're at the limits of your strength. Beyond the limits. In the end only one fear remains—of being ugly after death. A woman's fear . . . Not to be torn to pieces by a shell . . . I saw it happen . . . I picked up those pieces . . .

Liubov Ivanovna Osmolovskaya
PRIVATE, SCOUT

It rained and rained . . . We ran over the mud, people fell into this mud. Wounded, killed. I didn't want to die in that swamp. A black swamp. For a young girl to lie in such mud . . . And another time, this was already in Belorussia . . . in the Orsha forests, there were small bushes of bird cherry. Blue snowdrops. A whole clearing covered with blue flowers . . . To perish among such flowers! To lie there . . . I was a silly goose, seventeen years old . . . That's how I imagined death . . .

I thought that to die was like flying off somewhere. Once during the night we talked about death, but only once. We were afraid to pronounce the word . . .

Alexandra Semyonovna Popova
LIEUTENANT OF THE GUARDS, PILOT

Our regiment was all women . . . We flew to the front in May 1942 . . .

The planes they gave us were Po-2s. Small, slow. They flew only at a low level. Hedge-hopping. Just over the ground! Before the war young people in flying clubs learned to fly in them, but no one could have imagined they would have any military use. The plane was constructed entirely of plywood, covered with aircraft fabric. In fact, with cheesecloth. One direct hit and it caught fire and burned up completely in the air, before reaching the ground. Like a match. The only solid metal part was the M-11 motor.

Later on, toward the end of the war, we were issued parachutes, and a machine gun was installed in the pilot's cabin, but before there had been no weapon, except for four bomb racks under the wings—that's all. Nowadays they'd call us kamikazes, and maybe we were kamikazes. Yes! We were! But victory was valued more than our lives. Victory!

You ask how we could endure it? I'll tell you . . .

Before I retired, I became ill from the very thought of how I could possibly not work. Why then had I completed a second degree in my fifties? I became a historian. I had been a geologist all my life. But a good geologist is always in the field, and I no longer had the strength for it. A doctor came, took a cardiogram, and asked, "When did you have a heart attack?"

"What heart attack?"

"Your heart is scarred all over."

I must have acquired those scars during the war. You approach a target, and you're shaking all over. Your whole body is shaking, because below it's all gunfire: fighter planes are shooting, antiaircraft guns are shooting . . . Several girls had to leave the regiment; they couldn't stand it. We flew mostly during the night. For a while they tried sending us on day missions, but gave it up at once. A rifle shot could bring down a Po-2 . . .

We did up to twelve flights a night. I saw the famous ace Pokryshkin when he returned from a fighting mission. He was a sturdy man, not twenty and not twenty-three like us. But while his plane was refueled, a technician took his shirt off and wrung it out. It was soaked as if he had been in the rain. So now you can easily imagine what it was like for us. You come back and you can't even get out of the cabin; they used to pull us out. We couldn't carry the chart case; we dragged it on the ground.

And the work our girl armorers did! They had to attach four bombs to the aircraft by hand—that meant eight hundred pounds. They did it all night: one plane takes off, another lands. The body reorganized itself so much during the war that we weren't women . . . We didn't have those women's things . . . Periods . . . You know . . . And after the war not all of us could have children.

We all smoked. I also smoked. It made you feel as if you'd calmed down a little. You come back to earth shaking all over, you light a cigarette—and you calm down. We wore leather jackets, trousers, army shirts, plus a fur jacket in winter. Like it or not something masculine appeared in your gait and your movements. When the war was over, they made us khaki-colored dresses. We suddenly felt we were young girls . . .

Sofya Adamovna Kuntsevich

SERGEANT MAJOR, MEDICAL ASSISTANT IN AN INFANTRY COMPANY

They gave me a medal recently . . . from the Red Cross . . . The Florence Nightingale international gold medal. Everybody congratulates me and wonders, "How could you drag out 147 wounded men? You're such a diminutive girl in the wartime photos . . ." Well, maybe I dragged out two hundred, nobody was counting then. It never entered my head, we didn't understand it that way. A battle was going on, people were losing blood, so should I sit and take notes? I never waited for the attack to be over, I crawled around during the combat picking up the wounded. If a man had a shrapnel wound and I arrived an hour or two later, there would have been nothing for me to do, the man would have lost all his blood.

I was wounded three times and had a concussion three times. People dreamed of all sorts of things during the war: one of going back home, another of getting to Berlin, and I wished for just one thing—to live until my birthday, so as to turn eighteen. For some reason I was afraid to die without having lived at least eighteen years. I used to wear trousers, a forage cap, and I was always in tatters, because I always crawled on my knees, and under the weight of the wounded man. It was hard to believe that a day would come when I would be able to get up and walk, not crawl on the ground. That was my dream! One day a division commander arrived, saw me, and asked, "Who is this adolescent boy? Why do you keep him here? He should be sent to school . . ."

I remember when there weren't enough bandages . . . There were such terrible bullet wounds that each needed a whole package. I tore up all my underwear, and I told the boys, "Take off your long johns, your undershirts, I've got people dying here." They took everything off, tore it up. I wasn't embarrassed in front of them, they were like brothers to me, and I lived among them like a boy. We would march by three holding hands, and the middle one could sleep for an hour or two. Then we'd change places.

I got as far as Berlin. I put my signature on the Reichstag: "I, Sofya Kuntsevich, came here to kill war."

When I see a common grave, I kneel before it. Before every common grave . . . always on my knees . . .

OF A GIRLISH TREBLE AND
SAILORS' SUPERSTITIONS

Klara Semyonovna Tikhonovich
SERGEANT, ANTIAIRCRAFT GUNNER

I heard . . . words . . . Poison . . . Words like stones . . . It was men's desire—to go and fight. Can a woman kill?! Those were abnormal, defective women . . .

No! A thousand times no! No, it was a human desire. The war was going on, I lived my usual life. A girl's life . . . Then a neighbor received a letter: her husband was wounded and in the hospital. I thought, "He's wounded, and who will replace him?" One came without an arm—who will replace him? Another came back without a leg—who will go instead of him? I wrote letters, begged, pleaded to be taken into the army. That's how we were brought up, that nothing in our country should happen without us. We had been taught to love it. To admire it. Since there's a war, it's our duty to help in some way. There's a need for nurses, so we must become nurses. There's a need for antiaircraft gunners, so we must become antiaircraft gunners.

Did we want to resemble men at the front? At first we did, very much: we cut our hair short, we even changed our way of walking. But later, no, no way! Later we wanted to put on makeup, we saved sugar, instead of eating it, to stiffen our bangs. We were happy to get hold of a pot of water to wash our hair. During a long march we searched for soft grass. We tore up some grass and rubbed our legs . . . You see, we used the grass to wash off the . . . We were girls, we had our special needs . . . The army didn't think about it . . . Our legs were green . . . It was good if the sergeant major was an older man and understood everything, and didn't confiscate extra underwear from a kit bag. A young one was sure to throw it out. But it wasn't extra for a girl who had to change underwear twice a day. We used to tear sleeves from the undershirts, and we had only two, meaning only four sleeves . . .

Klara Vasilyevna Goncharova
PRIVATE, ANTIAIRCRAFT GUNNER

Before the war I loved everything military . . . Men's things . . . I wrote to the school of aviation requesting application forms. I looked good in a military uniform. I liked formation, precision, abrupt words of command. The response from the school was: "First finish high school."

Of course, when the war began, with my mood I couldn't stay home. But they wouldn't take me at the front. By no means, because I was sixteen. The military commissar said, Why, what will the enemy think of us, if the war has only just begun, and we're sending such children to the front—underaged girls!

"We must crush the enemy."

"We'll crush him without you."

I insisted that I was tall, that no one would know I was sixteen, that they'd think I was older. I stood in his office refusing to leave: "Write that I'm eighteen, not sixteen." "You say that now, and what will you think of me later?"

After the war I no longer wanted, I couldn't go into any sort of military specialization. I wanted to take off all the khaki color quickly . . . I detest trousers to this day. I won't wear them even to the forest to pick mushrooms or berries. I wanted to wear something ordinary, feminine . . .

Maria Nesterovna Kuzmenko
SERGEANT MAJOR, ARMORER

We felt the war at once . . . We graduated from professional school and the very same day the "buyers" came to us. That's what we called those who came to our school to recruit new people for the reorganized units. They were always men, and you could tell that they pitied us. We looked at them in one way, they looked at us in another. We tried to break the line, to step forward, to be taken, to be noticed, to show ourselves the sooner. They were tired and looked at us knowing where we were going to be sent. They understood everything.

Our regiment was all men, only twenty-two women. It was the 870th Long-range Artillery Regiment. We brought two or three changes of underwear from home, we couldn't take more. They bombarded us, and we were left with what we had on when we ran away. Men went to the depot and got a change of clothes. But there was nothing for us. They gave us footwraps, and we made panties and bras out of them. The commander found out and yelled at us.

Six months later . . . We were so overworked we ceased to be women . . . We stopped having . . . The biological cycle got thrown off . . . See? Very frightening! It's frightening to think that you'll never be a woman again . . .

Maria Semyonovna Kaliberda
SERGEANT, RADIO OPERATOR

We tried hard . . . We didn't want people to say of us, "Ah, these women!" And we made greater efforts than men did. We had to prove that we were no worse than men. For a long time there was this haughty, condescending attitude to us: "Some warriors, these women . . ."

But how could we be men? It was impossible. Our thoughts were one thing, our nature—another. Our biology . . .

We march . . . About two hundred girls, then about two hundred men. It's hot. A forced march of twenty miles. Twenty! We march, and leave these red spots behind us in the sand . . . red traces . . . The women's thing. How can you hide anything here? The soldiers come after us and pretend that they don't notice anything . . . don't look under their feet . . . Our trousers got dry on us and became sharp as glass. They'd cut us. We had wounds and there was always the smell of blood. The army didn't provide us with anything . . . We were on the lookout: when the soldiers hung their shirts on the bushes, we'd steal a couple . . . They figured it out and laughed. "Sergeant, give us spare underwear. The girls took ours." There wasn't enough cotton wool and bandaging for the wounded . . . And nothing for our . . . Women's underwear appeared maybe two years later. We wore men's underpants and tank tops. So, we march . . . In boots! Our feet are roasted, too. We march . . . To the crossing, where the ferries are waiting. We reach the crossing, and there the shelling begins. A dreadful shelling, the men all hide wherever they can. They call us . . . And we don't even hear the shelling, we can't be bothered, we quickly run to the river. Into the water . . . Water! Water! We sat in it till we soaked it off . . . Under the shrapnel . . . That's it . . . We were more afraid of shame than of death. Several girls were killed in the water . . .

Maybe for the first time then I wanted to be a man . . . For the first time . . .

Then—the Victory. At first I'd go down the street and not believe it was Victory. I'd sit at the table and not believe it was Victory. Victory! Our Victory . . .

Anna Nikolaevna Khrolovich

LIEUTENANT OF THE GUARDS, PARAMEDIC

We were already liberating Latvia . . . We were near Daugavpils. It was late at night, I was just about to lie down. I hear the sentinel call to someone, "Halt! Who goes there?" And literally ten minutes later

I'm summoned to the commander. I go to the commander's dugout, our comrades are there and some man in civilian dress. I remember this man well. All those years I saw only men in khaki, in army overcoats, and this one was in a black overcoat with a plush collar.

"I need your help," the man says to me. "My wife is giving birth a mile and a half from here. She's alone, there's no one in the house."

The commander hesitates. "It's in no-man's-land. You know it may be dangerous."

"A woman is giving birth. I must help her."

They gave me five riflemen. I packed a bag of bandage material, also a pair of new flannelette footwraps they issued me recently. We went. There was shelling all the time—now undershot, now overshot. And the forest was so dark, we couldn't even see the moon. Finally we saw the silhouette of some building. It was a farmstead. When we went into the house, I saw a woman. She was lying on the floor, all covered with some old rags. The husband at once began to curtain the windows. Two riflemen stood outside, two by the door, and one held the flashlight for me. The woman could barely keep from moaning; she was in great pain.

I kept begging her, "Bear with it, dearest. You mustn't cry. Bear with it."

It was no-man's-land. If the enemy noticed anything, they would rain shells down on us. But when the soldiers heard that the baby was born . . . "Hurray! Hurray!" Very soft, almost a whisper. A baby was born on the front line!

They brought water. There was nowhere to boil it, so I wiped the baby with cold water. Swaddled it in my footwraps. There was nothing in the house except the old rags the mother was lying on.

I slipped away to that farmstead for several nights. The last time I went was before we began to advance, and I said goodbye. "I can't come to you anymore, I'm leaving."

The woman asked her husband something in Latvian. He translated, "My wife asks what your name is."

"Anna."

The woman said something else. The husband translated again, "She says it's a very beautiful name. We'll call our daughter Anna in your honor."

The woman raised herself a little—she still couldn't get up—and handed me a beautiful mother-of-pearl powder box. This was obviously the thing she cherished most. I opened the powder box, and the smell of the powder, when there was shooting around, explosions . . . It was something . . . I want to weep even now . . . The smell of the powder, that little mother-of-pearl lid . . . The little baby, a girl . . . Something homey, something from a real woman's life . . .

Taissia Petrovna Rudenko-Sheveleva

CAPTAIN, COMPANY COMMANDER IN THE MOSCOW FLEET,
NOW A RETIRED LIEUTENANT COLONEL

A woman in the navy . . . That was something forbidden, even unnatural. People thought it would be bad luck for a ship. I was born near Fastov. In our village the women teased my mother to death: what did you give birth to—a girl or a boy? I wrote a letter to Voroshilov himself, asking to be accepted in the Leningrad Artillery School. They accepted me only on his personal order. The only girl.

When I finished the school, they still wanted me to stay on dry land. Then I stopped telling them that I was a woman. My Ukrainian last name, Rudenko, saved me.* But on one occasion I gave myself away. I was scrubbing the deck, suddenly heard a noise, and turned around: a sailor was chasing a cat that had ended up on the ship, no one knew how. There was a belief, probably from the earliest times, that cats and women bring bad luck at sea. The cat didn't want to quit the ship, and its dodges would have been the envy of a world-class football player. The whole ship was laughing. But when the cat nearly

---

* Most Russian family names have a feminine ending for women (Ivanov becomes Ivanova), but often Ukrainian names, such as Rudenko, do not.

fell into water, I got frightened and screamed. And it was evidently such a girlish treble that the men's laughter stopped at once. Silence fell.

I heard the commander's voice: "Watchman, is there a woman on board?"

"No, sir, Comrade Commander."

Panic again—there was a woman on board.

. . . I was the first woman to be a commissioned officer in the navy. During the war I was in charge of arming the ships and the naval infantry. Then an article appeared in the British press saying that some incomprehensible creature—neither man nor woman—was fighting in the Russian navy. And that no man would ever take this "lady with a dirk" for a wife. Not take me for a wife?! No, you're mistaken, my good sir, the most handsome officer will take me . . .

I was a happy wife and am still a happy mother and grandmother. It's not my fault that my husband was killed in the war. And I loved the navy all my life and still do . . .

Klavdia Vasilyevna Konovalova
JUNIOR SERGEANT, COMMANDER OF AN ANTIAIRCRAFT GUN

I worked in a factory . . . In a chain factory in our village of Mikhalchikovo, Kstovsky district, Gorki region. When men began to be recruited and sent to the front, I was transferred to a machine to do men's work. From there I was transferred to the forge shop as a hammerer, to make ship's chains.

I asked to be sent to the front, but the factory superiors used various pretexts to keep me there. Then I wrote to the district Komsomol committee and in March 1942 received a summons. I was leaving with several other girls, and the whole village came to see us off. We went on foot twenty miles to Gorki, and there they distributed us to various units. I was sent to the 784th Middle-caliber Antiaircraft Artillery Regiment.

Soon I was appointed number-one gunlayer. But that wasn't enough for me; I now wanted to become a loader. True, that was regarded as purely a man's job: you had to work with thirty-pound shells and carry out intense fire at a rate of one salvo every five seconds. It was not in vain that I had worked as a hammerer. Within a year I was promoted to the rank of junior sergeant and appointed commander of the second gun, which was serviced by two girls and four men. From the intense firing the gun barrels turned red-hot and it became dangerous to use them. We were forced, against all the rules, to cool them off with blankets moistened with water. The guns couldn't stand it, but people could. I was a tough, strong girl, but I know that in the war I was capable of doing more than in peaceful life. Even physically. An unknown strength surged up from somewhere . . .

Hearing about the Victory on the radio, I roused my team by sounding the alarm and gave my last command: "Azimuth—fifteen zero-zero. Angle of elevation—ten-zero. Detonator—hundred and twenty, pace—ten!"

I myself went to the breechblock and began a four-round salute in honor of our Victory after four years of war.

At these shots, everybody who was at the battery position came running, along with the battery commander, Slatvinsky. He ordered me put under arrest for the unauthorized action, but then canceled his decision. And we all went on saluting together from personal weapons, embracing and kissing each other. Drank vodka, sang songs. And then wept all night and all day . . .

Galina Yaroslavovna Dubovik

PARTISAN OF THE 12TH STALIN MOUNTED
PARTISAN BRIGADE

I carry a handheld machine gun on my shoulder . . . I'll never admit it's heavy. Otherwise who would keep me as number two? Inadequate fighter, to be replaced. They'd send me to the kitchen. That's a disgrace. God forbid I should spend the whole war in the kitchen. I'd just cry . . .

Were women sent on missions equally with men?

They tried to spare us. You had to ask to be sent on a combat mission, or somehow to deserve it. To prove yourself. For that you needed boldness, desperateness of character. Not every girl was capable of it. We had a girl, Valya, working in the kitchen. She was so gentle, timid, you couldn't imagine her with a rifle. She would, of course, shoot in extremity, but she never yearned for action. Me? I yearned. I dreamed!

Yet in school I was a quiet girl . . . Inconspicuous . . .

Elena Ivanovna Variukhina

NURSE

The order: be in place within twenty-four hours . . . Assignment: to the 713th Mobile Field Hospital . . .

I remember I appeared in the hospital in a black marquisette dress and sandals, and over it I was wearing my husband's cape. They issued me a military uniform, but I refused to put it on, because everything was three or four sizes too big for me. They reported to the head of the hospital that I was insubordinate to army discipline. He didn't take any measures—let's just wait, in a few days she'll change clothes herself.

In a few days we were moving to another place, and came under heavy bombardment. We hid in a potato field, and it had rained just before. Can you imagine what became of my marquisette dress and what my sandals turned into? The next day I was dressed like a soldier. In full uniform.

Thus began my military path . . . All the way to Germany . . .

In the first days of January 1942 we entered the settlement of Afonevka, in the Kursk region. There was heavy frost. Two school buildings were chock-full of the wounded: they lay on stretchers, on the floor, on straw. There weren't enough trucks and fuel to evacuate them to the rear. The head of the hospital decided to make up a train of horse-drawn wagons from Afonevka and the neighboring settlements.

The next morning the train arrived. The horses were driven only by women. In the sledges lay hand-woven blankets, sheepskin coats, pillows. Some even brought featherbeds. To this day I can't remember without tears what happened then . . . Those scenes . . . Each woman chose a wounded man and began preparing him for the road and murmuring over him: "My dear little son!" "There, my dearest!" "There, my pretty one!" Each woman brought along a bit of home-cooked food, even warm potatoes. They wrapped the wounded in their homey things, put them carefully into the sledges. To this day it sits in my ear, this prayer, this soft women's murmuring: "There, my dearest," "There, my pretty one . . ." I'm sorry, and even feel remorse, that we didn't ask these women's last names then.

I also remember how we moved through liberated Belorussia and didn't meet any men in the villages. Only women met us. There were only women left . . .

OF THE SILENCE OF HORROR AND
THE BEAUTY OF FICTION

Anastasia Ivanovna Medvedkina
PRIVATE, MACHINE GUNNER

Can I find the right words? I can tell about how I shot. But about how I wept, I can't. That will be left untold. I know one thing: in war a human being becomes frightening and incomprehensible. How can one understand him?

You're a writer. Think up something yourself. Something beautiful. Without lice and filth, without vomit . . . Without the smell of vodka and blood . . . Not so frightening as life . . .

Anna Petrovna Kalyagina
SERGEANT, MEDICAL ASSISTANT

I don't know . . . No, I understand what you're asking about, but words fail me . . . I have no words . . . How can I describe it? I need . . . In order to . . . A spasm suffocated me, as it does now: at night I lie in the stillness and I suddenly remember. I suffocate. In shivers . . . Like this . . .

The words are somewhere . . . We need a poet . . . Like Dante . . .

Olga Nikitichna Zabelina
ARMY SURGEON

Sometimes I hear music . . . Or a song . . . a woman's voice . . . And there I find what I felt then. Something similar . . .

But I watch films about the war—not right. I read a book—not right. No, not it. It doesn't come off. I start talking, myself—that's also not it. Not as frightening and not as beautiful. Do you know how beautiful a morning at war can be? Before combat . . . You look and you know: this may be your last. The earth is so beautiful . . . And the air . . . And the dear sun . . .

Liubov Eduardovna Kresova
UNDERGROUND FIGHTER

We lived in the ghetto behind barbed wire . . . I even remember that this happened on a Tuesday. For some reason, I paid attention later that it had been Tuesday. Tuesday . . . I don't remember the date or the month. But it was Tuesday. I went up to the window by chance. Across the street from our house a boy and girl were sitting on a bench kissing. There were pogroms around, shootings. And they were kissing! I was astounded by this peaceful picture . . .

At the other end of the street, which was short, a German patrol appeared. They, too, saw it all, they had good eyesight. I had no time to think about anything. Of course I didn't . . . Shouting. Racket. Gunshots . . . I . . . No thoughts . . . The first feeling—fear. I only saw that the boy and the girl stood up—and had already fallen. They fell down together.

And then . . . A day passed, a second . . . a third . . . I was still thinking about it. You must understand: they didn't kiss at home, but outside. Why? They wanted to die like that . . . They knew they would die in the ghetto anyway, and they wanted to die differently.

Of course, this was love. What else? What else could it have been . . . Only love.

So, I've told you . . . And, true, it came out well—beautiful. But in reality? In reality I was horrified . . . Yes . . . What else? It just occurred to me . . . They were fighting . . . They wanted to die beautifully. That was their choice, I'm sure . . .

Irina Moiseevna Lepitskaya
PRIVATE, RIFLEMAN

Me? I don't want to talk . . . Although . . . In short . . . these things can't be talked about . . .

Antonina Albertovna Vyzhutovich
PARTISAN NURSE

A mad woman wandered around the town . . . She never washed, never combed her hair. Her five children had been killed. All of them. And killed in different ways. One had been shot in the head, another in the ear . . .

She used to come up to people in the street . . . anybody . . . And say, "I'll tell you how my children were killed. Which one to begin with? With Vasenka . . . They shot him in the ear! And Tolik in the head . . . Well, which one?"

Everybody fled from her. She was crazy, that's why she could tell . . .

Anna Mikhailovna Perepelka

SERGEANT, NURSE

I remember just one thing: the cry—victory! All day the cry rang out . . . Victory! Victory! Brothers! At first I didn't believe it, because we were already used to the war—as if that was life. Victory! We won . . . We were happy! Happy!

"YOUNG LADIES! DO YOU KNOW: THE COMMANDER OF A SAPPER PLATOON LIVES ONLY TWO MONTHS . . ."

———

I talk about the same thing all the time . . . In one way or another I keep coming back to it . . .

Most often I talk about death. About their relationships with death—it constantly circled around them. As close and as habitual as life itself. I try to understand, how was it possible to survive amid this endless experience of dying? To look at it day after day. To think. To try it on despite yourself.

Is it possible to talk about it? What lends itself to words and to our feelings? And what is ineffable? More and more questions arise for me, and fewer and fewer answers.

Sometimes I come home after these meetings with the thought that suffering is solitude. Total isolation. At other times it seems to me that suffering is a special kind of knowledge. There is something in human life that it is impossible to convey and preserve in any other way, especially among us. That is how the world is made; that is how we are made.

I met one of the heroines of this chapter in the auditorium of the Belorussian State University. The students were noisily and happily putting away their notebooks after the lecture.

"How were we then?" she replied to my first question with a question. "The same as these students of mine. Only dressed differently, and girls' jewelry was simpler. Steel rings, glass beads. Rubber sneakers. We didn't have these jeans and tape recorders."

I followed the hurrying students with my eyes, and the story was already beginning . . .

Stanislava Petrovna Volkova

SECOND LIEUTENANT, COMMANDER OF A SAPPER PLATOON

A girlfriend and I finished university before the war, and sapper's school during the war. We came to the front as officers . . . second lieutenants. They met us like this: "Good for you, girls! It's fine that you've come, girls. But we're not sending you anywhere. You'll be with us at headquarters." That was how they met us at the headquarters of the corps of engineers. We about-faced and went looking for Malinovsky, commander in chief of the front. While we went around, a rumor spread through the settlement that two girls were looking for the commander in chief.

An officer came up to us and said, "Show me your papers."

He examined them. "Why are you looking for the commander in chief? You're supposed to go to the headquarters of the corps of engineers."

"We were sent as commanders of sapper platoons, and they want to keep us at headquarters. But we insist on being only commanders of sapper platoons, and only at the front line."

Then this officer took us back to the headquarters of the engineer corps. For a long time they all talked and talked, there was a whole cottage full of people, and everybody gave advice and some laughed. But we held our ground, that we had an assignment, that we are supposed to be only commanders of sapper platoons.

Then the officer who brought us there got angry. "Young ladies! Do you know how long the commander of a sapper platoon lives? The commander of a sapper platoon lives only two months . . ."

"We know. That's why we want to go to the front line."

There was nothing to be done; they wrote out the assignment. "Well, all right, we'll send you to the 5th Shock Army. What a shock army is you probably know, the name itself tells you. Constantly on the front line . . ."

And they told us all sorts of horrors. We were glad.

"Agreed!"

We came to the headquarters of the 5th Shock Army. A cultivated captain was sitting there. He received us very nicely, but when he heard that we wanted to be commanders of sapper platoons, he clutched his head.

"No, no! What are you saying? We'll find work for you here at headquarters. Are you joking? There are only men there, and suddenly the commander's a woman—it's crazy. No, no!"

For two days they worked on us like that. I'm telling you . . . Persuading . . . We didn't budge: only commanders of sapper platoons. We didn't give an inch. That wasn't the end of it. Finally . . . Finally we got our assignments. I was brought to my platoon . . . The soldiers looked at me, one mockingly, another even angrily, yet another just shrugged his shoulders, which made everything clear at once. When the battalion commander said, "I present to you your new platoon commander," they suddenly howled: "Hoo-o-o . . ." One even spat: "Pfui!"

A year later, when I was awarded the Order of the Red Star, these same boys, those who were still alive, carried me on high to my dugout. They were proud of me.

If you ask what color war is, I'll tell you—the color of earth. For a sapper . . . The black, yellow, clayey color of earth . . .

We're on a march somewhere . . . Spend the night in the forest. We make a bonfire, and the bonfire burns, and everybody sits very quietly, some are already asleep. I'm falling asleep, looking at the fire. I sleep with my eyes open: some moths, some bugs fly into the fire, they fly all night long, without a sound, without a rustle, they silently disappear into this big fire. Others come flying after them . . . I'm telling you . . . Just like us. We marched and marched. Rolling like a stream.

Two months later I wasn't killed, I was wounded. My first wound was light. And I stopped thinking about death . . .

Appolina Nikonovna Litskevich-Bairak

SECOND LIEUTENANT, COMMANDER
OF A SAPPER-MINER PLATOON

In my childhood . . . I'll begin with my childhood . . . During the war I was afraid most of all to remember my childhood. Precisely childhood. One shouldn't recall the most tender things during a war . . . Not the most tender things . . . It's a taboo.

Well, so . . . In my childhood my father used to give me a crew cut with an electric hair clipper. I recalled it when we got our haircuts and suddenly turned into young soldiers. Some girls were frightened . . . But I easily got used to it. My element. Not for nothing did my father say, "It's a boy I've got here, not a girl." The blame for it all went to a passion of mine, for which I often got yelled at by my parents. In winter I used to jump down from a steep bank onto the snow-covered river Ob. After classes I would put on my father's old cotton-padded trousers and tie them over my felt boots. Tucked my thick jacket into the trousers and tightened the belt. On my head was a long-eared hat, tied under the chin. Bundled up like that, waddling clumsily like a bear, I went to the river. I ran as fast as I could and jumped off the cliff . . .

Ah! What a sensation, when you fell into the abyss and sank over your head in the snow! It takes your breath away! Other girls tried to do it with me, but they couldn't get it right: they'd sprain a leg, or hit their nose against the snow, or something else would happen. I was more adroit than the boys.

I mentioned childhood . . . Because I don't want to begin with blood . . . But I understand—of course it's important, of course. I like to read books. I understand . . .

We arrived in Moscow in September 1942 . . . For a whole week they drove us around the ring rail line. We stopped at the Kuntsevo, Perovo, Ochakovo stations, and everywhere some girls were taken off the train. The "buyers," that is, the commanders of various units and combat branches, came and persuaded us to become snipers, medical assistants, radio operators . . . None of it tempted me. Finally there were only thirteen girls left of the whole convoy. We were all put into one freight car. Just two cars stood on the side track: ours and the staff car. For two days no one came to us. We laughed and sang the song "Forgotten, Abandoned." At the end of the second day, toward evening, we saw three officers coming to our car together with the chief of the convoy.

The "buyers"! They were tall, trim, tightly belted. Spanking new overcoats, gleamingly polished boots with spurs. Really something! We hadn't seen their like yet. They went into the staff car, and we pressed up to the wall to hear what they were going to say. The chief showed them the list and gave a brief description of each of us: so-and-so, where from, education. In the end we heard: "They'll all do."

Then the chief came out of the car and ordered us to line up. They asked, "Do you want to study the art of war?" How could we not, of course we wanted to. Very much so! It was our dream! Not one of us even asked: study where and what? The order was: "First Lieutenant Mitropolsky, take the girls to the school." We shouldered our kit bags, formed a column of two, and the officer led us through the streets of Moscow. My beloved Moscow . . . the capital . . . Beautiful even in this difficult time. Our own . . . The officer walked quickly, with big strides, we could barely keep up with him. It was only at the thirtieth anniversary of the Victory, at the reunion in Moscow, that Sergei Fyodorovich Mitropolsky confessed to us, the former students of the Moscow Military-Engineering School, how ashamed he had been to lead us through Moscow. He tried to keep as far as possible from us, so as not to attract attention. To this herd of girls . . . We didn't know that and almost ran after him. We must have been quite a sight!

Well, so . . . In the first few days of studies I got extra duty twice: first I protested against the cold auditorium, then it was something else. Schoolgirl habits. So I got what I deserved: one extra duty, then another . . . More followed. Whenever I was posted in the street, the boys noticed me and began to laugh: our staff orderly. It was funny for them, of course, but I missed classes, didn't sleep nights. I spent the whole day standing by the door at the orderly post, and at night I polished the floors in the barrack with mastic. How did we do it then? I'll explain at once . . . In detail . . . It was not like now, when we have all sorts of brushes, floor polishers, and the like. Back then . . . After lights out you take your boots off, so you don't muck them up with mastic, wrap your feet in pieces of old overcoat, making a sort of peasant shoe tied with string. You scatter mastic over the floor and spread it with a brush, not a synthetic brush, but a natural one, so the clumps of hair stick to the floor, and only after that you start working with your feet. You have to polish it so it shines like a mirror. There's a whole night's dancing for you! Your feet are sore and numb, you can't straighten your back, sweat streams down your face and gets into your eyes. In the morning you're so tired you can't even shout "On your feet!" to your company. And during the day you can't sit down, because the orderly has to stand by the post all the time.

Once I had a mishap . . . It was funny . . . I had just finished cleaning the barrack and was standing by the orderly post. I was so sleepy, I felt I'd fall down any minute. I leaned on the post and dozed off. Suddenly I heard someone open the door to the barrack, I roused myself—the battalion duty officer was standing before me. I raised my hand in salute and reported, "Comrade First Lieutenant, the company is resting." He stared at me and I saw he could barely keep from laughing. Then I realized that, being left-handed and in a hurry, I had saluted him with my left hand. I quickly tried to switch to the right hand, but it was too late. Again I had made a slip . . .

It took me a long time to realize that this was not some sort of game and not a simple school, but a military academy. Preparation for war. A commander's order is law for a subordinate.

I remember the last question on the last exam: "How many times in his life does a sapper make a mistake?"

"A sapper makes a mistake once in his life."

"That's right, girl . . ."

And then the familiar: "Student Bairak, you may go."

And now—war. Real war . . .

I was brought to my platoon. I order, "Platoon, attention!" and the platoon doesn't even think of standing up. One man is lying down, another sits and smokes, yet another stretches himself till his bones crack: "E-eh!" They pretended not to notice me. These men were insulted that they, seasoned male scouts, had to obey a twenty-year-old girl. I realized it very well and was forced to give the command, "As you were!"

Just then shelling began . . . I jumped down into a ditch, and my overcoat was new, so I lay down not in the mud, but to the side on the unmelted snow. That's how it happens when you're young—the overcoat is dearer than life. Foolish girl! And my soldiers laughed.

Well, so . . . What was the engineer scouting that we conducted? During the night the soldiers dug a double hole in no-man's-land. Before dawn one of the unit commanders and I crawled to this little trench, and the soldiers camouflaged us. And we lay like that all day, afraid to stir. In an hour or two our hands and feet began to freeze, even if we were wearing felt boots and sheepskin jackets. Four hours—and you turn into an icicle. It snows . . . You turn into a snowman. That's in winter . . . In summer we had to lie in the heat or the rain. We'd spend the whole day watching everything attentively and drawing up a map of the observed front line and marking the places where changes in the surface of the terrain appeared. If we saw bumps on the ground or lumps of soil, dirty snow, trampled grass or dew smeared on the grass, that was what we were after . . . our goal . . . It was clear that German sappers had placed mines there. If they set up a wire fence, it was necessary to find out the length and breadth of the fence. What sort of mines they had put there: antitroop, antitank, or surprise mines. We marked the enemy's firing points . . .

Before our troops advanced, we worked during the night. We felt the ground inch by inch. Made corridors in the mine fields. All the work was done crawling . . . On your belly . . . I shuttled from one unit to another. There were always more of "my" mines.

I can tell many incidents . . . Enough for a movie . . . A serial.

Some officers invited me for breakfast. I accepted. Sappers weren't always served hot food; we mostly lived on whatever grub we could get. When everybody sat down at the kitchen table, I paid attention to the Russian stove with a closed door. I went over and began to examine the door. The officers poked fun at me: "You women imagine mines even in pots and pans." I joked back and then noticed that at the very bottom, to the left of the door, there was a small hole. I looked closer and saw a thin wire going into the stove. I quickly turned to those around the table: "The house is mined, I ask you to quit the premises." The officers fell silent and stared at me with mistrust; no one wanted to leave the table. It smelled of meat, fried potatoes. I repeated, "Clear the premises immediately." I set to work with the sappers. First we removed the door. Cut the wire with scissors. And there . . . There . . . In the stove lay several liter-sized enamel mugs tied together with string. A soldier's dream! Better than a mess tin. Then, in the depths of the stove, two big packages wrapped in black paper. About forty pounds of explosives. There's pots and pans for you . . .

We moved through Ukraine and came to the Stanislavskaya, now the Ivano-Frankovsky, region. Our platoon was given a mission: to urgently demine a sugar factory. Every minute counted: we didn't know how the factory had been mined. If there was a time bomb, we could expect an explosion at any moment. So we set out at quick march on our mission. The weather was warm, we traveled light. As we were passing a long-range artillery position, one of the soldiers suddenly ran out of the trench and shouted, "Heads up! What a chassis!" I raised my head and began to look for a "chassis" in the sky. There was no plane to be seen. Everything was quiet, not a sound. Where was the "chassis"? One of my sappers asked permission to leave the ranks. I saw him go to that artillerist and give him a good slap. Before I could figure anything out, the artillerist shouted, "Boys, they're beating us!" Other artillerists jumped out of the trench and surrounded our sapper. My platoon, without thinking for long, dropped their probes, mine detectors, kit bags, and rushed to help him. A fight began. I couldn't understand what was happening. Why did my platoon get mixed up in a fight? Every minute counted, and there they were scuffling.

I gave the order: "Platoon, fall in!" Nobody paid any attention to me. Then I drew my pistol and fired into the air. Some officers ran out of the blindage. It took quite a while to quiet everybody down. A captain came up to my platoon and asked, "Who is the senior officer here?" I saluted. He rolled his eyes; even he was at a loss. Then he asked, "What happened here?" I was unable to answer, because I really did not know the reason. Then my subcommander stepped forward and explained how it had all come about. Thus I learned that the word "chassis" was very offensive for a woman. Something like "whore." A frontline obscenity . . .

And you know . . . We're having a candid conversation . . . I tried not to think about love or about my childhood during the war. Or about death . . . Hm-m-m . . . We're having a candid conversation . . . Well, so . . . As I said: I forbade myself many things in order to survive. Especially everything gentle and tender. Even to think about it. To recall. I remember how we were given a few free evenings for the first time in liberated Lvov. For the first time during the whole war . . . The battalion watched a film in the city movie theater. In the beginning it felt somehow unusual to sit in soft chairs, to see a beautiful interior, to feel cozy and quiet. An orchestra played before the film, artistes performed. There were dances in the foyer. We danced the polka, the krakoviak, the *pas d'Espagne,* and finished with the inevitable "Russian." I was particularly affected by the music . . . It seemed unbelievable that there was shooting somewhere and that we would soon be on the front line again. That death was somewhere near.

But already a day later an order came for my platoon to comb the irregular terrain between a hamlet and a railroad. Several trucks had blown up there on mines . . . Scouts with mine detectors started moving along the highway. Cold rain sprinkled. We were all soaked to the skin. My boots swelled up and became as heavy as if they had iron soles. I tucked the skirts of my overcoat under the belt, so that they wouldn't hinder my walking. Ahead of me on a leash ran my dog Nelka. When she found a shell or a mine, she sat next to it and waited for it to be cleared. My faithful friend. So Nelka sat down . . . she waited and whined a bit . . . Suddenly I heard a command passed down the line: "Lieutenant, to the general." I looked around: a jeep was standing on the country road. I jumped over a ditch, untucked the skirts of my overcoat, straightened my belt and forage cap. Despite all that I looked shabby.

I ran up to the car, opened the door, and began to report: "Comrade General, at your orders . . ."

Before I finished, I heard, "As you were . . ."

I paused and stood at attention. The general did not even turn toward me, but was looking at the road through the windshield. He was getting nervous and looked frequently at his watch. I stood there. He turned to his orderly: "Where's that sapper commander?"

I again tried to report: "Comrade General . . ."

He finally turned to me and said vexedly, "What the devil do I need you for!"

I figured out what was the matter and almost burst out laughing. Then his orderly realized, "Comrade General, maybe she is the sapper commander?"

The general stared at me. "Who are you?"

"The commander of the sapper platoon, Comrade General."

"You—the platoon commander?" he said indignantly.

"Yes, Comrade General!"

"These are your sappers at work?"

"Yes, Comrade General."

"Quit saying 'general, general' . . . "

He got out of the car, took a few steps, then came back to me. Stood there, measuring me with his eyes. Then said to his orderly, "See that?"

Then he asked me, "How old are you, Lieutenant?"

"Twenty, Comrade General."

"Where are you from?"

"Siberia."

He kept questioning me for a long time, offered to transfer me to their tank unit. Was indignant about me looking so shabby: he wouldn't allow that. They needed sappers desperately. Then he took me aside and pointed to a little wood.

"My little crates are standing there. I want to send them along this railroad. The rails and the sleepers have been removed, but the road may be mined. Do my tankmen a favor, check the road. This is a closer and more convenient way to the front line. Do you know what a surprise attack is?"

"Yes, Comrade General."

"Well, goodbye, Lieutenant. Make sure you live till the victory, it will come soon. Understand!"

The railroad indeed turned out to be mined. We checked it.

We all wanted to live till the victory . . .

In October 1944 our battalion, being a part of the 210th demining Detachment, together with the troops of the 4th Ukrainian Front, entered the territory of Czechoslovakia. We were met joyfully everywhere. They threw us flowers, fruit, packs of cigarettes . . . Spread rugs on the pavement . . . The fact that a girl was commander of a platoon of men, and was herself a sapper-miner, became a sensation. I had a boy's haircut, wore trousers and an army jacket. I had adopted some male ways. In short, I looked like an adolescent boy. Sometimes I rode into a village on horseback, and then it was very hard to tell who I was, but women's intuition told them and they observed me attentively. Women's intuition . . . It was funny . . . Great! I'd come to the quarters where I was to be billeted, and the owners would be told that their lodger was an officer, but not a man. Many were so surprised that they just stood gaping . . . A silent movie! But I . . . Hmm-m-m . . . I even enjoyed it. I enjoyed surprising people that way. It was the same in Poland. I remember in one little village an old woman patted me on the head. I understood: "Is the *pani* trying to see if I have horns?" I asked in Polish. She became embarrassed and said she simply wanted to show pity for me, "such a young *panenka*."

And there were mines at every step. Many mines. Once we went into a house, and someone saw a pair of calfskin boots standing by a wardrobe. He was already reaching out to take them. "Don't you dare touch them!" I shouted. When I came up and began to study them, they turned out to be mined. There were mined armchairs, chests of drawers, sideboards, dolls, chandeliers . . . Peasants asked us to demine the rows of tomatoes, potatoes, cabbage. Once, in order to sample some dumplings, our platoon went to a village to demine a field of wheat and even the flail for threshing the sheaves . . .

Well, so . . . I went through Czechoslovakia, Poland, Hungary, Romania, Germany . . . But few impressions have remained in my memory. Mostly I remember only visual images of the lay of the land. Boulders . . . Tall grass . . . Either it was really tall or it only seemed so to us because it was unbelievably difficult to go through it and work with our probes and mine detectors. Old grass . . . Burdock higher than bushes . . . I also remember many brooks and ravines. Dense forests, continuous wire fences with rotted stakes, overgrown minefields. Flowerbeds gone to seed. There were always mines hiding there; the Germans loved flowerbeds. Once there were people digging potatoes in a field, and next to them we were digging mines . . .

In Romania, in the town of Dej, I stayed in the house of a young Romanian woman who spoke good Russian. It turned out her grandmother was Russian. The woman had three children. Her husband had been killed at the front, in the Romanian volunteer division. Still, she liked to laugh and have fun. Once she invited me to go dancing with her. She offered me her outfits. The temptation was great. I put on trousers, an army shirt, calfskin boots, and on top of it all the Romanian national costume: a long embroidered linen blouse and a tight checkered skirt. Tied a black belt around my waist, threw a colorful shawl with long fringe over my head. To this should be added that, from crawling in the mountains all summer, I had a dark tan, only blond strands stuck out on my temples, and my nose was peeling—still it was hard to distinguish me from a real Romanian. A Romanian girl.

There was no club, the young people gathered in somebody's house. When we came, music was already playing, people were dancing. I saw almost all the officers of my battalion. At first I was afraid to be recognized and exposed, and so I sat in a far corner, without attracting attention, even covering myself with the shawl a little. At least I could see everything . . . From a distance . . . But after one of our officers invited me several times to dance without recognizing me with my lips and eyebrows painted, I began laughing and having fun. I was having a very good time . . . I liked to hear that I was beautiful. I heard compliments . . . I danced and danced . . .

The war ended, but we spent another whole year demining fields, lakes, rivers. During the war people dumped everything into the water; the main thing was to go ahead, to make it to the goal in time . . . But now we had to think about other things . . . About life . . . For the sappers the war ended several years later; they fought longer than everybody else. And what is it to wait for an explosion after the Victory? To wait for that moment . . . No, no! Death after the Victory was the most terrible. A double death.

Well, so . . . As a New Year's present in 1946 I was issued ten yards of red sateen. I laughed: "What do I need that for? Unless I make myself a red dress after demobilization. A Victory dress." As if I was reading the future . . . Soon the order came for my demobilization. As was customary, the battalion organized a festive farewell party for me. At the party the officers offered me a big, finely knitted dark blue shawl as a present. I had to redeem the shawl by singing a song about a blue shawl. I sang for them the whole evening.

On the train I developed a high fever. My face was swollen; I couldn't open my mouth. My wisdom teeth were growing . . . I was returning from the war . . .

"TO SEE HIM JUST ONCE . . ."

———

And now there will be a story about love . . .

Love is the only personal event in wartime. All the rest is common—even death.

What came unexpectedly for me? The fact that they spoke about love less candidly than about death. There was always this reticence, as if they were protecting themselves, stopping each time at a certain line. Guarding it vigilantly. There was an unspoken agreement among them—no further. The curtain fell. I understood what they were protecting themselves against: postwar insults and slander. And there was plenty of it! After the war they had to fight another war, no less terrible than the one they had returned from. If one of them resolved to be totally sincere, if a desperate confession escaped them, there was always a request at the end: "Change my last name," or "In our time it wasn't acceptable to talk about it aloud . . . indecent . . ." I heard more about the romantic and the tragic.

Of course, it is not the whole of life and not the whole truth. But it is their truth. As one of the writers of the war generation admitted honestly: "Cursed be the war—our stellar hour!" That is the watchword, the general epigraph to their lives.

But all the same, what was love like there? Near death . . .

OF A DAMNED WENCH AND
THE ROSES OF MAY

Efrosinya Grigoryevna Breus
CAPTAIN, DOCTOR

The war took my love from me . . . My only love . . .

The city was being bombed. My sister Nina came running to say goodbye. We thought we weren't going to see each other again. She said to me, "I'll join the medical volunteers, if only I can find them." I remember looking at her. It was summertime, she was wearing a light dress, and I saw a small birthmark on her left shoulder, here, by the neck. She was my sister, but it was the first time I noticed it. I looked and thought, "I'll recognize you anywhere."

And such a keen feeling . . . Such love . . . Heartrending . . .

Everybody was leaving Minsk. The roads were being shelled; we went through the forests . . . Somewhere a girl cried, "Mama, it's war!" Our unit was in retreat. We marched past a vast, wide field, the rye had come into ear, and there was a low peasant cottage by the road. It was already the Smolensk region . . . A woman was standing by the road, and it seemed as if this woman was taller than her house. She was wearing a linen dress embroidered with a national Russian pattern. Her arms were crossed on her chest; she kept bowing low. The soldiers marched past her, and she bowed to them and repeated, "May the Lord bring you home." She bowed to each of them and said the same thing. Everybody had tears in their eyes . . .

I remembered her all through the war . . . And another thing, this was in Germany, when we drove the Germans back. In some village . . . Two German women wearing bonnets were sitting in a courtyard having coffee . . . It looked as if there was no war . . . And

I thought, "My God, our country is in ruins, our people live in dug-outs and eat grass, and you sit here having coffee." Our trucks drive by, carrying our soldiers . . . And they drink coffee . . .

Then I rode through our land. And what did I see? All that remains of a village is a single stove. An old man sits there and three grandchildren stand behind him. He has evidently lost his son and daughter-in-law. The old woman collects dead coals to start the stove. She has hung up her coat, meaning she came from the forest. And there is nothing cooking in this stove . . .

And such a keen feeling . . . Such love . . .

. . . Our train stopped. I don't remember what it was—railroad repairs, or they changed the engine. I sit there with a nurse and next to us two soldiers are cooking kasha. From somewhere two German prisoners come to us and ask for food. We had some bread. We took a loaf, divided it and gave them some. I hear the soldiers who are cooking say, "Look how much bread our doctors gave to the enemy!" And then something like, "Ah, as if they know what real war is, they sit in their hospitals, how would they know . . ."

Some time later other prisoners came to those same soldiers who were cooking kasha. And the same soldier who disapproved of us just before says to a German, "What—want some grub?"

The man stands there . . . Waits. Our other soldier gives a loaf to his friend and says, "All right, cut him some."

The other cut them a slice each. The Germans take the bread and stand there—they see that there's kasha cooking.

"Well, all right," the one soldier says, "give him some kasha."

"It's not ready yet."

"You hear?"

And the Germans stand there as if they understand the language. Waiting. The soldiers added some lard to the kasha and gave it to them in empty tin cans.

There's the soul of a Russian soldier for you. First they denounced us, then they themselves gave the Germans bread and kasha as well, and only after adding some lard. I remember that . . .

And such a keen feeling . . . So strong . . .

The war was long over . . . I was going to a resort . . . Just then came the Caribbean crisis.* Again the world was uneasy. Everything became unstable. I packed my suitcase, put in dresses, blouses. So, did I forget anything? I fetched a folder with my papers in it and took out my army card. I thought, "If anything happens, I'll go straight to the recruiting office."

I was already on the seashore, resting, and I happened to tell some-one at the table in the dining room that, in preparing to come here, I took along my army card. I said it without any ulterior motive or wish to show off. But a man at our table got all excited: "No, only a Russian woman can take her army card with her as she leaves for a resort, and think that if anything happens she'll go straight to the re-cruiting office."

I remember the man's ecstasy. His admiration. He looked at me the way my husband used to. With the same eyes . . .

Forgive me the long introduction . . . I don't know how to tell it in good order. My thoughts always jump, my feelings burst out . . .

My husband and I went to the front. The two of us together.

There's a lot I've forgotten. Though I think about it every day . . .

The end of a battle . . . It was so quiet, we could hardly believe it. He caressed the grass with his hands, it was so soft . . . and he looked at me. Looked . . . With those eyes . . .

He left with a reconnaissance team. We waited two days for them . . . I didn't sleep for two days . . . I dozed off. I woke up because he was sitting next to me and looking at me. "Go to sleep."

"It's a pity to sleep."

And such a keen feeling . . . Such love . . . Heartrending . . .

I've forgotten a lot, almost everything. I thought I wouldn't for-get. Not for anything.

We were already passing through East Prussia, everybody was al-

---

* Known in the West as the Cuban Missile Crisis, a two-week standoff between the United States and the Soviet Union over the stationing of Soviet ballistic missiles in Cuba.

ready talking about Victory. He was killed . . . killed instantly . . . by shrapnel . . . An instant death. In a second. I was told they had all been brought, I came running . . . I put my arms around him, I wouldn't let them take him away. To be buried. They buried quickly during the war: the battle is over, they gather all those who were killed and dig a big hole. They cover them with earth. Another time it was just dry sand. And if you look at this sand for a long time, you think it's moving. Quivering. The sand heaves. Because there . . . For me they're alive, these people had just been alive . . . I see them, I talk with them . . . I don't believe . . . We go on walking, and don't believe yet that they're there . . . Where?

So I didn't allow them to bury him at once. I wanted us to have one more night. To sit next to him. To look . . . To caress . . .

Morning . . . I decided I would take him home. To Belarus. Several thousand miles away. War roads . . . Confusion . . . Everybody thought I'd lost my mind from grief. "You must calm down. Get some sleep." No! No! I went from one general to another and got as far as Rokossovsky, the commander in chief of the front.* At first he refused . . . Some sort of abnormal creature! So many men had been buried in common graves, in foreign lands . . .

I managed to obtain another meeting with him.

"Do you want me to kneel before you?"

"I understand you . . . But he's already dead . . ."

"We had no children. Our house burned down. No photographs are left. There's nothing. If I bring him home, there will at least be a grave. And I'll have somewhere to go back to after the war."

He said nothing. Paced the office. Paced.

"Have you ever loved, Comrade Marshal? I'm not burying my husband, I'm burying my love."

* Konstantin Rokossovsky (1896–1968) was a Polish-born Soviet officer. After serving with great distinction, he was arrested during the Great Purge and accused of treason. After being tortured and sent to the Gulag, he was rehabilitated, and during World War II became a key strategist in the major battles against the Germans. He was promoted to Marshal of the Soviet Union, and led the victory parade in Moscow in 1945.

He said nothing.

"Then I, too, want to die here. Why should I live without him?"

He said nothing for a long time. Then came up to me and kissed my hand.

I was given a special plane for one night. I boarded the plane . . . Put my arms around the coffin . . . And fainted . . .

Liubov Fominichna Fedosenko

PRIVATE, NURSE-AIDE

We were separated by the war . . . My husband was at the front. I was evacuated first to Kharkov, then to Tataria. Found a job there. Once I discovered they were looking for me. My maiden name was Lisovskaya. Everybody was shouting, "Sovskaya! Sovskaya!" I shouted, "It's me!" They told me, "Go to the NKVD, take a pass and go to Moscow." Why? Nobody told me anything, and I knew nothing. It was wartime . . . I thought maybe my husband had been wounded and they were summoning me to see him. I hadn't had any letters from him for four months. I was determined that if I found him crippled, without arms, without legs, I'd take him and go back home. We'd live somehow.

I arrived in Moscow and went to the appointed address. It says: CCCPB (Central Committee of the Communist Party of Belorussia) . . . That is, it was our Belorussian government, and there were many women there like myself. We asked, "What? Why? What had they summoned us for?" They said, "You'll find everything out." We were gathered in a big auditorium. Ponomarenko, the secretary of our Central Committee, is there, and other leaders. They ask me, "Do you want to go back where you come from?" Well, where I come from is Belorussia. Of course I want to. And they send me to a special school. To prepare me for going to the enemy's rear.

Today we finish training, tomorrow they put us in trucks and drive us to the front line. Then we walk. I didn't know what the front was and what "no-man's-land" meant. The order: "Ready! Fire number one." Bang! Flares were fired off. I saw the snow, very, very white, and then a row of people—it was us all suddenly lying down. There were lots of us. The flares died out, there was no shooting. A new command: "Run!" and we ran . . . And so we went through . . .

While I was in the partisan unit, I received a letter from my husband by some miracle. This was such a joy, so unexpected, because for two years I had heard nothing from him. And then a plane dropped some food, ammunition . . . And the mail . . . And in the mail, in this canvas bag, there was a letter—for me. Then I wrote a letter to the Central Committee. I wrote that I would do anything so long as my husband and I were together. I gave this letter to a pilot in secret from the commander of our unit. Soon there was news, sent by radio—once our mission was accomplished, our group was expected in Moscow. Our entire special group. We'd be sent to another place . . . Everybody must be on the flight, and especially Fedosenko.

We waited for the plane, it was nighttime and pitch-dark. And some sort of plane was circling over us, and then it dumped bombs on us. It was a Messerschmitt. The German had spotted our camp and circled back again. And at the same time our plane, a U-2, arrived and landed just by the fir tree where I was standing. The pilot barely landed and immediately began to take off again, because he saw that the German was circling back and would start shooting again. I took hold of the wing and shouted, "I must go to Moscow, I have permission." He even swore: "Get in!" And we flew together, just the two of us. There were no wounded . . . Nobody.

I was in Moscow in May and I went around in felt boots. I came to a theater in felt boots. It was wonderful anyway. I wrote to my husband: How are we going to meet? I'm in the reserves for now . . . But they promise . . . I ask everywhere: send me where my husband is, give me at least two days, just to look at him once, and then I'll come back, and you can send me wherever you like. Everybody shrugs. Still, I figured out from the postal code where my husband was fighting, and I went to him. First I go to the regional party committee, show my husband's address, the papers showing I'm his wife, and say that I want to see him. They tell me it's impossible, he's on the front line, go back, but I was so beaten down, so hungry, what was this—go back? I went to the military commandant. He looked at me and gave an order to issue me some sort of clothes. They gave me an army shirt, put a belt on me. And he began to talk me out of it.

"You know, it's very dangerous where your husband is . . ."

I sat there and wept, so he took pity on me and gave me the pass.

"Go out to the highway," he said. "There'll be a traffic controller, he'll tell you how to go."

I found the highway, found the traffic controller. He put me on a truck, and I went. I arrive at the unit, everybody's surprised, they're all military. "Who are you?" they ask. I couldn't say I was a wife. How could I say it? There were bombs exploding . . . I tell them—his sister. I don't even know why I said it. "Wait," they tell me, "it's a four-mile walk there." How could I wait, since I'd already traveled so far. Just then a car came from there to pick up food. There was a sergeant major with them, red-haired, freckled. He says, "Oh, I know Fedosenko. But he's in the trenches."

Well, I insisted and he took me. We drive, I can't see anything anywhere . . . There's a forest . . . A forest road . . . A new thing for me: the front line. But nobody anywhere. Only some shooting somewhere from time to time. We arrive. The sergeant asks, "Where's Fedosenko?"

They reply, "They went on a scouting mission yesterday. They stayed till daylight, and now they're waiting it out."

But they had communications. They told him that his sister had arrived. What sister? They say, "The redhead." His sister had black hair. So he figured out at once what sister. I don't know how he managed to crawl out of there, but he came soon, and he and I met. What joy . . .

I stayed one day, then two, and then decided: "Go to headquarters and report. I'm staying here with you."

He went to the superiors, and I held my breath: what if they tell me to clear out within twenty-four hours? It's the front, I know that. Suddenly I see the superiors coming to the dugout: the major, the colonel. Everybody shakes my hand. Then, of course, we sat down in the dugout, drank, and each of them said something about a wife finding her husband in the trenches. That's a real wife, she has papers. What a woman! Let me set eyes on such a woman! They said things like that, and they all wept. I'll remember that evening all my life . . . What else have I got left?

They enlisted me as a nurse-aide. I went on scouting missions with him. A mortar fires, I see him fall down. "Killed or wounded?" I think. I run there, the mortar goes on firing, and the commander shouts, "Where do you think you're going, you damned wench!" I crawled to him—he was alive . . . Alive!

By the Dnieper, on a moonlit night, they gave me the Order of the Red Banner. The next day my husband was wounded, badly wounded. We ran together, we waded together through some swamp, we crawled together. The machine guns kept rattling, and we kept crawling, and he got wounded in the hip. With an exploding bullet, and try bandaging that—it was in the buttock. It was all torn open, and mud and dirt all over. We were encircled and tried to break out. There was nowhere to take the wounded, and there were no medications. When we did break through, I took my husband to the hospital. By the time we got there, he had a general blood infection. It was the New Year . . . 1944 was beginning. He was dying . . . I knew he was dying . . . He had many decorations; I took all his medals and put them next to him. The doctor was making his rounds, and he was asleep.

The doctor came up. "You should leave here. He's already dead."

I reply, "Quiet, he's still alive."

My husband opened his eyes just then and said, "The ceiling has turned blue."

I looked: "No, it's not blue, Vasya. The ceiling's white." But he thought it was blue.

His neighbor says to him, "Well, Fedosenko, if you survive, you'll have to carry your wife in your arms."

"And so I will," he agrees.

I don't know, he probably felt he was dying, because he took me by the hands, pulled me to him and kissed me. The way one kisses for the last time.

"Liubochka, what a pity, everybody's celebrating the New Year, and you and I are here . . . But don't be sorry, we'll still have everything . . ."

And when he had only a few hours left to live . . . He had an accident, and I had to change his bed . . . I gave him a clean sheet, bandaged his leg, but I had to pull him up to lay him on the pillow, and he was a man, he was heavy. I was pulling him up, I bent very low, and I felt that that was it, another minute or two and he'd be no more . . . It was in the evening. A quarter past ten . . . I remember it to the minute. I wanted to die myself . . . But I was carrying our child under my heart, and only that held me back. I survived those days. I buried him on January 1, and thirty-eight days later I gave birth to a son. He was born in 1944; he has children himself now. My husband's name was Vassily, my son is Vassily Vassilyevich, and I have a grandson, Vasya . . . Vassilek . . .

Vera Vladimirovna Shevaldysheva
FIRST LIEUTENANT, SURGEON

I saw . . . Every day . . . But I couldn't be reconciled to that. A young, handsome man dies . . . I wanted to hurry up and, well . . . and kiss him. To do something feminine, since I couldn't do anything as a doctor. At least to smile. To caress him. To take his hand . . .

Many years after the war a man confessed to me that he remembered my young smile. For me he was an ordinary wounded man, I didn't even remember him. He told me that my smile brought him back to life, from the other world, as they say . . . A woman's smile . . .

Sofya Krigel
SERGEANT MAJOR, SNIPER

We arrived at the 1st Belorussian Front . . . Twenty-seven girls. Men looked at us with admiration: "Not laundresses, not telephone operators, but sniper girls. It's the first time we've seen such girls. What girls!" The sergeant major composed a poem in our honor. The sense of it was that girls should be delicate, like roses in May, and the war shouldn't cripple their souls.

As we were leaving for the front, each of us gave an oath: there will be no romances there. It would all happen, if we survived, after the war. Before the war we didn't have time even to kiss. We looked at these things more strictly than young people nowadays. For us to kiss meant love for the rest of your life. At the front, love was forbidden. If the superiors found out about it, one of the couple as a rule was transferred to another unit. They were simply separated.

We cherished our love and kept it secret. We didn't keep our childish oaths . . . We loved . . .

I think that if I hadn't fallen in love at the war, I wouldn't have survived. Love saved us. It saved me . . .

Sofya K—vich
MEDICAL ASSISTANT

You ask about love? I'm not afraid of telling the truth . . . I was what's called a field campaign wife. A war wife . . . A second one. An unlawful one.

The first commander of the battalion . . .

I didn't love him. He was a good man, but I didn't love him. But I went to his dugout after several months. What else could I do? There were only men around, so it's better to live with one than to be afraid of them all. It was less frightening in battle than after battle, especially if we pulled back for a rest or re-formation. When there's shooting, gunfire, they call out, "Nurse! Dear nurse!" But after the battle each of them lies in wait for you . . . You can't get out of the dugout at night . . . Did other girls talk to you about that or did they not confess? They were ashamed, I think . . . Kept quiet. Proud! All sorts of things happened, because we didn't want to die. It's too bad to die when you're young . . . And for men it was hard to live for four years without women . . . There were no bordellos in our army, and there weren't any pills. Maybe somewhere they took care of those things. Not here. Four years . . . Commanders could allow themselves something, but not simple soldiers. Discipline. But no one talks about it . . . It's not done . . . I, for instance, was the only woman in the battalion. I lived in a common dugout with the men. They gave me a separate space, but what kind of space was it, if the whole dugout was twenty square feet. I used to wake up at night because I waved my arms—I'd slap one on the cheek, or the hands, then another. I was wounded and got into a hospital. I waved my arms there, too. A floor attendant woke me up in the night: "What's the matter?" How could I tell her?

The first commander was killed by a mine fragment.

The second commander of the battalion . . .

I loved him. I went into combat with him, I wanted to be near him. I loved him, and he had a beloved wife, two children. He showed me their photographs. And I knew that after the war, if he stayed alive, he would go back to them. To Kaluga. So what? We had such happy moments! We lived such happiness! Once we came back . . . A terrible battle . . . And we were alive. He wouldn't have had the same thing with anyone else! It wouldn't have worked! I knew it . . . I knew that without me he wouldn't be happy. He wouldn't be happy with anyone as we were happy together in the war. He wouldn't . . . Never!

At the end of the war I got pregnant. I wanted it . . . But I raised our daughter by myself, he didn't help me. Didn't lift a finger. Not a single present or letter . . . or postcard. The war ended, and love ended. Like a song . . . He went to his lawful wife and the children.

He left me his photo as a memento. I didn't want the war to end . . . It's a terrible thing to say . . . to open my heart . . . I'm crazy. I was in love! I knew that love would end together with the war. His love . . . But even so I'm grateful to him for the feeling he gave me, and that I had known with him. I've loved him all my life, I've kept my feeling through the years. I have no need to lie. I'm an old woman. Yes, through my whole life! And I don't regret it.

My daughter reproached me: "Mama, why do you love him?" Yet I love him . . . I recently found out that he died. I wept a lot. Because of it I even quarreled with my daughter: "Why do you weep? He's been long dead for you." But I love him even now. I remember the war as the best time of my life, I was happy then . . .

Only, please, don't give my last name. For my daughter's sake . . .

Ekaterina Nikitichna Sannikova
SERGEANT, RIFLEMAN

During the war . . .

I was brought to the unit . . . To the front line. The commander met me with the words, "Take your hat off, please." I was surprised . . . I took it off . . . In the recruiting office we were given crew cuts, but while we were in the army camps, while we were going to the front, my hair grew back a bit. It began to curl, I had curly hair. Tight curls . . . You can't tell now, I'm already old . . . And so he looks and looks at me: "I haven't seen a woman for two years. I just want to look."

After the war . . .

I lived in a communal apartment. My neighbors were all married, and they insulted me. They taunted me: "Ha-ha-ha . . . Tell us how you whored around there with the men . . ." They used to put vinegar into my pot of boiled potatoes. Or add a tablespoon of salt . . . Ha-ha-ha . . .

My commander was demobilized. He came to me and we got married. We went and got registered, that's all. Without a wedding. And a year later he left me for another woman, the director of our factory canteen: "She wears perfume, and you smell of army boots and foot-wraps."

So I live alone. I don't have anybody in the whole wide world. Thank you for coming . . .

Anastasia Leonidovna Zhardetskaya

CORPORAL, MEDICAL ASSISTANT

And my husband . . . It's good he isn't here, he's at work. He told me strictly . . . He knows I like to talk about our love . . . How I made my wedding dress out of bandages overnight. By myself. My friends and I spent a month collecting bandages. Trophy bandages . . . I had a real wedding dress! I still have a picture: I'm in this dress and boots, only you can't see the boots. But I remember I wore boots. I concocted a belt out of an old forage cap . . . An excellent little belt. But what am I . . . going on about my own things . . . My husband told me not to say a word about love—no, no, but to talk about the war. He's strict. He taught me with a map . . . For two days he taught me where each front was . . . Where our unit was . . . I'll tell you, I wrote it down. I'll read it . . .

Why are you laughing? What a nice laugh you have. I also laughed . . . What kind of historian am I! I'd better show you that photo, where I'm in that dress made of bandages.

I like myself so much in it . . . In a white dress . . .

OF A STRANGE SILENCE FACING
THE SKY AND A LOST RING

Maria Selivestrovna Bozhok
NURSE

I left Kazan for the front as a nineteen-year-old girl . . .

Six months later I wrote my mother that people thought I was twenty-five or twenty-seven. Every day is spent in fear, in terror. Shrapnel flies, you think your skin is torn off. And people die. They die every day, every hour, it feels like every minute. We didn't have enough sheets to cover them. We laid them out in their underwear. There was a strange silence in the wards. I don't remember such silence anywhere. When a man dies he always looks up, never to the side or at you, if you're next to him. Only up . . . At the ceiling . . . But as if he's looking into the sky . . .

And I kept telling myself that I wouldn't hear a single word of love in that hell. I wouldn't believe it. The war went on for so many years, and I don't even remember a single song. Not even the famous "Dugout." Not a single one . . . I only remember: when I was leaving home for the front, there were cherry trees blossoming in the garden. I walked and kept looking back . . . Later I probably came across gardens along the way, they must have blossomed during the war. But I don't remember . . . In school I was such a laugher, but here I never smiled. If I saw a girl pluck her eyebrows or use lipstick, I was indignant. I was categorically against it: how was it possible, how could she want to be attractive at such a time?

There were wounded around, there was moaning . . . Dead people have such yellow-green faces. How could I think of joy? Of my happiness? I didn't want to combine love with that. With those things . . .

It seemed to me that there, in those surroundings, love would perish instantly. What love can there be without festivity, without beauty? Once the war ends, there'll be a beautiful life. And love. But here . . . Here, no. What if I suddenly die, and the man who loves me suffers? Such a pity. That's how I felt . . .

My present husband courted me there; we met at the front. I didn't want to hear him: "No, no, when the war's over, only then will we be able to talk about it." I'll never forget how once, on returning from a battle, he asked me, "Do you have some nice little blouse? Please put it on. Let me see you in a blouse." But all I had was an army shirt.

I used to tell my girlfriend who got married at the front, "He didn't bring you flowers. Didn't court you. And suddenly—marriage. What kind of love is that?" I didn't approve of her feelings.

The war ended . . . We looked at each other and didn't believe that the war had ended and we were still alive. Now we were going to live . . . We were going to love . . . But we had forgotten all that, we didn't know how to do it. I came home, I went with mama to have a dress made. My first postwar dress.

My turn came and they asked me, "What kind of dress do you want?"

"I don't know."

"You come to a dressmaker, and you don't know what kind of a dress you want?"

"No, I don't . . ."

I hadn't seen a single dress in five years. I'd even forgotten how a dress is made. That there are all sorts of tucks, slits . . . Low waist, high waist . . . Incomprehensible to me. I bought a pair of high-heeled shoes, walked up and down the room, and took them off. I put them in the corner, thinking, "I'll never learn to walk in them . . ."

Elena Viktorovna Klenovskaya
PARTISAN

I want to remember . . . I want to tell what an extraordinarily beautiful feeling I brought away from the war. Almost no words can convey with what rapture and admiration men regarded us. I lived in the same dugouts with them, slept on the same bunks, went on the same missions, and when I froze so that I felt my spleen freeze in me, my tongue freeze in my mouth, a little longer and I'd faint, I begged, "Misha, undo your coat, warm me up." He'd do it: "Well, is that better?" "It is."

I've never met with anything like it in my life. But it was impossible to think of anything personal when the Motherland was in danger.

But there was love?

Yes, there was. I encountered it . . . But you must forgive me, maybe I'm not right, and this isn't quite natural, but in my heart I disapproved of those people. I thought that it wasn't the time to be concerned with love. Around us was evil. Hatred. It seems many thought the same way . . .

And how were you before the war?

I liked to sing. To laugh. I wanted to be a pilot. I didn't even think about love! It wasn't the main thing in my life. The main thing was—the Motherland. Now I think we were naïve . . .

Svetlana Nikolaevna Liubich
MEDICAL VOLUNTEER

In the hospital . . . They were all happy. They were happy because they were still alive. There was a twenty-year-old lieutenant who was upset that he had lost a leg. But then, in the midst of universal grief, it seemed like happiness: he was alive, and, just think, he was only missing one leg. The main thing was—he was alive. He'd have love, and he'd have a wife, and everything. Nowadays it's an awful thing to find yourself without a leg, but then they all hopped around, and smoked, and laughed. They were heroes and all that! Just think!

Did you fall in love there?

Of course, we were so young. As soon as the new wounded arrived, we always fell in love with somebody. My girlfriend fell in love with a first lieutenant, he was wounded all over. She pointed him out—there he is. So I, too, decided to fall in love with him. When he was taken away, he asked me for a photo. I had one photo taken somewhere at a train station. I took this photo to give to him, but then I thought: what if this isn't love, and I've given him the photo? They were already taking him away. I gave him my hand in which I clutched the photo, but I couldn't bring myself to open my fist. That's the whole of my love . . .

Then there was Pavlik, also a lieutenant. He was in great pain, so I put a chocolate under his pillow. And when we met, this was after the war, already twenty years after, he began to thank my friend, Lilya Drozdova, for this chocolate. Lilya said, "What chocolate?" Then I confessed that it was me . . . And he kissed me . . . After twenty years he kissed me . . .

<u>Lilya Alexandrovskaya</u>

ART SINGER

Once after a concert . . . In a big evacuation hospital . . . The head doctor came up to me and asked, "We have a badly wounded tankman here in a separate room. He reacts to almost nothing, maybe your singing will help him." I went to the ward. As long as I live, I'll never forget this man, who by some miracle got out of a burning tank, burned from head to foot. He lay motionless, stretched out on the bed, his face black, eyeless. My throat was seized with a spasm, and for a few moments I couldn't get hold of myself. Then I began to sing quietly . . . I saw the man's face stir slightly. He whispered something. I bent over and heard, "Sing more." I sang for him more and more, all my repertoire, till the doctor said, "It seems he's fallen asleep . . ."

Nina Leonidovna Mikhai

SERGEANT MAJOR, NURSE

Our battalion commander and the nurse Liuba Silina . . . They loved each other! Everybody could see that. He went to battle and she . . . She said she wouldn't forgive herself if he didn't die before her eyes, and she didn't see him in his last moment. "Let them kill us together. With the same shell." They wanted to die together or to live together. Our love was not divided into today and tomorrow, there was only today. Each of us knew that you love now, and the next moment either you or this man would be no more. In war everything happens more quickly: both life and death. In those few years we lived a whole life. I've never been able to explain it to anybody. Time is different there . . .

In one battle the commander was badly wounded, and Liuba lightly, just a scratch on a shoulder. He was sent to the rear, and she stayed on. She was pregnant, and he gave her a letter, "Go to my parents. Whatever happens to me, you're my wife. And we'll have our son or our daughter."

Later Liuba wrote to me that his parents didn't accept her and didn't recognize the child. And the commander died.

For many years I've been meaning . . . I wanted to go and visit her, but it didn't work out. We had been bosom friends. But to go so far—to the Altai. Recently a letter came telling me she had died. Now her son invites me to come and visit her grave . . .

I'd like to go . . .

Lilya Mikhailovna Butko
SURGICAL NURSE

Victory Day . . .

We gathered for our traditional reunion. I came out of the hotel, and the girls said to me, "Where have you been, Lilya? We cried our eyes out."

It turned out that a man had approached them, a Kazakh, and asked, "Where are you from, girls? What hospital?"

"Who are you looking for?"

"I come here every year looking for a nurse. She saved my life. I fell in love with her. I want to find her."

My girls laughed.

"You're looking for a nurse, but she's a granny by now."

"No . . ."

"You must have a wife? Children?"

"I have grandchildren, and I have children, and I have a wife. I've lost my soul . . . I have no soul . . ."

The girls told me that, and together we recalled: might he be that Kazakh of mine?

. . . They brought a young Kazakh boy. Really very young. We operated on him. He had seven or eight intestinal ruptures and was considered hopeless. He lay there so indifferently that I noticed him at once. Each time I had a spare moment I'd run to see him: "How are you doing?" I gave him intravenous injections, took his temperature, and he made it. He began to recover. Our hospital was on the front line, we didn't keep the wounded for long. We rendered first aid, tore them from the clutches of death, and sent them on. He was supposed to be taken away with the next party.

He lay on a stretcher, and they told me he had asked for me.

"Nurse, come closer to me."

"What is it? What do you want? You're fine. They're sending you to the rear. Everything will be all right. Count yourself among the living."

He says, "I beg you. I'm an only son. You've saved me." And he gave me a present—a ring, a small ring.

I didn't wear rings, for some reason I didn't like them. So I refused.

"I can't. I really can't."

He insisted. The wounded men supported him.

"Take it, it's from a pure heart."

"It's just my duty, don't you see?"

They persuaded me. To tell the truth, I lost that ring later on. It was too big for me, and once I fell asleep in a car, there was a jolt, and it fell off somewhere. I was very sorry.

Did you find that man?

No, we didn't meet. I don't know whether it was the same one. But the girls and I spent the whole day looking for him.

. . . In 1946 I returned home. They asked me, "Will you wear army clothes or civilian?" Army clothes, of course. It never even occurred to me to take them off. One evening I went to the Officers' House to a dance. Now you're going to hear what the attitude toward army girls was.

I put on shoes and a dress, and left the overcoat and boots at the cloakroom.

An officer comes up to me and invites me to dance.

"You must be from other parts," he says. "You're a very cultivated girl."

He spent the whole evening with me. Didn't let me get away. The dances were over, he says to me, "Give me your token."

He goes on ahead. They give him the boots and the overcoat from the cloakroom.

"These aren't mine . . ."

I come up: "No, they're mine."

"You didn't tell me you were at the front."

"Did you ask me?"

He was at a loss. Couldn't raise his eyes to me. He himself had just come back from the war . . .

"Why are you so surprised?"

"I couldn't imagine you had been in the army. You see, a girl at the front . . ."

"You're surprised that I was alone? Without a husband and not pregnant? Not wearing a padded jacket, not blowing strong cigarette smoke, and not using foul language?"

I didn't allow him to take me home.

I was always proud that I had been at the front. Defending the Motherland . . .

Liubov Mikhailovna Grozd
MEDICAL ASSISTANT

My first kiss . . .

Second Lieutenant Nikolai Belokhvostik . . . Ah, see, I'm blushing all over, and I'm already a grandmother. We were young then. Very young. I thought . . . I was sure . . . That . . . I didn't confess even to my girlfriend that I was in love with him. Head over heels. My first love . . . Maybe my only love? Who knows . . . I thought no one in our company had guessed. I had never liked anyone like that before! If I liked someone, it was not so much. But he . . . I walked around and thought about him all the time, every minute. That . . . It was real love. I felt it. By all the signs . . . Ah, see, I'm blushing . . .

We were burying him . . . He was lying on a tarpaulin; he had just been killed. The Germans were shelling us. We had to bury him quickly . . . Right away . . . We found some old birches; we chose one that stood a short way from an old oak. The biggest one. Next to it . . . I tried to remember, so I could come back and find this place afterward. The village ended there, there was a fork in the road . . . How to remember? How to remember if one of those birches was already burning right in front of our eyes . . . How? We began to take leave of him . . . They told me, "You go first." My heart leaped, I realized . . . That . . . It turned out everybody knew about my love. Everybody . . . The thought struck me: maybe he knew, too? See . . .

He's lying here . . . They'll put him into the ground now . . . a hole. They'll cover him with sand . . . But I was terribly glad at the thought that maybe he knew, too. And what if he liked me? As if he were alive and would now answer me . . . I remembered how he gave me a German chocolate bar for the New Year. I didn't eat it, I spent a month carrying it around in my pocket.

I've remembered it all my life . . . That moment . . . There were bombs falling around . . . He lay on a tarpaulin . . . That moment . . . I was happy . . . I stood smiling to myself. Crazy. I was happy that maybe he knew about my love . . .

I went up and kissed him. I'd never kissed a man before . . . That was the first time . . .

OF THE LONELINESS OF A BULLET AND A HUMAN BEING

Klavdia S—va
SNIPER

My story is a particular one . . . Prayers console me. I pray for my daughter . . .

I remember a saying of mama's. Mama liked to say, "A bullet's a fool; fate is a villain." She had this saying for all sorts of troubles. A bullet is alone, and man is alone; a bullet flies wherever it likes, and fate twists a man however it likes. This way and that, this way and that. A man is a feather, a sparrow's feather. You can never know your future. It's not given to us . . . We can't penetrate this mystery. When we were returning from the war, a Gypsy told me my future. She came up to me at the train station, called me aside . . . She predicted I would have a great love . . . I had a German watch; I took it off and gave it to her for this great love. I believed her.

And now I can't weep enough over that love . . .

I was going to the war happily. As a Komsomol girl. Along with everybody else. We traveled in freight cars. There were inscriptions on them in black mazut: "Forty persons/eight horses." There were a hundred of us stuffed in each car.

I became a sniper. I could have been a radio operator. It's a useful profession—both in the army and in peacetime. A woman's profession. But they told me they needed people to shoot, so I shot. I did it well. I have two Orders of Glory and four medals. For three years of war.

They shouted to us—Victory! They announced—Victory! I remember my first feeling—joy. And at once, that same moment—fear! Panic! Panic! How to live from here on? Papa had been killed at Stalingrad. My two older brothers had been missing in action since the beginning of the war. Mama and I were left. Two women. How were we to live? All our girls fell to thinking . . . We'd get together in the evening in a dugout . . . We discussed how our lives were only beginning. There was joy and fear. Before we had been afraid of death, and now—of life . . . It was equally frightening. It's true! We talked and talked, then sat and said nothing.

Will we get married or won't we? For love or without love? We told fortunes with daisies . . . We threw flower wreaths into the river, we melted wax . . . I remember in one village they showed us where a sorceress lived. We all rushed to her, even several officers. And all the girls. She told fortunes in water. By palm reading. Another time an organ-grinder had us draw paper lots. Tickets. I used to have lucky tickets . . . Where is that luck of mine?

How did the Motherland meet us? I can't speak without sobbing . . . It was forty years ago, but my cheeks still burn. The men said nothing, but the women . . . They shouted to us, "We know what you did there! You lured our men with your young c——! Army whores . . . Military bitches . . ." They insulted us in all possible ways . . . The Russian vocabulary is rich . . .

A fellow took me home from a dance; I suddenly felt really bad, my heart started fluttering. I walked and walked and then sat down in a snowdrift. "What's the matter?" "Never mind. Too much dancing." It was because of my two wounds. Because of the war . . . I had to learn to be tender. To be weak and fragile. But my feet were used to size ten boots. I wasn't used to being embraced. I was used to being responsible for myself. I waited for tender words, but I didn't understand them. To me they seemed childish. Among men at the front there were foul Russian curses. I was used to that. My girlfriend who worked in the library kept telling me, "Read poetry. Read Esenin."*

I quickly got married. A year later. To our factory engineer. I dreamed of love. I wanted to have a home and a family. I wanted my home to smell of small children. I smelled my first baby's diapers and was happy. The smell of happiness . . . A woman's happiness . . . In war there are no women's smells, they're all men's. War smells of men.

I have two children . . . A boy and a girl. First I had a boy. A good, intelligent boy. He finished university. An architect. But the girl . . . My girl . . . She began to walk when she was five, said her first word, "mama," at seven. Even now it comes out not "mama" but "moomo," not "papa" but "poopo." She . . . To this day I think it can't be true. It's some kind of a mistake. She's been in an insane asylum . . . For forty years. Since I retired, I go there every day. It's my sin . . .

For many years now, at the beginning of the school year I buy her a new primer. We spend a whole day reading the primer. Sometimes I come home from her, and it feels as if I've lost the ability to read and write. To talk. I don't need any of that. What for?

I've been punished . . . For what? Maybe for having killed people? I sometimes think so . . . You have a lot of time when you're old . . . I

---

* Sergei Esenin (1895–1925) was one of the major Russian lyric poets of the twentieth century.

think and think. In the morning I go on my knees, I look out the window. And I pray to God . . . I pray for everybody . . . I don't have a grudge against my husband, I forgave him long ago. The girl was born . . . He looked at us . . . He stayed for a while and left. Left with a reproach: "Would a normal woman have gone to the war? Learned to shoot? That's why you're unable to give birth to a normal child." I pray for him . . .

Maybe he's right? I sometimes think so . . . It's my sin . . .

I loved the Motherland more than anything in the world. I loved . . . Who can I tell it to now? To my girl . . . To her alone . . . I recall the war, and she thinks I'm telling her fairy tales. Children's fairy tales. Scary children's fairy tales . . .

Don't write my last name. No need to . . .

"ABOUT TINY POTATOES . . ."

————

There was yet another war . . .

In this war no one marked on the map where no-man's-land was, where the front line began. No one could count up all the soldiers. The numbers of weapons. People shot from antiaircraft batteries, machine guns, hunting rifles. From old Berdan rifles. There were no pauses, no general advances. Many fought single-handed. Died single-handed. It was not an army fighting—divisions, battalions, companies—but people, partisans and underground fighters: men young and old, women, children. Tolstoy called this many-faced surge "the cudgel of the people's war" and "the hidden warmth of patriotism," and Hitler (like Napoleon before him) complained to his generals that "Russians don't fight according to the rules."

To die in this war was not the most frightening thing. There was something else . . . Picture to yourself a soldier at the front, surrounded by his family—children, wife, old parents. He must be ready at every moment to sacrifice them, too. To send them to the slaughter. Courage, as well as betrayal, often had no witnesses.

In our villages on Victory Day there is weeping, not rejoicing. Many weep. They grieve. "It was so horrible . . . I buried all my family, I buried my soul in the war" (V. G. Androsik, underground fighter).

They begin to talk softly, and in the end almost all of them shout.

———

I am a witness . . .

I'll talk about the commander of our partisan unit . . . I won't name him, because his relations are still alive. It will pain them to read it . . .

The liaisons sent a message to the unit: the commander's family had been taken by the Gestapo—his wife, two small daughters, and the old mother. There were notices hanging everywhere, and distributed in the market: if the commander did not surrender, the family would be hanged. He was given two days to think it over. The *polizei* went around the villages and agitated among the people, saying that the Red commissars didn't pity their own children. They were monsters. Nothing was sacred for them. They scattered leaflets from a plane over the forest . . . The commander wanted to surrender, wanted to shoot himself. He wasn't left alone all this time, he was watched. He was capable of killing himself . . .

His unit got in touch with Moscow and reported the situation. They received instructions . . . The same day a party meeting of the unit was convened. The decision was made: not to yield to German provocation. As a Communist, our commander submitted to party discipline . . .

Two days later scouts were sent to the town. They brought terrible news: the whole family had been hanged. The commander was killed in the first battle after that . . . Killed somehow incomprehensibly. Accidentally. I think he wanted to die . . .

Instead of words I have tears . . . How can I persuade myself that I must speak? Who will believe it . . . People want to have a calm and pleasant life, not to listen to me and suffer . . . (V. Korotaeva, partisan).

I, too, try to persuade myself that I must go on . . .

OF A MINE AND A STUFFED TOY
IN A BASKET

Antonina Alexeevna Kondrashova
SCOUT FOR THE BYTOSHSKY PARTISAN BRIGADE

I carried out my mission . . . After that I couldn't stay in the village
and went to join the detachment. A few days later my mother was
taken by the Gestapo. My brother managed to escape, but my mother
was taken away. They tortured her there, questioned her about her
daughter's whereabouts. For two years she was held there. For two
years, along with our other women, the fascists made her lead the way
during their operations: they feared the partisan mines and always
drove local people ahead of them—if there were mines, those people
would be blown up, and the German soldiers would remain un-
harmed. A living shield. For two years they used my mother that way.

More than once, while waiting in ambush, we suddenly saw
women followed by fascists. Once they came closer, you could see
that your mother was there among them. And most frightful of all
was waiting for your commander to give the order to fire. Everyone
waited in fear for that order, because one would whisper, "There's my
mother," another "And there's my sister," or someone would see their
own child . . . My mama always went around in a white kerchief. She
was tall, she was always the first to be noticed. Before I had time to
notice her, someone would already report, "There goes your
mother . . ." When they give the order to shoot, you shoot. And I
myself didn't know where I was shooting; there was one thing in my
head: "Don't lose sight of that white kerchief—is she alive, has she
fallen?" A white kerchief . . . They all run away, fall down, and you
don't know whether your mother has been killed or not. For the next

two days or more, I walk around, beside myself, until the liaisons come back from the village to tell me she's alive. I can live again. Until the next time. I don't think I could stand it now . . . I hated them . . . My hatred helped me . . . To this day the scream of a child who is thrown down a well still rings in my ears. Have you ever heard that scream? The child is falling and screaming, screaming as if from somewhere under the ground, from the other world. It's not a child's scream, and not a man's either. And to see a young fellow cut up with a saw . . . Our partisan . . . After that, when you go on a mission, your heart seeks only one thing: to kill them, kill as many as possible, annihilate them in the cruelest way. When I saw fascist prisoners, I wanted to sink my claws into them one by one. To strangle them. To strangle them with my hands, to tear them with my teeth. I wouldn't have killed them, it would have been too easy a death for them. Not with weapons, not with a rifle . . .

Before their retreat, this was already in 1943, the fascists shot my mother. My mother was like this, she gave us her blessing: "Go, children, you have to live. Rather than just die. It's better not to just die . . ." Mama didn't say big words, she found simple women's words. She wanted us to live and study, especially to study.

The women who shared her cell said that each time she was led away, she begged, "Oh, my dears, I weep only for this: if I die, help my children!"

After the war, one of those women took me into her home, her family, even though she had two young children. The fascists burned our cottage, my younger brother died fighting with the partisans, my mother was shot, my father had been at the front. He came back from the front wounded, sick. He didn't survive much longer, he died soon. So, of my whole family, I was the only one left. That woman was poor herself, and what's more she had two young children. I decided to leave, to go away somewhere. But she wept and wouldn't let me.

When I discovered my mother had been shot, I lost my mind. I didn't know what to do with myself, I had no peace. I had to find her . . . But they had been shot and their grave, in a big antitank trench, had been leveled out by tractors. I was shown approximately where she stood, and I ran, dug there, turning corpses over. I recognized my mother by the ring on her hand . . . When I saw that ring, I cried out, and I remember nothing more. I remember nothing . . . Some women pulled her out, washed her from a tin can, and buried her. I still have that can.

At night I sometimes lie and think: my mother died because of me. No, not because of me . . . If, in fear for my loved ones, I hadn't gone to fight, and if another, a third and a fourth hadn't either, what is now wouldn't be. But to say to myself . . . To forget . . . How my mother walked . . . The sound of the order . . . I shot in the direction she came from. Her white kerchief. You can't imagine how hard it is to live with. And the longer I live, the harder it gets. Sometimes, at night, there's a sudden young laughter or voice outside the window, and you shudder, it suddenly sounds like a child crying, shouting. Sometimes you suddenly wake up feeling like you can't breathe. The smell of burning chokes you . . . You don't know the smell of a burning human body, especially in the summer. An anxious and sweet smell. With the job I have now, if there's a fire, I have to go there, write a report. But if they say that a farm is on fire, that there are dead animals, I never go, I'm not able . . . It reminds me . . . That smell . . . Like burning people . . . And so you wake up at night, run and fetch your cologne, and it seems that in the cologne, too, there's that smell. Everywhere . . .

For a long time I was afraid to get married. Afraid to have children. What if there's war suddenly, and I leave for the front? What about the children? Now I like to read books about life after death. What's there? Who will I meet? I want to meet mama, and I'm afraid of it. When I was young I wasn't afraid, but now I'm old . . .

Yadviga Mikhailovna Savitskaya

UNDERGROUND FIGHTER

My first impression . . . I saw a German . . . As if I'd been hit, my whole body hurt, every cell—how is it they're here? Hatred—it was stronger than fear for our near ones, our loved ones, and fear of our own death. Of course, we thought of our families, but we had no choice. The enemy had come with evil to our land . . . With fire and sword . . .

For instance, when it became known that they were going to arrest me, I left for the forest. To the partisans. I left, leaving at home my seventy-five-year-old mother, and alone at that. We agreed she would pretend to be blind, deaf, and they wouldn't harm her. Obviously, that was how I comforted myself.

The day after I left, fascists burst into my house. Mama pretended she was blind and couldn't hear, as we had agreed. They beat her badly, trying to extort from her where her daughter was. My mother was ill for a long time . . .

Alexandra Ivanovna Khramova

SECRETARY OF THE UNDERGROUND REGIONAL PARTY COMMITTEE OF ANTOPOL

I'll stay this way till the end . . . The way we used to be then. Yes, naïve; yes, romantic. Till my hair turns gray . . . But—that's me!

My friend Katya Simakova was a partisan liaison. She had two girls. Both girls were small—well, how old were they? Six or seven years old. She took those girls by the hands, went through the town and memorized what equipment stood where. A sentry would yell at her, and she would open her mouth, pretending to be simpleminded. She did it for several years . . . The mother sacrificed her daughters . . .

There was another woman, Zajarskaya. She had a daughter, Valeria; the girl was seven years old. We had to blow up the mess hall. We decided to plant a mine in the stove, but it had to be carried there. And the mother said her daughter would bring the mine. She put the mine in a basket and covered it with a couple of children's outfits, a stuffed toy, two dozen eggs, and some butter. And so the little girl brought the mine to the mess hall. People say that maternal instinct is stronger than anything. No, ideas are stronger! And faith is stronger! I think . . . I'm even certain that if it weren't for such a mama and such a girl, and they hadn't carried that mine, we wouldn't have been victorious. Yes, life—is a good thing. Excellent! But there are things that are dearer . . .

Paulina Kasperovich

PARTISAN

We had the Chimuk brothers in our detachment . . . They ran into an ambush in their village, took refuge in some barn, there was shooting, the barn was set on fire. They went on shooting till they ran out of cartridges . . . Then they came out, burned . . . They were driven around the villages in a cart to see who would recognize them as their own. So that people would give themselves away . . .

The entire village stood there. Their father and mother stood there, nobody made a sound. What a heart the mother must have had not to cry out. Not to call. She knew that if she began to weep, the whole village would be burned down. She wouldn't be killed alone. Everybody would be killed. For one German killed they used to burn an entire village. She knew . . . There exist awards for everything, but no award, not even the highest Star of the Hero of the Soviet Union is enough for that mother . . . For her silence . . .

Valentina Mikhailovna Ilkevich

PARTISAN LIAISON

I came to the partisans together with my mama . . . She did laundry for everyone and cooked. If she had to, she also stood watch. One day I left on a mission, and my mother was told I had been hanged. When I returned a few days later and my mother saw me, she became paralyzed; for several hours she couldn't speak. All of that had to be lived through . . .

We picked up a woman on the road. She was unconscious. She couldn't walk, she crawled and thought she was already dead. She felt blood streaming over her, but decided that she felt it in the other world, not in this one. When we shook her, and she regained some consciousness, we heard . . . She told us how they had been shot; she had been led out to be shot, she and her five children. As they were being led to the barn, the children were killed. They shot them and had fun doing it . . . Only one remained, a nursing baby boy. A fascist pointed at him: "Toss him up, I'm going to shoot him." The mother threw the child so as to kill him herself . . . Her own child . . . So the German wouldn't have time to shoot . . . She said she didn't want to live, that she couldn't live in this world after that, only in the other one . . . She didn't want to . . .

I didn't want to kill, I wasn't born to kill. I wanted to be a teacher. But I saw how they burned a village . . . I couldn't scream, I couldn't weep loudly: we were on a scouting mission and came close to that village. I could only bite my hands; I still have the scars; I bit them till they bled. Till the raw flesh showed. I remember how the people screamed . . . The cows screamed . . . The chickens screamed . . . It seemed to me they were all screaming with human voices. All of them alive. Burning and screaming . . .

This isn't me speaking, it's my grief speaking . . .

Valentina Pavlovna Kozhemyakina

PARTISAN

We knew . . . Everybody knew we had to win . . .

Later on people thought my father had stayed on an assignment from the Party. Nobody left him with any assignment. We ourselves decided to fight. I don't remember any panic in our family. There was great sorrow, yes. But no panic. We all believed that victory would be ours. On the first day the Germans entered our village, my father played "The Internationale" on his violin. He wanted to do something like that. Some sort of protest . . .

Two months went by, or three . . . Or . . .

There was a Jewish boy . . . A German leashed him to his bicycle, and the boy ran after him like a dog: *"Schnell! Schnell!"* He rode and laughed. A young German . . . Soon he grew tired of it, got off the bicycle, and gestured to the boy to kneel in front of him . . . On all fours . . . And creep like a dog . . . Leap . . . *"Hundik! Hundik!"* He threw a stick: fetch it! The boy stood up, ran, and brought the stick in his hands. The German got angry . . . Started beating him. Yelling at him. He showed him: leap on all fours and fetch it in your teeth. The boy fetched it in his teeth . . .

The German played with this boy for two hours. Then he leashed him to his bicycle again and they went back. The boy ran like a dog . . . Toward the ghetto . . .

And you ask why we began to fight? Why we learned to shoot . . .

Alexandra Nikiforovna Zakharova

PARTISAN COMMISSAR OF THE
225TH REGIMENT OF GOMEL PROVINCE

How could I forget . . . Wounded soldiers ate salt by the spoonful . . . A name is called, a soldier steps out of the ranks and collapses with his rifle from weakness. From hunger.

The people helped us. If they hadn't helped us, the partisan movement couldn't have existed. The people fought together with us. At times with tears, but still they gave: "Dear children, let's grieve together. Wait for victory."

They'd bring out the last tiny potatoes; they'd give us bread. Prepare sacks to take to the forest. One would say: "I'll give this much," another "This much." "How about you, Ivan?" "And you, Maria?" "I'll give, like everybody else, but I have children . . ."

What are we without our people? An entire army in the forest, but without them we would have died. They sowed, plowed, took care of us and of the children, clothed us all through the war. They plowed at night, when there was no shooting. I remember how we came to a village where an old man was being buried. He had been killed at night. Sowing wheat. He gripped the grain so hard we couldn't straighten his fingers. He was put in the ground with the grain . . .

We had weapons, we could defend ourselves. But they? For giving a loaf of bread to a partisan, they were shot. I stayed overnight and left, but if anyone gave away that I had spent the night in this cottage, they would all be shot. There was a woman there alone, without her husband, but with her three little children. She never drove us away when we came, but lit the stove and cleaned our clothes . . . She gave us all she had left, "Eat, lads." And the potatoes in spring are as tiny as peas. We're eating, and the children are sitting on the stove crying. Those were their last peas . . .

Vera Grigoryevna Sedova
UNDERGROUND FIGHTER

My first mission . . . They brought me leaflets. I sewed them into my pillow. Mama was making the bed and felt them. She ripped open the pillow and saw the leaflets. She began to cry. "You'll destroy yourself and me." But later she helped me.

The partisan liaisons came to us often. They'd unhitch the horses and come in. Do you think the neighbors didn't see? They saw and guessed. I said it was from my brother, from the country. But everybody knew very well that I had no brother in the country. I'm grateful to them; I should bow down to my entire street. One single word would have been enough for us all to die, my entire family. All they needed was to point a finger at us. But no one . . . Not a single person . . . During the war I came to love the people so much that I'll never be able to stop loving them . . .

After the liberation, I'd walk down the street and look around: I couldn't help being afraid, I couldn't calmly walk the streets. I counted the cars as I went, counted the trains at the station . . . It took me a while to get rid of that habit . . .

<u>Vera Safronovna Davydova</u>
PARTISAN

I'm already crying . . . The tears are pouring down . . .

We entered a house, there was nothing in it, just two bare, planed benches and a table. There wasn't even a mug, I think, to drink water. The people had nothing left but an icon in the corner, and an embroidered cloth draped over it.

An old man and an old woman were sitting there. One of our partisans took off his boots, his footwraps were so torn that he couldn't use them anymore. And the rain, and the dirt, and the torn boots. And this old woman goes to the icon, takes the embroidered cloth, and gives it to him: "Take it, child, or how can you go on?" There was nothing else in this cottage . . .

Vera Mitrofanovna Tolkacheva
PARTISAN LIAISON

In the early days . . . I picked up two wounded men outside the village . . . One was wounded in the head, and the other soldier had shrapnel in his leg. I pulled out the shrapnel myself, and poured kerosene in the wound. I didn't find anything else . . . I knew by then that kerosene was a disinfectant . . .

I took care of them and got them back on their feet. First one went off into the woods, then the other. The latter, as he was leaving, suddenly fell at my feet. He wanted to kiss my feet.

"Dear sister! You saved my life."

There were no names, nothing. Just sister and brother.

In the evening, the women gathered in my house. "They say the Germans have taken Moscow."

"Never!"

With these same women, after the war, we organized a kolkhoz, and I was appointed the chairwoman. There were also four old men and five boys, from ten to thirteen years old. Those were my plowmen. We had twenty horses. They all had scabies and needed treatment. That was all I had for farming. There were no wheels or yokes. The women turned the soil with shovels and did the harrowing with cows and bulls. The bullocks would lie down and refuse to get up—unless you all but tore their tails off. The boys harrowed by day, and in the evening, when they opened their little bundles, they all had the same food—potato prasnaki. You don't know what it is. Sorrel seeds, turnsole . . . You don't know it? There is such an herb. We picked clover. We ground it all in a mortar. And we cooked these prasnaki. A sort of bread . . . Bitter—very bitter . . .

In the fall came instructions: cut down 580 cubic meters of timber. Who with? I took my twelve-year-old boy and a ten-year-old girl with me. So did the other women. We delivered the timber . . .

———

Iosif Georgievich Yasukevich and his daughter Maria, partisan liaisons of the Petrakov Unit of the Rokossovsky Brigade during the war, tell the following story:

Iosif Georgievich

I gave away everything for the victory . . . My dearest things. My sons fought at the front. My two nephews were executed for communicating with the partisans. The fascists burned my sister, their mother. In their own house . . . People said that until the smoke covered her, she stood upright like a candle, holding an icon. After the war, whenever the sun goes down, I think something's burning . . .

Maria

I was young, thirteen years old. I knew my father helped the partisans. I understood. People would show up at night. They would leave something, take something. Often my father would take me along, put me onto the cart: "Sit and don't move from here." Once we got to the right place, he would pull out guns or leaflets.

Later he began sending me to the station. He taught me what I should remember. I would quietly sneak into the bushes and hide there until night, counting how many trains passed by. I memorized what they transported, you could see it: guns, tanks, or soldiers. Two or three times a day the Germans would shoot into the bushes.

But weren't you scared?

I was small, I always slipped through, and nobody would notice me. But that day . . . I remember it very well. My father tried twice to leave the farmstead where we lived. The partisans were waiting for him in the woods. Twice he went off and twice he was sent back by the patrols. It was getting dark. He called me: "Marika . . ." And my mother shouted, "I won't let our child go." She pulled me away from my father . . .

Still I ran through the woods, as he told me to. I knew all the paths by heart, but to tell the truth, I was afraid of the dark. I found the partisans, they were waiting, and I reported everything my father had told me. On my way back, it was already growing light. How was I to get around the German patrols? I circled through the forest, fell into the lake; my father's jacket and boots, everything sank. I got out of the hole in the ice . . . Ran barefoot over the snow . . . I fell ill and took to my bed and never got up. My legs were paralyzed. There were no doctors or medications. Mama treated me with herb infusions. Applied clay . . .

After the war they took me to doctors. But it was already too late. I remained bedridden . . . I can sit up a little, then I lie and look out the window . . . Remembering the war . . .

Iosif Georgievich

I carry her in my arms . . . For forty years. Like a little child . . . My wife died two years ago. "I forgive you everything," she said to me. "The sins of youth . . . Everything . . ." But not Marika. I saw it in her eyes . . . I'm afraid to die, because Marika will be left alone. Who will carry her? Who will cross her before going to bed? Who will ask God . . .

OF MOMMIES AND DADDIES

The village of Ratyntsy, Volozhinsky district, Minsk region. An hour's drive from the capital. An ordinary Belorussian village—wooden houses, flowers in the front gardens, chicken and geese in the streets. Children in sandboxes. Old women on the benches. I came to see one of them, but the whole street gathered. They started talking. Loudly, all at the same time.

Each about herself, but all about the same thing. How they plowed, sowed, baked bread for the partisans, took care of the children, went to diviners and Gypsies to interpret their dreams, and asked God to protect them. Waited for their husbands to come back from the war.

I wrote down the first three names: Elena Adamovna Velichko, Yustina Lukyanovna Grigorovich, Maria Fyodorovna Mazuro. After that I could no longer make them out because of the weeping . . .

—Ah, my darling daughter! My golden one! I don't like Victory Day. I weep! Ah, how I weep! Whenever I think, it all comes back. Happiness is beyond the mountains, but grief is just over your shoulder . . .

The Germans burned us down, picked us clean. We were left on a bare rock. We came back from the woods, there was nothing. Only the cats were still there. What did we eat? In the summer I went and gathered berries, mushrooms. The house was full of children.

When the war was over, we went to the kolkhoz. I reaped, and mowed, and threshed. We pulled the plow in place of horses. There were no horses; the Germans killed them. They shot all the dogs. My mother used to say: when I die, I don't know about my soul, but my hands will get some rest. My little girl was ten; she reaped with me. The brigadier came to see how such a little thing fulfilled the norm before evening. We reaped and reaped; the sun went down behind the forest, but we wanted it to stay higher. One day wasn't enough. We did two norms. We weren't paid anything; they just put down marks that counted as workdays. We spent the whole summer in the field and in the fall didn't get even a sack of flour. We raised the children on nothing but potatoes . . .

—So the war was over. I was alone. I was the cow, and the bull, and the woman, and the muzhik. Aie, aie, aie . . .

—War was woe . . . Only children in my cottage. Not a bench, not a trunk. Total nakedness. We ate acorns, in spring it was grass . . . When my girl went to school, I bought her her first pair of shoes. She slept in them, she didn't want to take them off. That's how we lived! Life is over, but there's nothing to remember. Only the war . . .

—A rumor went around that the Germans had brought our prisoners to a hamlet, and those who recognized their own could take them. Our women got up and ran! In the evening some brought back their own, others brought strangers, and what they told us was beyond belief: people were rotting alive, starving to death, ate all the leaves off trees . . . Ate grass . . . Dug roots from the ground . . . I ran there the next day, didn't find mine, and thought I might save someone else's son. I took a fancy to a swarthy one, his name was Sashko, like my little grandson. He was probably about eighteen years old. I gave the German some lard, eggs: "My brother." Crossed my heart. We came back home. He couldn't eat a whole egg, he was so weak. Before the month was out, a bastard turned up. He lived like all of us, married, two children . . . He went to the commandant's office and reported that we had taken in strangers. The next day the Germans came on their motorcycles. We begged and fell on our knees, but they deceived us by saying they would take them closer to their homes. I gave Sashko my grandfather's suit . . . I thought he would live . . .

But they were driven out of the village . . . All mowed down with machine guns . . . All of them. To a man . . . They were so young, young and good! And we decided, those who had taken them in—nine of us—to bury them. Five of us dragged them out of the pit, the other four looked around so the Germans wouldn't fall on us. We couldn't use our hands; it was very hot, and they had been lying there for four days . . . We were afraid of cutting them with our shovels . . . We put them on tablecloths and pulled . . . We drank water and covered our noses. So as not to faint . . . We dug a grave in the woods, and laid them down side by side. Covered their heads with sheets . . . Their feet . . .

For a year we never stopped mourning them. And each of us thought: Where is my husband or son? Are they alive? Because men do come back from war, but from under the sand—never . . . Aie, aie, aie . . .

—My husband was nice, kind. We only lived together for a year and a half. When he was leaving, I bore our baby in my bosom. But he didn't get to see our daughter, I gave birth to her without him. He left in the summer, and I gave birth to her in the fall.

I was still giving her the breast; she was less than a year old. I was sitting on the bed nursing her . . . A knock on the window: "Lena, a notice has come . . . About your husband . . ." (The women didn't let the postman come, they came to tell me themselves.) As I stood there holding my little girl to my breast, the milk spurted straight on the floor. My girl cried out, she got scared. She never took my breast again. It was precisely on the eve of Palm Sunday that I was told. In April . . . The sun was shining . . . I read in the notice that my Ivan had been killed in Poland. His grave is near the city of Gdansk. He died on March 17, 1945 . . . Such a small, thin scrap of paper . . . We were already expecting the Victory, our men were about to come home. The gardens were in bloom . . .

After this scare my girl was sick for a long time, till she went to school. A hard knock on the door or a shout—and she got sick. Cried during the night. I suffered over her for a long time, maybe for seven years I didn't see the sun, it didn't shine for me. Everything was dark in my eyes.

Victory!—they said. The men began to come home. But fewer returned than we sent out. Less than half. My brother Yusik came back first. Crippled, though. And he had a daughter just like mine. Four years old, or five . . . My daughter used to go to their house, but one day she came back crying: "I won't go anymore." "Why are you crying?" I asked. "Her daddy takes Olechka on his knees" (their daughter was called Olechka) "and comforts her. But I don't have a daddy. I only have a mommy." We hugged each other . . .

And so it went for two or three years. She would run home from outside: "Can I play at home? Or else daddy will come, and I'll be outside with the other kids. He won't recognize me. He's never seen me . . ." I couldn't chase her out of the house to the other kids. She sat at home for days. Waiting for daddy. But daddy never returned . . .

—Mine, as he was leaving for the war, cried so hard about leaving his little children. He was sorry. The children were so young they didn't know they had a father. Above all, they were all boys. I was carrying the smallest of them in my arms. He took him and pressed him to himself. I ran after him. They were already shouting "Fall in!" But he couldn't let go of him, he stood in the column with him . . . The commander yelled at him, and he was flooding the baby with tears. All the swaddling clothes got wet. We ran out of the village with the children; we ran for another three miles. Other women also ran along. My children were falling down, and I was barely able to carry the little one. And Volodya, that's my husband, turned to look, and I kept running. I was the last . . . The children stayed behind on the road. I was running with the little one . . .

A year later a notice came: your husband Vladimir Grigorovich was killed in Germany, near Berlin. I've never even seen his grave.

One of our neighbors came home perfectly healthy, another came home missing a leg. I grieved so much: let mine come back, even without legs, but alive. I'd have carried him in my arms . . .

—I was left with three little sons. I carried sheaves on my back, and wood from the forest, and potatoes and hay . . . All alone . . . I pulled the plow by myself, on my back, dragged the harrow. So what? In every second cottage of our village there was a widow or a soldier's wife. We were left without men. Without horses. The horses were also taken to the war. So I . . . I even received two awards as "best worker," and was once given ten yards of cotton. I was so happy! I sewed shirts for my boys, all three of them.

—After the war . . . The sons of those who had been killed were just becoming adolescents. Growing up. The boys were thirteen or fourteen years old, but they thought they were already adults. Wanted to marry. There weren't any men, but the women were all young . . .

If I had been told: give up your cow and there won't be any war, I'd have given it up! So that my children wouldn't have to endure what I have. Day and night I feel my sorrow . . .

—I look out the window, it's as if he's sitting there . . . Sometimes in the evening something seems to be there . . . I'm already old, but I always see him young. The way he was when he left. If I dream of him, he's also young. And I'm young, too . . .

The women all got death notices, but I got a scrap of paper—"Missing in action." Written in blue ink. For the first ten years I waited for him every day. I wait for him even now. As long as we live we can hope for anything . . .

———

—And how can a woman live alone? A man came, helped me or didn't. It's bad either way. Anyone can say what he likes . . . People talk, dogs bark . . . But if only Ivan had seen his five grandsons. Every once in a while I stand by his portrait and show him their photographs. I talk to him . . .

—Aie, aie, aie . . . Dear God . . . Merciful one . . .

—Just after the war I had a dream: I go out into the yard, and my husband is walking there . . . In a uniform . . . And he calls me, he keeps calling me. I leaped from under the blanket, opened the window . . . All's quiet. Even the birds aren't singing. They're asleep. Wind passes over the leaves . . . Whistling softly . . .

In the morning I took a dozen eggs and went to the Gypsy woman. "He's no more," she laid out the cards. "Don't wait in vain. It's his soul walking near the house." There had been love between us. Great love . . .

—A Gypsy woman taught me: "When everybody falls asleep, put on a black shawl and sit down by a big mirror. He'll appear in it . . . You shouldn't touch either him or his clothes. Just talk to him . . ." I sat up all night . . . Before morning he came . . . He said nothing, and his tears flowed. He appeared like that three times. I called him and he came. He wept. I stopped calling him. I felt sorry . . .

—And I'm waiting to meet mine . . . I'll tell him things day and night. I need nothing from him, only—let him listen. He's probably also grown old there. Like me.

———

—It's my native soil . . . I dig up potatoes, beetroots . . . He's there somewhere, and I'll come to him soon . . . My sister tells me: "Don't look in the ground, look at the sky. Upward. They're there." That's my cottage . . . Nearby . . . Stay with us. If you stay overnight you'll learn more. Blood isn't water, it's a pity to spill it, but it keeps flowing. I see it on television . . . every day . . .

You don't have to write about us . . . Better to remember . . . How you and I talked together. Wept. When you take leave of us, turn to look at us and our cottages. Not once, like a stranger, but twice, like our own. No need for anything more. Turn to look . . .

OF LITTLE LIFE AND A BIG IDEA

Thecla Fedorovna Struy
PARTISAN

I always believed . . . I believed Stalin . . . I believed the Communists. I myself was a Communist. I believed in Communism . . . I lived for that, I stayed alive for that. After Khrushchev's report at the Twentieth Congress, when he told about Stalin's errors, I became ill, I took to my bed. I couldn't believe it was true. During the war I also shouted, "For the Motherland! For Stalin!" Nobody made me do it . . . I believed . . . It's my life . . .

Here it is . . .

I fought with the partisans for two years . . . In my last battle, I was wounded in the legs, lost consciousness. It was freezing cold. When I came to, I felt my hands were frostbitten. Now they're alive, good hands, but then they were black . . . My feet, of course, were also frostbitten. If it weren't for the frost, it would have been possible to save my legs, but they were bloody and I lay there for a long time. When they found me, they put me with the other wounded; many of us were brought to one place, and the Germans encircled us again. Our unit escaped . . . Broke through . . . They stacked us onto sledges like firewood. There was no time for looking, for pitying; we were driven deeper into the forest. To hide. They drove and drove, and then reported to Moscow about my injury. You see, I was a deputy of the Supreme Soviet. A big person; they were proud of me. I was from the lowest, from a simple peasant family. I joined the Party very early . . .

My legs were gone . . . They amputated them . . . They did the surgery right there in the forest. The conditions were the most primitive. They put me on a table to operate, and there was no iodine; they sawed my legs off with a simple saw, both legs . . . They drove for four miles to get iodine from another village, while I lay on the table. Without anesthesia. Without . . . Instead of anesthesia—a bottle of moonshine. There was nothing but an ordinary saw . . . A carpenter's saw . . .

They contacted Moscow to request a plane. The plane flew over three times, circled and circled, but couldn't land. There was shooting all around. The fourth time, it landed, but both my legs were already amputated. Later, in Ivanovo and Tashkent, they performed four re-amputations; four times the gangrene came back. They cut away bit by bit, and it ended very high up. At first I wept . . . I sobbed . . . I imagined how I'd go crawling on the ground. I wouldn't be able to walk again, only crawl. I myself don't know what helped me, what held me back from . . . How I persuaded myself. Of course, I met good people. Many good people. We had a surgeon, also with no legs. He said this about me, the other doctors told me: "I admire her. I've operated on so many men, but I haven't seen anyone like her. She never made a sound." I controlled myself . . . I was used to being strong in front of people . . .

Then I went back to Disna. My native town. I came back on crutches.

Now I walk poorly, because I'm old, but back then I ran around town and went everywhere on foot. I ran around on my wooden legs; I traveled to the kolkhozes. They gave me the post of vice chairman of the district party committee. A big job. I never stayed in my office. I went around to the villages, the fields. I would get offended if I sensed some indulgence. There were few competent kolkhoz chairmen at the time, and if there was some responsible work, they sent representatives from the district committee. And so, every Monday we were summoned to the committee and dispatched here and there. I'd sit there in the morning, looking out the window; people kept coming to the committee, but I wasn't called. And it somehow pained me; I wanted to be like everybody else.

And at last the phone rings, the first secretary calls, "Thecla Fedorovna, report." How happy I was then, though it was very very hard for me to go from village to village. They would send me fifteen or twenty miles away, and sometimes I rode, sometimes I walked. I'd go somewhere through the forest, fall down, and be unable to get up. I'd steady myself against my bag, or cling to a tree, get up, and go on. And I received a pension, I could have lived for myself, for myself alone. But I wanted to live for others. I'm a Communist . . .

I have nothing of my own. Only orders, medals, and certificates of honor. My house was built by the state. It's a big house, because there are no children in it, so it seems quite big . . . And the ceilings are quite high . . . I live with my sister. She's my sister, my mama, my nurse. I'm old now . . . In the morning I can't get up by myself . . .

We live together, live by our past. We have a beautiful past. It was a hard life, but beautiful and honest, and I have no grudges. On account of my life . . . I lived honestly . . .

Sofya Mironovna Vereshchak
UNDERGROUND FIGHTER

Our time made us the way we were. We proved ourselves. There won't be another time like that. It won't be repeated. Our idea was young then, and we were young. Lenin had died recently. Stalin lived . . . How proud I was to wear a Pioneer neckerchief. A Komsomol badge . . .

And then—the war. And we were like that . . . Of course, we quickly organized an underground group in Zhitomir. I joined it at once, there was no discussion: to go or not to go, be afraid or not afraid. It wasn't even discussed . . .

After a few months our underground group was tracked down. It had been betrayed. I was seized by the Gestapo . . . Of course I was afraid. For me it was even more frightening than to die. I was afraid of torture . . . What if I couldn't stand it? We all thought that way . . . Alone . . . Since childhood, for instance, I had borne physical pain poorly. But we didn't know ourselves, we didn't know how strong we were . . .

At my last interrogation, after which for the third time I was put on the list to be shot . . . Here's what happened with my third interrogator, who told me he was a historian by education . . . This fascist wanted to understand why we were such people, why our ideas were so important to us. "Life is above any ideas," he said. I, of course, disagreed with that. He shouted, he beat me. "What? What makes you be this way? To calmly accept death? Why do Communists believe that Communism should conquer the whole world?" he asked. He spoke excellent Russian. So I decided to speak everything out, since I knew they'd kill me anyway—at least it would not be for nothing, and let him know that we were strong. For about four hours he questioned, and I answered, what I knew, what I had managed to learn in courses of Marxism-Leninism at school and at the university. Oh, what it did to him! He clutched his head, he ran around the room, stopped as if rooted to the spot and looked at me, but for once he didn't beat me . . .

I stood facing him . . . Half my hair had been torn out; I used to have two thick braids. Starving . . . At first I dreamed of a little, tiny piece of bread, then—at least of a crust, and later—of finding at least a few crumbs . . . So I stood facing him like that . . . With burning eyes . . . He listened to me for a long time. Listened and didn't beat me . . . No, he was not afraid yet, it was only 1943. But he already felt something . . . some kind of danger. He wanted to know—what kind? I answered him. But when I left, he put me on the list to be shot . . .

On the night before the execution, I looked back over my life, my short life . . .

The happiest day of my life was when my father and mother, after driving away from home under bombardment for several dozen miles, decided to come back. Not to leave. To stay home. I knew then that we would fight. It seemed to us that the victory would come so soon. Absolutely! The first thing we did was find and rescue the wounded. They were in the fields, in the grass, in the ditches, or had crept into someone's barn. I stepped out one morning to dig some potatoes and found one in our kitchen garden. He was dying . . . A young officer, he didn't even have enough strength to tell me his name. He whispered some words . . . I couldn't make them out . . . I remember my despair. But I think I've never been so happy as during those days. I acquired my parents for a second time. I used to think my father was not concerned with politics. He turned out to be a non-Party Bolshevik. My mother—an uneducated peasant, she believed in God. She prayed all through the war. But how? She fell on her knees before an icon: "Save the people! Save Stalin! Save the Communist Party from that monster Hitler." Every day while I was being interrogated by the Gestapo, I expected the door to open and my parents to come in. Papa and mama . . . I knew where I had come to, and I'm happy that I didn't betray anyone. We were more afraid to betray than to die. When

I was arrested, I understood that the time of suffering had come. I knew my spirit was strong, but what about my body?

I don't remember my first interrogation. I didn't lose consciousness . . . I only lost consciousness once, when they twisted my arms with some sort of wheel. I don't think I screamed, though they had shown me earlier how others screamed. During the following interrogations, I lost the sense of pain, my body became numb. Made of plywood. There was only one thought: no! I won't die in front of them. No! Only after it was over and they dragged me back to my cell, then I began to feel pain, I turned into a wound. I was a wound all over . . . My whole body . . . But I had to hold out. To hold out! So that my mother would know I died a human being, I betrayed no one. Mama!

They beat me, they hung me up. Always completely undressed. They photographed me. I could only cover my breasts with my hands . . . I saw people go mad. I saw how little Kolenka, he wasn't even a year old, we were teaching him to say "mama," when they were taking him from his mother, he understood in some supernatural way that he was losing her forever and shouted for the first time in his life, "Mama!" It wasn't a word, or wasn't only a word . . . I want to tell you . . . Tell you everything . . . Oh, such people I met there! They died in the basements of the Gestapo, and their courage was known only to the walls. And now, forty years later, I mentally kneel to them. "Dying is easiest of all," they used to say. But to live . . . How we wanted to live! We believed victory would come, we were only doubtful about one thing—would we survive until that great day?

In our cell there was a small window with a grille on it; somebody had to lift you up to look out of it—not even at a piece of sky, but at a piece of roof. But we were all so weak, we couldn't lift each other up. But we had Anya, a paratrooper. She was captured when they were being dropped from a plane in the rear, and her group was ambushed. And now, all bloodied up, battered, she suddenly asked, "Push me up, I'll look out at freedom. I want to be there!"

I want to—that's all. We lifted her together, and she shouted, "Girls, there's a little flower . . ." Then each of us started asking, "And me . . . And me . . ." And we found the strength somewhere to help each other. It was a dandelion. How it got to the roof and managed to stay there, I have no idea. And we all made a wish over this flower. I now think everyone's wish was: "Please get me out of this hell alive."

I used to love the spring so much . . . I loved it when the cherry trees were in bloom and near the lilac bushes there was the fragrance of lilac . . . Don't be surprised by my style, I used to write poetry. But now I don't like the spring. The war stands between us, between me and nature. When the cherry trees were in bloom, I saw fascists in my native Zhitomir . . .

I stayed alive by a miracle. I was saved by people who were grateful to my father. My father was a doctor. At the time that was a big thing. They pushed me out of the column, in the dark, as we were led out to be shot. I remembered nothing on account of the pain; I walked as if in sleep . . . I went where I was led . . . Then driven . . . They brought me home. I was all wounds. I immediately developed eczema from the stress. I couldn't even hear a human voice. I heard it and felt pain. Mama and papa talked in a whisper. I kept screaming, and fell silent only in hot water. I didn't allow my mother to leave me even for a second. She asked, "My dear, I have to go to the oven. To the garden . . ." But I clung to her. The moment I let go of her hand, it all descended on me again. Everything that had happened to me. To distract me, they brought me flowers. My favorite bluebells . . . Chestnut leaves . . . The smells distracted me . . . My mother kept the dress I wore when I was with the Gestapo. When she was dying, it was under her pillow. Until her last hour . . .

The first time I got up was when I saw our soldiers. Suddenly I, who had been lying in bed for over a year, leaped up and ran outside: "My dear ones! My darlings . . . You're back . . ." The soldiers carried me into the house. In my enthusiasm, on the second and third day, I ran to the recruitment office: "Give me a job!" They told my father, and he came for me: "My baby, how did you get here? Who helped you?" I held out for a few days . . . Then the pain came back . . . The suffering . . . I screamed for days. People passed by our cottage and begged, "Lord, either take her soul, or help her, so that she stops suffering."

The curative mud of Tskaltubo saved me. The will to live saved me. To live, live—nothing else. I went on living. I lived, like everybody else . . . Lived . . . For fourteen years I worked in a library. Those were happy years. The happiest. Now my life has become a continuous struggle with illnesses. Old age, whatever you say, is a nasty thing. Also the solitude. I remained completely alone. Papa and mama are long gone. These long sleepless nights . . . So many years have gone by, but my most frightening dream—I wake up in cold sweat. I don't remember Anya's last name . . . I don't remember whether she was from the Bryansk or the Smolensk region. I remember how she didn't want to die! She would put her plump white hands behind her head, look out the window through the grille, and shout, "I want to live!"

I never found her parents . . . I don't know who I should tell this story to . . .

Klara Vasilyevna Goncharova
ANTIAIRCRAFT GUNNER

After the war we learned about Auschwitz, Dachau . . . How to give birth after that? But I was already pregnant . . .

I was sent to a village to take subscriptions for a loan. The government needed money to rebuild plants and factories.

I arrived, there was no village, everybody was underground . . . Living in dugouts . . . A woman came out in some kind of terrible-looking clothing. I went into the dugout; three children were sitting there, all hungry. She was grinding something in a mortar for them, some kind of grass.

She asked me, "You came to take subscriptions for a loan?"

I said, "Yes."

She: "I have no money, but I have a chicken. Yesterday the neighbor wanted it. I'll go and ask her. If she buys it, I'll give you the money."

Even as I tell you this, I get a lump in my throat. Such people there were! Such people! Her husband was killed at the front. She was left with her three children, nothing else, just that chicken, and she was selling it to give me money. We were collecting cash then. She was ready to give away everything, just to have peace, for her children to stay alive. I remember her face. And all her children . . .

How did they grow up? I'd like to know . . . I'd like to find them and meet them . . .

"MAMA, WHAT'S A PAPA?"

—

I don't see the end of this road. The evil seems infinite to me. I can no longer treat it only as history. Who will answer me: what am I dealing with—time or human beings? Times change, but human beings? I think about the dull repetitiveness of life.

They've spoken as soldiers. As women. Many of them were mothers . . .

OF BATHING BABIES AND OF
A MAMA WHO LOOKS LIKE A PAPA

Lyubov Igorevna Rudkovskaya
PARTISAN

I run . . . Several of us are running. Running away . . . We're being chased. Shot at. And there's my mother already under fire. But she sees us running . . . And I hear her voice, she's shouting. People told me later how she was shouting. She shouted, "It's good that you put on a white dress . . . My dear daughter . . . There'll be no one to dress you . . ." She was convinced I'd be killed, and she was glad that I would lie all in white . . . Before this happened we were preparing to visit the neighboring village. For Easter . . . To see our relatives . . .

It was so quiet . . . They stopped firing. There was only my mother shouting . . . Maybe they were firing? I didn't hear . . .

My entire family was killed during the war. The war is over, and I have no one to wait for . . .

Raissa Grigoryevna Khosenevich

PARTISAN

They began to bomb Minsk.

I rushed to the kindergarten to get my son. My daughter was out of town. She had just turned two; she was at the day nursery, and they went out of town. I decided to pick up my son and bring him home, and then run for her. I wanted to gather them all quickly.

I reached the kindergarten, planes were flying over the city, bombing somewhere. I heard my son's voice over the fence; he was not quite four years old: "Don't worry, my mother says the Germans will be crushed."

I looked through the gate. There were many of them there, and he was reassuring the others like that. But when he saw me, he began to tremble and cry. It turned out he was terrified.

I brought him home, asked my mother-in-law to look after him, and went to get my daughter. I ran! I found no one where the nursery was supposed to be. The village women told me the children had been taken somewhere. Where? Who? Probably to the city, they said. There were two teachers with them; they didn't wait for the car and left on foot. The city was seven miles away . . . But they were such little children, from one to two years old. My dear, I looked for them for two weeks . . . In many villages . . . When I entered a house and they told me it was that very nursery, those kids, I didn't believe them. They were lying, forgive me, in their own excrement, feverish. As if dead . . . The director of the nursery was a very young woman; her hair had turned gray. It turned out that they had walked all the way to the city, got lost on the way, several children had died.

I walked among them and didn't recognize my daughter. The director comforted me, "Don't despair, look around. She must be here. I remember her."

I found my Ellochka only thanks to her shoes . . . Otherwise I would have never recognized her . . .

Then our house burned down . . . We were left on the street, in what we had on. German units had already entered the city. We had nowhere to go. I walked around the streets with my children for several days. I met Tamara Sergeevna Sinitsa; we had been slight acquaintances before the war. She heard me out and said, "Let's go to my place."

"My children are sick with whooping cough. How can I go with you?"

She also had little children; they might get infected. That's how it was then . . . There were no medications, hospitals no longer worked.

"No, let's go."

My dear, how could I ever forget it? They shared potato peelings with us. I sewed pants out of my old skirt for my son, to give him something for his birthday.

But we dreamed of fighting . . . Inactivity tormented us . . . What a joy it was when the opportunity came to join the underground workforce, and not sit around with folded arms, waiting. Just in case, I sent off my son, the older boy, to my mother-in-law. She made one condition: "I'll take my grandson, but you should no longer be seen in the house. We'll all get killed on account of you." For three years I didn't see my son; I was afraid to go near the house. And when the Germans already had an eye on me and picked up my trail, I took my daughter and we both went to the partisans. I carried her for thirty miles . . . Thirty miles. We walked for two weeks . . .

She stayed there with me for over a year . . . I often think: how did we survive that? If you asked me, I couldn't tell you. My dear, such things are impossible to endure. Even today my teeth chatter at the words "partisan blockade."

May 1943 . . . I was sent off with a typewriter to the neighboring partisan zone. Borisovskaya. They had our typewriter, with Russian characters, but they needed one with German characters, and we were the only ones to have such a typewriter. This was the typewriter I had carried out of occupied Minsk, following the underground committee's orders. When I got there, to Lake Palik, after a few days the blockade began. That's where I ended up . . .

I didn't come alone, I came with my daughter. When I went on a mission for a day or two, I left her with other people, but there was nowhere to leave her for longer periods. So of course I took my child with me. And we got caught in the blockade . . . The Germans encircled the partisan zone . . . They bombed us from the sky and shot at us from the ground . . . The men went around carrying rifles, but I carried a rifle, the typewriter, and Ellochka. As we walked, I tripped, she fell over me into a swamp. We went on, she fell again . . . And so on, for two months! I swore to myself, if I survived, I wouldn't go near that swamp again, I couldn't look at it anymore.

"I know why you don't lie down when they shoot. You want us both to get killed." That's what my four-year-old child would say to me. But I didn't have the strength to lie down; if I did, I'd never get up again.

Other times the partisans felt sorry for me.

"Enough. Let us carry your daughter."

But I didn't trust anyone. What if they start shelling, what if she gets killed without me, and I don't hear it? What if she gets lost . . .

I met the brigade commander Lopatin.

"What a woman!" He was amazed. "In those circumstances she carried her child, and didn't let go of the typewriter. Not every man could do that."

He took Ellochka in his arms, hugged her, kissed her. He emptied out all his pockets, gave her bread crumbs. She downed them with water from the swamp. And following his example, other partisans emptied their pockets and gave her crumbs.

When we got out of the encirclement, I was completely sick. I was covered with boils, my skin was peeling off. And I had a child on my hands . . . We were waiting for a plane from the mainland. They said that if it came, they would send off the most badly wounded, and they could take my Ellochka. And I remember that moment when I was sending her away. The wounded reached out for her: "Ellochka, to me." "Come to me. There's enough room . . ." They all knew her; in the hospital she sang for them: "Ah, if only I live till my wedding bells."

The pilot asked, "Who are you here with, little girl?"

"With mama. She stayed outside the cabin . . ."

"Call your mama, so she can fly with you."

"No, my mama can't leave. She has to fight the fascists."

That's how they were, our children. And I looked at her face and had spasms—will I see her again someday?

Let me tell you how my son and I were reunited . . . This was already after the liberation. I was walking to the house where my mother-in-law lived. My legs were like cotton wool. The women from the brigade, they were older, warned me, "If you see him, no matter what, don't reveal to him straightaway that you're his mother. Do you realize what he's lived through without you?"

A neighbor girl runs by: "Oh! Lenya's mother. Lenya's alive . . ."

My legs won't go any further: my son is alive. She told me that my mother-in-law had died of typhus, and a neighbor woman had taken Lenya in.

I walked into their yard. What was I wearing? A German army shirt, a patched-up, black padded jacket, and old boots. The neighbor immediately recognized me, but she said nothing. And my son sits there, barefoot, ragged.

"What's your name, boy?" I ask.

"Lenya . . ."

"And who do you live with?"

"I used to live with my grandmother. When she died, I buried her. I came to her every day and asked her to take me into her grave. I was afraid to sleep alone . . ."

"Where are your mama and papa?"

"My papa's alive, he's at the front. But mama was killed by the fascists. So my grandmother said . . ."

Two partisans were with me; they had come to bury their comrades. They listened to how he was answering, and wept.

I couldn't stand it any longer.

"Why don't you recognize your mama?"

He rushed to me. "Papa!!" I was wearing men's clothes and a hat. Then he hugged me and screamed, "Mama!!!"

It was such a scream! Such hysterics . . . For a month he didn't let me go anywhere, not even to work. I took him with me. It wasn't enough for him to see me, to see I was nearby, he had to hold on to me. If we sat down for lunch, he held me with one hand and ate with the other. He only called me "Mamochka." He still does . . . Mamochka . . . Mamulenka . . .

When we were reunited with my husband, a week wasn't enough to tell everything. We talked day and night . . .

Larissa Leontyevna Korotkaya
PARTISAN

War—it's always funerals . . . We often had to bury partisans. Either a group fell into an ambush, or they died in battle. I'll tell you about one funeral . . .

There was very heavy fighting. In that fighting we lost many people, and I was wounded. And after the battle came the funeral. Usually we gave short speeches over the grave. First came the commanders, then the friends. But here, among the dead, was a local fellow, and his mother had come to the funeral. She began to lament: "My little son! We prepared the house for you! You promised you would bring a young wife home! But you are marrying the earth . . ."

The unit stood there, silent, no one touched her. Then she lifted her head and saw that not only her son had been killed, but many other young ones were lying there, and she began to cry over those other sons: "My sons, my dear ones! Your mothers don't see you, they don't know you're being put in the ground! And the ground is so cold. The winter cold is cruel. I will weep instead of them, and pity all of you . . . My dear ones . . . Darlings . . ."

She just said, "I will pity all of you" and "my dear ones"—all the men began weeping aloud. No one could help it, no one had strength enough. The unit wept. Then the commander shouted, "Fire the salute!" And the salute silenced everything.

And I was so struck that I think of it even now, the greatness of a mother's heart. In such great grief, as her son was buried, she had enough heart to mourn for the other sons . . . Mourn for them like her own . . .

Maria Vasilyevna Pavlovets
PARTISAN DOCTOR

I went back to my village . . .

Children are playing outside our house. I look and think: "Which one is mine?" They all look alike. Shorn as sheep used to be—in rows. I didn't recognize my daughter and asked which one was Lusya. And I saw one of the kids in a long shirt up and run into the house. It was hard to tell who was a girl and who was a boy because of their clothing. I asked again, "So which one of you is Lusya?"

They pointed their fingers, meaning the one who ran off. And I realized that she was my daughter. After a moment my grandmother, my mother's mother, brought her out by the hand. She led her to meet me: "Come, come. We're going to give it to this mother now for leaving us."

I was wearing men's military clothes, a forage cap, and was riding a horse, and my daughter, of course, pictured her mother like a grandmother, like the other women. And here a soldier had arrived. For a long time she wouldn't come to my arms, she was scared. There was no point in feeling hurt—I hadn't raised her, she had grown up with grandmothers.

I had brought soap as a gift. At the time it was a fancy gift, and when I began washing her, she bit it with her teeth. She wanted to try and eat it. That's how they lived. I remembered my mother as a young woman, but it was an old woman who greeted me. They told her that her daughter had come back, and she flew out of her garden into the street. She saw me, spread her arms and ran. I recognized her and ran to her. She was a few steps away from me, and she fell down, exhausted. I fell next to her. I kissed my mother. I kissed the ground. I had so much love in my heart, and so much hatred.

I remember a wounded German soldier lying on the ground and clutching at it from pain, and our soldier came up to him: "Don't touch, this is my ground! Yours is there, where you came from . . ."

Antonina Grigoryevna Bondareva
LIEUTENANT OF THE GUARDS, SENIOR PILOT

I went to war after my husband . . .

I left my daughter with my mother-in-law, but she soon died. My husband had a sister, and she took my girl. And after the war, when I was demobilized, she didn't want to give my child back to me. She told me something like this: you can't have a daughter, since you abandoned her when she was little and went to war. How can a mother abandon her child, and such a helpless one at that? I came back from the war, my daughter was already seven years old; I had left her when she was three. I met a grown-up girl. When she was little, she didn't eat enough, didn't sleep enough. There was a hospital nearby; she would go there and act and dance, and they would give her some bread. She told me later . . . At first she waited for her papa and mama, but later—only for her mama. Her father had been killed . . . She understood . . .

I often remembered my daughter at the front, I never forgot her for a minute, I dreamed of her. I missed her a lot. I cried, knowing I wasn't the one telling her fairy tales at night. She fell asleep and woke up without me . . . Somebody else braided her hair . . . I wasn't upset with my sister-in-law. I understood . . . She was very fond of her brother. He was strong, handsome; it was unthinkable that such a man could be killed. But he died straight off, in the first months of the war . . . Their planes were bombed on the ground in the morning. In the first months and probably even in the first year of the war, the German pilots ruled the skies. And he died . . . She didn't want to let go of what was left from him. The last thing. She was one of those women for whom family, children, were the most important thing in life. Bombing, shelling, and all she can think of is, how come the child didn't get her bath today? I can't blame her . . .

She said I was cruel . . . had no woman's soul . . . But we suffered greatly at war. No family, no home, no children . . . Many of us left our children at home, I wasn't the only one. We would sit under a parachute, waiting for our assignment. The men smoked, played dominoes, and we, while waiting for a signal to take off, sat and embroidered handkerchiefs. We stayed women.

Here's something about my navigator. She wanted to send a picture home, so we tied a kerchief—someone had a kerchief—to hide her straps, and covered her army shirt with a blanket. And it was as if she was wearing a dress . . . And so we took the picture. It was her favorite picture . . .

My daughter and I became friends . . . We've been friends ever since . . .

OF LITTLE RED RIDING HOOD
AND THE JOY OF MEETING A CAT
DURING THE WAR

Lyubov Zakharovna Novik
NURSE

It took me a long time to get used to the war . . .

We were attacking. And when a wounded soldier came, bleeding from an artery . . . I had never seen such a wound, blood spurting out . . . I rushed for the doctor. But the wounded man shouted, "Where? Where are you going? Tie it with a belt!" Only then did I come to my senses . . .

What do I feel sorry about? One little boy . . . This seven-year-old kid was left without a mama. His mama had been killed. The boy was sitting on the road next to his dead mother. He didn't understand that she was already gone; he waited for her to wake up, and kept asking for food . . .

Our commander didn't leave the boy there, he took him along: "You have no mama, sonny, but you'll have lots of papas." So he grew up with us. As the son of the regiment. From the age of seven. He reloaded the cartridge disks of the PPSH-41 submachine gun.

When you leave, my husband will be angry. He doesn't like these kinds of conversations. He doesn't like the war. But he didn't go to war, he's young, younger than me. We don't have children. I always remember that boy. He could be my son . . .

After the war I felt sorry for everybody. For men . . . For roosters, for dogs . . . I still can't stand the pain of others. I worked in a hospital. The patients loved me because I was gentle. We have a big garden. I've never sold a single apple, a single berry. I just give them away, I

give them away to people . . . I remained like that after the war . . .
My heart's like that . . .

Lyudmila Mikhailovna Kashechkina
UNDERGROUND FIGHTER

I didn't cry then . . .

I was afraid of only one thing . . . When comrades were captured,
several days of unbearable waiting: would they stand firm under torture or not? If they didn't, there would be more arrests. After a certain
time, it became known that they would be executed. We had an assignment: to go and see who was to be hanged that day. You walk
down the street and you see: they're already preparing the rope . . .
You can't cry, you can't linger for an extra second, because there are
spies everywhere. And so much—this is the wrong word—courage,
so much mental strength was needed to keep silent. To pass by without tears.

I didn't cry then . . .

I knew what was coming, but I only understood, I only really felt
everything, when I was arrested. I was taken off to jail. They beat me
with boots, with whips. I learned what a fascist "manicure" was. Your
hands are put on a table and some sort of machine sticks needles under
your nails . . . Simultaneously under each nail . . . Hellish pain! You
immediately lose consciousness. I don't even remember, I know the
pain was horrible, but I don't remember it. I was drawn on logs.
Maybe that's not the word, maybe I've got it wrong. But this is what
I remember: there was a log here and a log there, and they put you in
between . . . Then some kind of machine is turned on . . . And you
hear how your bones crunch, get dislocated . . . Did it last long? I
don't remember that either . . . I was tortured on an electric chair . . .
That was when I spat in the face of one of the torturers . . . Young,
old, I don't remember anything. They stripped me naked, and that
one came up to me and grabbed me by the breast . . . I could only

spit . . . I couldn't do anything else. So I spat in his face. They sat me on the electric chair . . .

I've had very little tolerance for electricity ever since. I remember it just starts jolting you. Now I can't even iron my laundry . . . All my life it's been so. I start ironing, and I feel the current through my whole body. I can't do anything that's related to electricity. Maybe I needed some sort of psychotherapy after the war? I don't know. But I've already lived my life this way . . .

I don't know why I'm crying so much today. I didn't cry then . . .

They sentenced me to death by hanging. They put me in the cell for the condemned. There were two other women. You know, we didn't cry, we didn't panic: we knew what awaited us when we joined the underground fighters, and so we remained calm. We talked about poetry, remembered our favorite operas . . . We talked a lot about *Anna Karenina* . . . about love . . . We didn't even mention our children, we were afraid to mention them. We even smiled, cheered each other up. So we spent two and a half days . . . In the morning of the third day they called me. We said goodbye, kissed without tears. There was no fear. Apparently I was so used to the thought of death that the fear was already gone. And so were the tears. There was some sort of emptiness. I no longer thought of anyone . . .

We drove for a long time, I don't even remember how long. I was saying goodbye to life . . . But the truck stopped, and we . . . there were about twenty of us . . . We couldn't get out of the truck, we were so worn out. They threw us on the ground like sacks, and the commanding officer ordered us to crawl to the barracks. He urged us on with a whip . . . Near one of the barracks a woman was standing, breastfeeding her child. And somehow, you know . . . There were dogs and guards, all dumbfounded, standing there and not touching her. The commanding officer saw that scene . . . He rushed at her. He snatched the baby out of its mother's hands . . . And, you know, there was a pump there, a water pump, and so he smashed the child against that iron. His brains gushed out . . . Milk . . . And I see the mother fall . . . I understand, I'm a doctor . . . I understand that she's had heart failure . . .

. . . They led us to work. They led us through the city, through familiar streets. We just started to go down, there was a steep hill, and suddenly I hear a voice: "Mama, mamochka!" And I see my aunt Dasha standing there, and my daughter is running from the sidewalk. They happened to be walking down the street and saw me. My daughter ran and immediately threw herself on my neck. And just imagine, there were dogs, they were specially trained to attack people, but not a single dog moved from its place. They're trained to tear you to pieces if you come close, but here none of them moved. My daughter ran up to me, and I didn't cry, I only said, "My little daughter! Natashenka, don't cry. I'll come home soon." The guards stood there, and the dogs. Nobody touched her . . .

And I didn't cry then . . .

At the age of five my daughter read prayers, not poems. Aunt Dasha taught her to pray. She prayed for her papa and mama, for us to stay alive.

In 1944, on the thirteenth of February, I was sent off to a fascist hard-labor camp . . . I wound up in the Croisette concentration camp, on the shores of the English Channel.

Spring . . . On the day of the Paris Commune, the French organized our escape. I left and joined the maquis.*

I was awarded the French Order of the Croix de Guerre . . .

After the war, I came back home . . . I remember . . . The first stop on our land . . . We all jumped off the train and kissed the ground, embraced it. I remember I was wearing a white smock. I fell to the ground, kissed it, and put whole handfuls in my bosom. I thought to myself, surely I won't ever part with it again, my very own land . . .

I arrived in Minsk, but my husband wasn't home. My daughter

---

* The rural French underground resistance forces during the German occupation, from the word for "bush" or "scrubland."

was at Aunt Dasha's. My husband had been arrested by the NKVD; he was in prison. I went there . . . And what do I hear there? . . . They tell me, "Your husband is a traitor." But my husband and I worked together in the underground. The two of us. He was a brave, honest man. I realized that someone had denounced him . . . Slander . . . "No," I say, "my husband can't be a traitor. I believe him. He's a true Communist." His interrogator . . . He started yelling at me, "Silence, French prostitute! Silence!" He had lived under the occupation, had been captured, had been taken to Germany, had been in a fascist concentration camp—it was all suspicious. One question: how did he stay alive? Why didn't he die? Even the dead were under suspicion . . . Even them . . . And they didn't take into consideration that we fought, we sacrificed everything for the sake of victory. And we won . . . The people won! But Stalin still didn't trust the people. That was how our Motherland repaid us. For our love, for our blood . . .

I went everywhere . . . I wrote to all the authorities. My husband was released after six months. They broke one of his ribs, injured his kidney . . . When he was captured by the fascists, they smashed his skull, broke his arm. He turned gray there, and in 1945 the NKVD made him an invalid for good. I took care of him for years; I pulled him out of his illnesses. But I wasn't allowed to say anything against them; he wouldn't hear of it . . . "It was a mistake," that's all. The main thing, he thought, was that we won. That's all—period. And I believed him.

I didn't cry. I didn't cry then . . .

Nadezhda Vikentyevna Khatchenko
UNDERGROUND FIGHTER

How do you explain to a child? How do you explain death to him . . .

I was walking down the street with my son, and dead people were lying there, on one side and the other. I was telling him about Little Red Riding Hood, and around us were dead people. It was when we were returning from the evacuation. We arrived at my mother's, and he wasn't well. He crawled under his bed and sat there for whole days. He was five years old, and I couldn't get him to go outside . . .

For a year I struggled with him. I couldn't figure out what was the matter. We lived in a basement—when someone walked by in the street, we could only see his boots. And so one day he came out from under the bed, saw someone's boots out the window, and began to scream . . . Afterward I remembered that a fascist had hit him with his boot . . .

Somehow, in the end, it passed. He was playing in the yard with other kids, came home one evening and asked, "Mama, what's a papa?"

I explained to him, "He's fair, handsome, he's in the army."

And when Minsk was liberated, the first to burst into the city were the tanks. And so my son came running home crying: "My papa's not there! They are all dark, none of them are fair . . ." It was in July, and the tank crews were all young, tanned.

My husband came back from the war an invalid. He came back not young, but old, and I was in trouble: my son was used to thinking that his father was fair, handsome, but a sick old man came back. And for a long time my son didn't accept him as his father. He didn't know what to call him. I had to get them accustomed to each other.

My husband came home from work late, and I met him: "Why are you so late? Dima was worried: 'Where's my daddy?'"

He, too, after six years of war (he had also fought against the Japanese), had lost touch with his son. With his home.

And when I bought something, I said to my son, "Daddy bought this, he cares about you . . ."

Soon they became closer . . .

Maria Alexandrovna Arestova
ENGINEER

My biography . . .

Since 1929 I worked on the railroad. I was an assistant engineer. At the time there were no female locomotive engineers in the Soviet Union. But I dreamed. The head of the locomotive depot threw up his hands: "This girl, she just wants a man's profession." But I persevered. And in 1931 I became the first one . . . I was the first female engineer. You wouldn't believe it, when I was driving the locomotive, people gathered in the stations: "A girl is driving the locomotive."

Our engine was just undergoing a blowdown—that is, it was getting repaired. My husband and I took turns driving, because we already had a baby, and we settled on this: if he drove, I stayed with the baby; if I drove, he stayed home. On that very day, my husband had returned, and I was supposed to go. I woke up in the morning and heard something abnormal in the street, noisy. I turned on the radio: "War!"

I told my husband, "Lenya, get up! War! Get up, it's war!"

He ran to the depot and came back in tears: "War! War! Do you know what it is—war?"

What are we to do? What do we do with the baby?

I was evacuated along with my son to Ulyanovsk, to the rear. They gave us a two-room apartment. The apartment was nice, even now I don't have one like that. They took my son in the kindergarten. All was well. Everyone loved me. What else! A female engineer, and the first one . . . You won't believe it, I lived there a short time, less than half a year. I couldn't stay longer: how is it, everyone's defending the Motherland, and I sit at home!

My husband came. "So, Marusya, are you going to sit here in the rear?"

"No," I said, "let's go."

At the time they were organizing a special reserve unit servicing the front. My husband and I asked to join it. My husband was a senior engineer, and I was an engineer. For four years we drove a freight car, and our son with us. He didn't even get to see a cat during the entire war. When he got hold of a cat near Kiev, our train was being heavily bombarded, five planes were attacking us. He hugged her and said, "Dear kitty, I'm so glad I got to see you. I never see anyone. Come and sit with me, let me kiss you." A child . . . Children need children's things . . . He fell asleep saying, "Mama, we have a cat. Now we have a real home." You can't make up something like that . . . Don't leave it out . . . Be sure to write about the cat . . .

We were constantly being bombarded, shot at by machine guns. Their target was the locomotive; their main objective was to kill the engineer, to destroy the locomotive. The planes flew down and hit the freight car and the locomotive. And my son was sitting in the freight car. Above all, I was afraid for my son. I can't describe it . . . When they bombed us, I took him with me from the freight car to the locomotive. I grabbed him, pressed him to my heart: "Let us die from the same shrapnel." But could that be? Clearly, that's why we stayed alive. Write that down as well . . .

My locomotive was my life, my youth, the most beautiful thing in my life. Even now I wish I could drive trains, but they won't let me—I'm old . . .

How frightening to have a single child. How foolish . . . Now we live together with my son's family. He's a doctor, the head of his department. We have a small apartment. But I never go anywhere on holidays, I never go away on vacation . . . I can't describe it . . . I don't want to be away from my son, from my grandchildren. I'm afraid to part with them even for a day. And my son doesn't go anywhere. He's been working for nearly twenty-five years, and never once has he used a travel voucher. At work, they noticed he never asked for one. "Mama, I'd rather stay with you"—that's what he says. And my daughter-in-law is the same. I can't describe it . . . We don't own a country place only because we can't part, even for a few days. I can't live without them even for a minute.

Whoever has been to war knows what it is to part even for a day. For a single day . . .

OF THE SILENCE OF THOSE WHO
COULD NOW SPEAK

Valentina Evdokimovna M—va

PARTISAN LIAISON

To this day I speak in a whisper . . . About . . . That . . . In a whisper. After more than forty years . . .

I've forgotten the war . . . Because even after the war I lived in fear. I lived in hell.

Here was the Victory, here was joy. Here we were already gathering bricks, metal, and starting to clean up the city. We worked day and night; I don't remember when we slept or what we ate. We worked and worked.

September . . . It was a warm September, I remember a lot of sun. I remember the fruit. A lot of fruit. They sold bucketloads of Antonovka apples at the market. And that day . . . I was hanging the laundry on the balcony . . . I remember everything in detail, because from that day, everything changed in my life. Everything was shattered. Turned upside down. I was hanging the laundry . . . White bedsheets—I always had white sheets. My mother taught me how to wash them with sand instead of soap. We would go to the river to get sand, I knew a spot there. And so . . . The laundry . . . My neighbor called me from downstairs, shouting in a voice not her own, "Valya!! Valya!!" I rushed downstairs. My first thought was: where is my son? Back then, you know, the boys ran around in the ruins, played war and found real grenades, real mines. They blew up . . . They were left with no hands, no legs . . . I remember how we wouldn't let them go away from us, but they were young boys, they were curious. We yelled: stay home—five minutes later they were gone. They were at-

tracted by weapons . . . Especially after the war . . . I rushed downstairs. I went out to the yard, and there was my husband . . . My
Ivan . . . My dearest little husband . . . Vanechka!! He had come
back . . . He had come back from the front! Alive! I kiss him, I touch
him. I stroke his shirt, his hands. He had come back . . . My legs were
weak . . . But he . . . He stands as if turned to stone. Well, he stands
stiff as cardboard. He doesn't smile, he doesn't hug me. As if frozen. I
got scared: he was probably shell-shocked, I thought. Maybe he's
deaf. But never mind, the main thing is he's back. I'll look after him,
I'll nurse him. I've seen so many other women living with such husbands, but everyone still envied them. All this flashed through my
head in a second. My legs were weak from happiness. They trembled.
He's alive! Oh, my dear, our women's lot . . .

The neighbors gathered at once. They were all happy, they all
hugged each other. And he—a stone figure. Silent. They all noticed.

I said, "Vanya . . . Vanechka . . ."

"Let's go inside."

All right, let's go. I clung to his shoulder . . . Happy! I was full of
joy and happiness. And proud! He sat down on a stool and remained
silent.

"Vanya . . . Vanechka . . ."

"You know . . ." And he couldn't speak. He wept.

"Vanya . . ."

We had one night. Just one night.

The next day they came for him, knocking on the door in the
morning. He was smoking and waiting; he already knew they would
come. He told me very little . . . He didn't have time . . . He had gone
through Romania, Czechoslovakia. He brought back honors, but he
came in fear. He had already been questioned, had been through two
government interrogations. He had been marked, because he had been
a prisoner. In the first weeks of the war . . . He was captured near
Smolensk, and was supposed to shoot himself. He wanted to, I know
he wanted to . . . They had run out of bullets—not only to shoot, he
had no bullets to kill himself. He was wounded in the leg, and was

captured wounded. Before his very eyes, the commissar smashed his own head with a stone . . . The last bullet misfired . . . Before his very eyes . . . A Soviet officer doesn't surrender, we don't have captives, we have traitors. Thus spoke Comrade Stalin, who renounced his own son who had been captured. My husband . . . Mine . . . The interrogators yelled at him, "Why are you alive? Why did you stay alive?" He escaped from captivity . . . He escaped to the woods, to the Ukrainian partisans, and when Ukraine was liberated, he asked to go to the front. He was in Czechoslovakia on Victory Day. He was recommended for a decoration . . .

We had one night . . . If only I had known . . . I wanted to have another child, I wanted a daughter . . .

In the morning he was taken away . . . They took him out of bed . . . I sat down at the table in the kitchen and waited for our son to wake up. Our son had just turned eleven. I knew he would wake up, and the first thing he would ask would be, "Where is our papa?" What answer could I give him? How was I to explain to the neighbors? To my mother?

My husband came home seven years later . . . My son and I waited for him, through four years of war, and after the Victory, through another seven years of Kolyma.* Labor camp. Eleven years we waited. Our son grew up . . .

I learned to keep silent . . . Where is your husband? Who is your father? In every questionnaire there was this question: were any of your relatives in captivity? The school didn't accept me as a cleaning woman when I applied, they didn't trust me to clean the floors. I became an enemy of the people, the wife of an enemy of the people. A traitor. My entire life was a waste . . . Before the war I was a teacher, I graduated from teachers' college, but after the war I carried bricks at construction sites. Eh, my life . . . If this comes out incoherent, confused, forgive me. I rush . . . Sometimes, at night . . . How many

---

*   The Kolyma region in far eastern Siberia, a vast, unsettled, subarctic territory, was made into a system of forced labor camps during the early 1930s. The prisoners were engaged in gold mining.

nights I spent lying alone and telling someone my story over and over. But in the daytime I kept silent.

Nowadays we can talk about everything. I want to . . . I want to ask: who is to blame that in the first months of the war millions of soldiers and officers were captured? I want to know . . . Who beheaded the army before the war, shooting and slandering the Red commanders—as German spies, as Japanese spies. I want to . . . Who trusted in the Budenny Cavalry back then, when Hitler was armed with tanks and planes? Who assured us, "Our border is secure . . ." Yet in the very first days, the army was counting its bullets . . .

I want . . . I can ask now . . . Where is my life? Our life? But I keep silent, and my husband keeps silent. We're afraid even now. We're frightened . . . And so we'll die scared. Bitter and ashamed . . .

"AND SHE PUTS HER HAND
TO HER HEART . . ."

———

And finally—Victory . . .

If life for them used to be divided into peace and war, now it was into war and Victory.

Again two different worlds, two different lives. After learning to hate, they now had to learn to love again. To recall forgotten feelings. Forgotten words.

The person shaped by war had to be shaped by something that was not war.

OF THE LAST DAYS OF THE WAR,
WHEN KILLING WAS REPUGNANT

Sofya Adamovna Kuntsevich
MEDICAL ASSISTANT

We were happy . . .

We crossed the border—the Motherland was free. Our land . . . I didn't recognize the soldiers, they were changed people. Everybody smiled. They put on clean shirts. They found flowers somewhere. I had never known such happy people. I had never seen it. I thought that when we entered Germany, I would have no pity for them, they would be shown no mercy. We had so much hatred stored up in our breasts! And hurt! Why should I feel sorry for his child? Why should I feel sorry for his mother? Why shouldn't I destroy his house? He didn't feel sorry . . . He killed . . . Burned . . . But I? I . . . I . . . I . . . Why? Why-y-y? I wanted to see their wives, their mothers, who had given birth to such sons. How would they look us in the eye? I wanted to look them in the eye . . .

I wondered: What will become of me? Of our soldiers? We all remember . . . How are we going to stand it? How much strength does it take to stand it? We came to some village; children were running around, hungry, miserable. Afraid of us . . . They hid . . . I, who swore I hated them all . . . I gathered from our soldiers all they had left of their rations, any piece of sugar, and gave it to the German children. Of course, I didn't forget . . . I remembered everything . . . But I couldn't calmly look into their hungry children's eyes. Early in the morning, German children stood in line near our kitchens, we gave them firsts and seconds.

Every child had a bag for bread slung over one shoulder, a can for soup at their belts, and something for seconds—kasha, peas. We fed them, treated them. We even caressed them . . . The first time I caressed one . . . I got scared . . . Me . . . Me! Caressing a German child . . .

My mouth went dry from agitation. But soon I got used to it. And they did too . . .

Nina Petrovna Sakova

LIEUTENANT, PARAMEDIC

I got to Germany . . . All the way from Moscow . . .

I was a senior paramedic in a tank regiment. We had T-34 tanks; they burned up quickly. Very scary. Before the war I had never even heard a gunshot. Once, when we were driving to the front, they were bombing some place very far away, and it felt to me as if all the ground was shaking. I was seventeen, I had just graduated from nursing school. And so it turned out, I just came and went straight into battle.

I got out of the tank . . . Fire . . . The sky was burning . . . The earth was burning . . . The metal was burning . . . Here were corpses, and there someone shouted, "Save me . . . Help me" . . . Such horror gripped me! I don't know how I didn't run away. How did I not flee the battlefield? It's so scary, there are no words, only feelings. Before I couldn't stand it, but now I can watch war movies, though I still cry.

I got to Germany . . .

The first thing I saw on German soil was a handmade sign, right by the road: "Here she is—accursed Germany!"

We entered a village . . . The shutters were all closed. They had dropped everything and fled on bicycles. Goebbels had persuaded them that the Russians would come and would hack, stab, slaughter. We opened the doors of the houses; there was no one, or they all lay killed or poisoned. Children lay there. Shot, poisoned . . . What did we feel? Joy, that we had defeated them, and that now they were suffering the way we did. A feeling of vengeance. But we felt sorry for the children . . .

We found an old woman.

I say to her, "We won."

She starts to cry: "I have two sons who died in Russia."

"And who is to blame? So many of us died!"

She answers, "Hitler . . ."

"Hitler didn't decide by himself. It's your children, husbands . . ."

Then she fell silent.

I got to Germany . . .

I wanted to tell my mother . . . But my mother died of starvation during the war. They had no bread, no salt, they had nothing. And my brother was lying in the hospital badly wounded. Only my sister waited for me at home. She wrote that when our troops entered Orel, she grabbed all the soldier girls by the overcoat. She thought I would surely be there. I had to come back . . .

Anastasia Vasilyevna Voropaeva
CORPORAL, SEARCHLIGHT OPERATOR

The roads of Victory . . .

You can't imagine the roads of Victory! Freed prisoners went with carts, bundles, national flags. Russians, Poles, French, Czechs . . . They all intermingled, each going his own way. They all embraced us. Kissed us.

I met some young Russian girls. I started talking to them, and they told me . . . One of them was pregnant. The prettiest one. She had been raped by the boss they worked for. He had forced her to live with him. She went along crying and beating her own stomach: "I won't bring a Fritz home! I won't!" They tried to reason with her . . . But she hanged herself . . . Along with her little Fritz . . .

It was back then that you should have listened to us—listened and recorded it. It's a pity that no one thought of hearing us out then; everyone just repeated the word "Victory," and the rest seemed unimportant.

One day a friend and I were riding bikes. A German woman was walking along; I believe she had three children—two in a baby carriage, one by her side, holding on to her skirt. She was so exhausted. And so, you see, she walks up to us, goes on her knees and bows. Like this . . . To the ground . . . We didn't understand what she said. And she puts her hand to her heart, and points at her children. We more or less understood, she was crying, bowing, and thanking us that her children had stayed alive . . .

She was somebody's wife. Her husband probably fought on the eastern front . . . In Russia . . .

A. Ratkina

JUNIOR SERGEANT, TELEPHONE OPERATOR

One of our officers fell in love with a German girl . . .

Our superiors heard about it . . . He was demoted and sent to the rear. If he had raped her . . . That . . . Of course, it happened . . . Not many write about it, but that's the law of war. The men spent so many years without women, and of course, there was hatred. When we entered a town or a village, for the first three days there was looting and . . . Well, in secret, naturally . . . You understand . . . After three days you could wind up in court. But in the heat of the moment . . . For three days they drank and . . . And here—love. The officer himself admitted it before the special section—love. Of course, that was treason . . . To fall in love with a German—the daughter or wife of the enemy? That's . . . And . . . Well, in short, they took away the photographs, her address. Of course . . .

I remember . . . Of course, I remember a German woman who had been raped. She was lying naked, with a grenade stuck between her legs . . . Now I feel ashamed, but then I didn't. Feelings change, of course. In the first days we had one feeling, and afterward another . . . After several months . . . Five German girls came to our battalion . . . To our commander. They were weeping . . . The gynecologist examined them: they had wounds. Jagged wounds. Their underwear was all bloody . . . They had been raped all night long. The soldiers stood in line . . .

Don't record this . . . Switch off the tape recorder . . . It's true! It's all true! . . . We formed up our battalion . . . We told those German girls: go and look, and if you recognize someone, we'll shoot him on the spot. We won't consider his rank. We're ashamed! But they sat there and wept. They didn't want to . . . They didn't want more blood. So they said . . . Then each one got a loaf of bread. Of course, all of this is war . . . Of course . . .

You think it was easy to forgive? To see intact . . . white . . . houses with tiled roofs. With roses . . . I myself wanted to hurt them . . . Of course . . . I wanted to see their tears . . . It was impossible to become good all at once. Fair and kind. As good as you are now. To pity them. That would take me dozens of years . . .

Aglaia Borisovna Nesteruk
SERGEANT, LIAISON

Our native land was liberated . . . Dying became totally unbearable, burials became totally unbearable. People died for a foreign land, were buried in a foreign land. They explained to us that the enemy had to be finished off. The enemy was still dangerous . . . We all understood . . . But it was such a pity to die . . . Nobody wanted to . . .

I remembered many signs along the road. They looked like crosses: "Here she is—accursed Germany!" Everybody remembered that sign . . .

And everybody was waiting for that moment . . . Now we'll understand . . . Now we'll see . . . Where do they come from? What is their land like, their houses? Could it be that they are ordinary people? That they lived ordinary lives? At the front, I couldn't imagine ever being able to read Heine's poems again. My beloved Goethe. I could never again listen to Wagner . . . Before the war, I grew up in a family of musicians, I loved German music—Bach, Beethoven. The great Bach! I crossed all of this out of my world. Then we saw, they showed us the crematoriums . . . Auschwitz . . . Heaps of women's clothing, children's shoes . . . Gray ash . . . They spread it on the fields, under the cabbage. Under the lettuce . . . I couldn't listen to German music anymore . . . A lot of time passed before I went back to Bach. Began to play Mozart.

Finally, we were on their land . . . The first thing that struck us was the good roads. The big farmhouses . . . Flowerpots, pretty curtains in the windows, even in the barns. White tablecloths in the houses. Expensive tableware. Porcelain. There I saw a washing machine for the first time . . . We couldn't understand why they had to fight if they lived so well. Our people huddled in dugouts, while they had white tablecloths. Coffee in small cups . . . I had only seen them in the museum. Those small cups . . . I forgot to tell you about one shocking thing, we were all shocked . . . We were attacking, and took the first German trenches . . . We jumped in, and there was still warm coffee in thermos bottles. The smell of coffee . . . Biscuits. White sheets. Clean towels. Toilet paper . . . We didn't have any of that. What sheets? We slept on straw, on sticks. Other times we went for two or three days without warm food. And our soldiers shot at those thermos bottles . . . At that coffee . . .

In German houses I saw coffee sets shattered by bullets. Flower-pots. Pillows . . . Baby carriages . . . But still we couldn't do to them what they had done to us. Force them to suffer the way we suffered.

It was hard for us to understand where their hatred came from. Ours was understandable. But theirs?

We got permission to send packages home. Soap, sugar . . . Some-one sent shoes. Germans have sturdy shoes, watches, leather goods. Everybody looked for watches. I couldn't, I was disgusted. I didn't want to take anything from them, though I knew that my mother and my sisters were living with strangers. Our house had been burned down. When I returned home, I told my mother, and she hugged me: "I, too, couldn't have taken anything from them. They killed our papa."

Only dozens of years after the war did I take a small volume of Heine in my hands. And the recordings of German composers that I had loved before the war . . .

Albina Alexandrovna Gantimurova

SERGEANT MAJOR, SCOUT

This was already in Berlin . . . This incident happened to me: I was walking down the street, and a boy came running toward me with a submachine gun—a Volkssturm.* The war was already over. The last days. My hand was on my submachine gun. Ready. He looked at me, blinked, and burst into tears. I couldn't believe it—I was in tears, too. I felt so sorry for him; there was this kid standing with his stupid submachine gun. And I shoved him toward a wrecked building, under the gateway: "Hide," I said. He was afraid I was going to shoot him right then—I was wearing a hat, it wasn't clear if I was a girl or a man. He took my hand. He cried! I patted his head. He was dumbstruck. It was war after all . . . I was dumbstruck myself! I had hated them for the entire war! Fair or unfair, it's still disgusting to kill, especially in the last days of the war . . .

Lilya Mikhailovna Butko
SURGICAL NURSE

I regret . . . I didn't fulfill one request . . .

They brought a wounded German to our hospital. I think he was a pilot. His thigh was crushed, and gangrene had set in. Some kind of pity took hold of me. He lay there and kept silent.

I understood a little German. I asked him, "Do you want to drink?"

"No."

The other wounded men knew there was a wounded German in the ward. He was lying separately. I went to him, and they got indignant: "So you bring water to the enemy?"

"He's dying . . . I have to help him . . ."

His leg was all blue, nothing could be done. Infection devours a man in no time; the man burns out overnight.

I gave him water, and he looked at me and suddenly said, *"Hitler kaputt!"*

That was in 1942. We were encircled near Kharkov.

---

* The Volkssturm was a national militia organized by the Nazi Party during the last months of World War II. It drafted males between the ages of sixteen and sixty.

I asked, "Why?"

"*Hitler kaputt!*"

Then I answered, "That's what you say and think now, because you're lying here. But there you were killing . . ."

He: "I didn't shoot, I didn't kill. They made me. But I didn't shoot . . ."

"Everybody makes excuses like that when they're captured."

And suddenly he asks me, "I really . . . really . . . beg of you, Frau . . ." and he hands me a packet of photographs. He shows me: there is his mother, himself, his brother, sisters . . . A beautiful picture. He writes down an address on the other side. "You will get there. You will!" This was a German speaking, in 1942, near Kharkov. "So please drop this in the mailbox."

He wrote the address on one photograph, but he had an envelope full of them. And I carried those photographs around for a long time. I was upset when I lost them during a heavy bombardment. By the time we got to Germany, the envelope was gone . . .

Nina Vasilyevna Ilinskaya
NURSE

I remember a battle . . .

In that battle we captured many Germans. Some of them were wounded. We bandaged their wounds; they moaned like our lads did. And it was hot . . . Scorching hot! We found a teapot and gave them water. In the open. We were under fire. An order: quickly entrench and camouflage yourselves.

We started digging trenches. The Germans stared. We explained to them: so, help us dig, get to work. When they understood what we wanted from them, they looked at us with horror; they took it that once they dug those pits, we would stand them by those pits and shoot them. They expected . . . You should have seen their horrified looks as they dug . . . Their faces . . .

And when they saw that we bandaged them, gave them water, and told them to hide in the trenches they had dug, they couldn't come to their senses, they were at a loss . . . One German started crying . . . He was an older man. He cried and didn't hide his tears from anyone . . .

OF A COMPOSITION WITH CHILDISH MISTAKES AND COMIC MOVIES

Vera Iosifovna Khoreva
ARMY SURGEON

The war was ending . . .

The political commissar called me. "Vera Iosifovna, you will have to work with the German wounded."

By that time my two brothers had already been killed. "I won't."

"But, you understand, it's necessary."

"I'm unable. I lost two brothers. I can't stand them, I'm ready to kill them, not treat them. Try to understand me . . ."

"It's an order."

"If it's an order, I'll obey. I'm a soldier."

I treated those wounded, did everything I had to, but it was hard for me. To touch them, to ease their pain. That's when I got my first gray hair. Right then. I did everything with them: operated, fed, anesthetized—everything I was supposed to. One thing only I couldn't do—that was the evening rounds. In the morning you had to bandage the wounded, take their pulse—in short, you proceeded like a doctor—but during the evening rounds you had to talk to the patients, ask how they felt. That I couldn't do. Bandage, operate—that

I could do, but talk with them—no. I warned the commissar straight off: "I won't do the evening rounds for them . . ."

Ekaterina Petrovna Shalygina
NURSE

In Germany . . . In our hospitals we already had many wounded Germans . . .

I remember my first wounded German. He had gangrene; we amputated his leg . . . And he lay in my ward . . .

In the evening, they said to me, "Katya, go check on your German."

I went. Maybe a hemorrhage, or something. He lay there, awake. He had no temperature, nothing. He just stared and stared, and then pulled out such a tiny pistol: "Here . . ."

He spoke German. I don't remember now, but back then I understood as much as I'd kept from my school lessons.

"Here . . ." he said. "I wanted to kill you, but now you kill me."

Meaning that we had saved him. He killed us, and we saved him. But I couldn't tell him the truth, that he was dying . . .

I left the ward and noticed unexpectedly that I was in tears . . .

Maria Anatolyevna Flerovskaya
POLITICAL WORKER

I might have had an encounter . . . I was afraid of that encounter . . .

When I was in school . . . I studied in a school with a German orientation . . . German school children would come to visit us. In Moscow. We went with them to the theater, we sang together. One of those German boys . . . He sang so well. We became friends. I even fell in love with him . . . And so, all through the war I thought: what if I meet him and recognize him? Could he also be among them? I'm very emotional, ever since I was a child, I'm very impressionable. Terribly!

One day I was walking in the field, the battle had just ended . . . We picked up our dead, only Germans were left . . . It seemed to me he was lying there . . . A similar-looking young man . . . On our land . . . I stood over him for a while . . .

A. C—va
ANTIAIRCRAFT GUNNER

You want to know the truth? I'm scared of it myself . . .

One of our soldiers . . . How can I explain this to you? His whole family had died. He . . . Nerves . . . Maybe he was drunk? The closer victory came, the more they drank. There was always wine to be found in the houses and basements. Schnapps. They drank and drank. He grabbed a submachine gun and ran into a German house . . . He unloaded the entire magazine . . . Nobody had time to stop him. We ran . . . But in the house, only corpses were left . . . Children lay there . . . They took away his submachine gun and tied him up. He cursed his head off: "Let me shoot myself!"

He was arrested and tried—and shot. I felt sorry for him. Everybody felt sorry for him. He had fought the entire war. As far as Berlin . . .

Are you allowed to write about this? Before, you weren't . . .

Xenia Klimentyevna Belko
LABOR-FRONT FIGHTER

The war waited for me . . .

Just as I turned eighteen . . . They brought me a written notice: present yourself to the district committee, bring three days' worth of food, a set of underwear, a mug, a spoon. It was called mobilization for the labor front.

They brought us to the town of Novotroitsk, in the Orenburg region. We started working in a factory. It was so freezing cold that my coat would freeze in our room; you took it and it was heavy as a log. We worked for four years without a vacation, without holidays.

We waited and waited for the war to end. Full stop. At three o'clock in the morning, there was noise in the dormitory; the director of the factory came, along with the other superiors. "Victory!" I didn't have the strength to get up from my bunk. They sat me up, but I fell back. For the whole day they couldn't get me up. I was paralyzed from joy, from strong emotions. I only stood up the next day . . . I went outside, I wanted to hug and kiss each and every one . . .

Elena Pavlovna Shalova
KOMSOMOL LEADER OF AN INFANTRY BATTALION

What a beautiful word—victory . . .

I wrote my name on the Reichstag . . . I wrote with charcoal, with what was at hand: "You were defeated by a Russian girl from Saratov." Everybody left something on the wall, some words. Confessions and curses . . .

Victory! My girlfriends asked me, "What do you want to be?" And we were so hungry during the war . . . Unbearably . . . We wanted to eat our fill at least once. I had a dream—when I got my first postwar salary, I would buy a big box of cookies. What do I want to be after the war? A cook, of course. I still work in the public food industry.

A second question: "When will you get married?" As soon as possible . . . I dreamed of kissing. I wanted terribly to kiss . . . I also wanted to sing. To sing! There . . .

Tamara Ustinovna Vorobeykova
UNDERGROUND FIGHTER

I learned how to shoot, throw grenades . . . Lay mines. Give first aid . . .

But in four years . . . During the war I forgot all the rules of grammar. The entire school program. I could disassemble a submachine gun with my eyes closed, but I wrote my application essay to the institute with childish mistakes and barely any commas. I was saved by my military decorations; I was accepted at the institute. I began to study. I read books and didn't understand them, read poems and didn't understand them. I'd forgotten those words . . .

At night I had nightmares: SS officers, dogs barking, cries of agony. When dying, men often whisper something, and that is even more frightening than their cries. Everything came back to me . . . A man was being led out to execution . . . In his eyes there was fear. You could see that he didn't believe it, until the last moment he didn't believe it. And curiosity, there was curiosity as well. He stood facing the submachine gun, and at the last moment he covered himself with his hands. He covered his face . . . In the mornings, my head was swollen from the shouting . . .

During the war I never thought about anything, but after it I began to think.

Going over it all . . . It all came back again and again . . . I couldn't sleep . . . The doctors forbade me to study. But the girls—my roommates in the dormitory—told me to forget about the doctors, and took me under their patronage. Every night they took turns dragging me to the movies to watch a comedy. "You have to learn to laugh. To laugh a lot." Whether I wanted or not, they dragged me. There weren't many comedies, and I watched each one a hundred times, a hundred times at a minimum. At first when I laughed it was like crying . . .

But the nightmares went away. I was able to study . . .

OF THE MOTHERLAND,
STALIN, AND RED CLOTH

Tamara Ivanovna Kuraeva
NURSE

It was spring . . .

Young boys died, they died in the spring . . . In March, in April . . .

I remember that in spring, at the time when the gardens were in bloom and everyone was waiting for victory, burying people was harder than ever. Even if others have already said it, write it down again. I remember it so well . . .

For two and a half years I was at the front. My hands bandaged and washed thousands of wounds . . . Bandages and more bandages . . . Once, as I went to change my headscarf, I leaned against the window frame and dozed off. I came to myself feeling refreshed. I ran into the doctor, and he started scolding me. I didn't understand anything . . . He went off, after giving me two extra assignments, and my workmate explained to me what it was about: I had been absent for over an hour. It turned out I had fallen asleep.

Nowadays I'm in poor health, my nerves are weak. When someone asks me, "What decorations did you receive?" I'm embarrassed to admit I don't have any decorations; there was no time to give me decorations. Maybe there was no time because many of us fought in the war and we each did what we could . . . We each did our best . . . How could everyone receive decorations? But we all received the greatest decoration of all—the ninth of May. Victory Day!

I remember an unusual death . . . At the time, no one could figure it out. We were busy with other things . . . But I remember . . . One of our captains died on the first day we set foot on German soil. We knew that his entire family had died during the occupation. He was a brave man, he was so looking forward to . . . He was afraid to die before that. Not to live till the day when he would see their land, their misery, their sorrow. See them cry, see them suffer . . . See broken stones in place of their homes . . . He died just like that, not wounded, nothing. He got there, looked—and died.

Even now, when I remember it, I wonder: why did he die?

Maria Yakovlevna Yezhova

LIEUTENANT OF THE GUARDS, COMMANDER OF A MEDICAL PLATOON

I asked to go to the front straight from the train . . . At once . . . A unit was leaving—I joined it. At the time, I figured that from the front, I would come home sooner, if only by a day, than from the rear. I left my mother at home. Even now, our girls remember: "She wouldn't stay at the medical platoon." And it's true, I would come to the medical platoon, wash up, grab some clean clothes—and go back to my trench. At the front line. I didn't think about myself. You crawl, you run . . . Only the smell of blood . . . I couldn't get used to the smell of blood . . .

After the war, I became a midwife in a maternity ward—but I didn't stay there for long. Not for long . . . For a short while . . . I'm allergic to the smell of blood; my body simply wouldn't accept it . . . I had seen so much blood during the war that I couldn't stand it anymore. My body wouldn't accept it anymore. I left Maternity and went to Emergency Aid. I got nettle rash, I was suffocating.

I sewed a blouse from a piece of red cloth, and by the next day some sort of red spots had spread all over my hands. Blisters. No red cloth, no red flowers—roses or carnations, my body wouldn't accept it. Nothing red, nothing that had the color of blood . . . Even now I have nothing red in my house. You won't find anything. Human blood is very bright, I have never seen such a bright color, not in nature, not in any painting. Pomegranate juice is somewhat similar, but not entirely. Ripe pomegranate . . .

Elena Borisovna Zvyagintseva
PRIVATE, ARMORER

Oh, oh, oh . . . Ah, ah, ah . . . Everybody oh'd and ah'd at how colorful I was. Jewelry all over. Even during the war I was like that. Not warlike. I wore all kinds of baubles . . . It's a good thing our commander was, as we'd say now, a democrat. Not from the barracks, but from the university. Just imagine, an assistant professor. With good manners. At that time . . . A rare bird . . . A rare bird had flown to us . . .

I love wearing rings, even cheap ones, so long as there are lots of them, on both hands. I like good perfume. Fashionable. All kinds of trinkets. Various and many. In our family they always laughed, "What should we give to our crazy Lenka for her birthday? A ring, of course." After the war, my brother made me my first ring out of a tin can. And a pendant out of a piece of green bottle glass that he polished. And another one of light brown glass.

I hang everything shiny on myself, like a magpie. Nobody believes that I was in the war. I myself can't believe it anymore. At this very moment, as we sit and talk, I don't believe it. But in that box lies the Order of the Red Star . . . The most elegant medal . . . Isn't it pretty? They gave it to me on purpose. Ha, ha, ha . . . To be serious . . . For history, right? This thing of yours is recording . . . So, it's for history . . . I'll say this: if you're not a woman, you can't survive war. I never envied men. Not in my childhood, not in my youth. Not during the war. I was always glad to be a woman. People say that weapons—submachine guns, pistols—are beautiful, that they conceal many human thoughts, passions, but I never found them beautiful. I've seen the admiration of men looking at a fine pistol; I find it incomprehensible. I'm a woman.

Why did I stay single? I had wooers. Wooers enough . . . But here I am single. I have fun by myself. All my friends are young. I love youth. I'm afraid of growing old more than of the war. You came too late . . . I think about old age now, not about the war . . .

So that thing of yours is recording? For history?

Rita Mikhailovna Okunevskaya

PRIVATE, SAPPER-MINER

I'm home . . . At home everybody is alive . . . Mama saved everybody: grandpa and grandma, my little sister and my brother. And I came back . . .

A year later our papa came back. Papa returned with great decorations; I brought back a decoration and two medals. But in our family we agree on this: the greatest hero was mama. She saved everybody. She saved our family, saved our home. She fought the most terrible war. Papa never wore his decorations and ribbons; he considered it shameful to show off in front of mama. Embarrassing. Mama doesn't have any awards . . .

Never in my life did I love anyone as I did my mama . . .

Bella Isaakovna Epstein

SERGEANT, SNIPER

I came back different . . . For a long time I had an abnormal relation with death. Strange, I would say . . .

They were inaugurating the first streetcar in Minsk, and I rode on that streetcar. Suddenly the streetcar stopped, everybody shouted, women cried, "A man's been killed! A man's been killed!" And I sat alone in the car. I couldn't understand why everybody was crying. I didn't feel it was terrible. I had seen so many people killed at the front . . . I didn't react. I got used to living among them. The dead were always nearby . . . We smoked near them, we ate. We talked. They were not somewhere out there, not in the ground, like in peacetime, but always right here. With us.

And then that feeling returned, again I felt frightened when I saw a dead man. In a coffin. After several years, that feeling returned. I became normal . . . Like the others . . .

Natalia Alexandrovna Kupriyanova
SURGICAL NURSE

This happened before the war . . .

I was at the theater. During the intermission, when the lights went on, I saw . . . Everyone saw him . . . There was a burst of applause. Thunder! Stalin was sitting in the government loge. My father had been arrested, my elder brother had disappeared in the camps, but despite that I felt so ecstatic that tears poured from my eyes. I was swooning with happiness! The whole room . . . The whole room stood up! We stood and applauded for ten minutes.

I came to the war like that. To fight. But during the war I heard quiet conversations . . . At night, the wounded smoked in the corridors. Some slept, some didn't sleep. They talked about Tukhachevsky, about Yakir . . . * Thousands had disappeared! Millions of people! Where? The Ukrainians told . . . How they had been driven into the kolkhozes. Forced to obey . . . How Stalin had organized famine; they themselves called it the "Death-by-Hunger." Golodomor. Mothers went mad and ate their own children . . . And the soil was so rich there that if you planted a twig, a willow would grow. German prisoners would put some in parcels and send it home. That soil was so rich. Meters deep of black earth. Of fertile soil. The conversations were quiet . . . In low voices . . . Those conversations never occurred

* Mikhail Tukhachevsky (1893–1937) and Iona Yakir (1896–1937) were two of the most important Soviet military leaders, theorists, and reformers. Both were arrested and shot during the purges of 1937.

in groups. Only if there were two people. A third was too many, the third one would have denounced . . .

I'll tell a joke . . . I'm telling it so as not to cry. It goes like this . . . It's nighttime. In the barracks. Prisoners are lying and talking. They ask each other, "Why were you locked up?" One says—for telling the truth. A second—because of my father . . . And a third answers, "For being lazy." What?! They're all surprised. He tells them, "We were sitting at a party in the evening, telling jokes. We got home late. My wife asked me, 'Should we go and denounce them now, or tomorrow?' 'Let's go tomorrow. I want to sleep.' But in the morning they came to take us . . ."

It's funny. But I don't feel like laughing. We should weep. Weep.

After the war . . . Everyone waited for their relatives to come back from the war, but we waited for them to come back from the camps. From Siberia . . . Of course! We were victorious, we had proved our loyalty, our love. Now they would believe us.

My brother came back in 1947, but we never found my father . . . Recently I visited my war friends from the front in Ukraine. They live in a big village near Odessa. Two obelisks stand in the center of the village: half the village died of starvation, and all the men died in the war. But how can we count them in all of Russia? People are still alive, go and ask them. We need hundreds like you, my girl, to tell our story. To describe all our sufferings. Our countless tears. My dear girl . . .

"SUDDENLY WE WANTED DESPERATELY TO LIVE . . ."

———

The phone keeps ringing. I write down new addresses, receive new letters. And it's impossible to stop, because each time the truth is unbearable.

Tamara Stepanovna Umnyagina
JUNIOR SERGEANT IN THE GUARDS, MEDICAL ASSISTANT

Ah, my precious one . . .

All night I was remembering, collecting my memories . . .

I ran to the recruiting office: I had a hopsack skirt, white rubber sneakers on my feet—they were like shoes, with a buckle. All the fashion then. Here I was in that skirt, those sneakers, volunteering to go to the front, so they sent me there. I got into some sort of vehicle. I reached the unit, it was an infantry division, stationed near Minsk, but they told me I wasn't needed there. The men would be ashamed, they said, if seventeen-year-old girls started fighting. And anyhow we would soon crush the enemy. Go back to your mama, little girl. I was upset, of course, that they wouldn't let me fight. So what did I do? I went to see the commander in chief. He was sitting with that same colonel who had dismissed me, and I said, "Comrade even higher superior, allow me to disobey the comrade colonel. I won't go home anyway, I'll retreat with you. Where would I go, the Germans are already close." And after that they all called me "Comrade Even Higher Superior." It was the seventh day of the war. We began to retreat . . .

Soon we were drenched in blood. There were many wounded, but they were so calm, so patient, they wanted so much to live. Everybody wanted to survive until the day of victory. We waited: any day now . . . I remember, I was all soaked with blood—up to, up to, up to . . . My sneakers were torn; I already went barefoot. What did I see? The train station near Mogilev was being bombarded. And there was a train carrying children. They started throwing them out through the windows, little children—three or four years old. There was a forest nearby, so they ran toward the forest. The German tanks immediately drove out, and the tanks drove over the children. There was nothing left of those children . . . Even now you could lose your mind from that scene. But during the war, people held on. They lost their minds after the war. They got sick after the war. During the war gastric ulcers healed over. We slept in the snow, we had flimsy overcoats, and in the morning we didn't even have runny noses.

Later, our unit was encircled. I had so many wounded, and not a single truck was willing to stop. The Germans were right on our heels; any moment now they would trap us in their circle. Then a wounded lieutenant handed me his pistol: "Can you shoot?" How could I? I had only watched them shoot. But I took the pistol and went with him to the road, to stop trucks. There, for the first time, I cursed. Like a man. A nice, well-rounded curse . . . All the trucks passed by . . . I fired a first shot in the air . . . I knew that we couldn't carry the wounded in our arms. Impossible. They begged us, "Listen, boys, finish us off. Don't leave us like this." A second shot . . . I pierced the hood . . . "You fool!! Learn to shoot first." They stepped on the brakes. Helped us to load them.

But the most terrible was ahead of us, the most terrible—Stalingrad. What sort of battlefield is that? It's a city—streets, houses, basements. Try dragging the wounded out of there! My whole body was one single bruise. And my pants were covered with blood. Completely. The first sergeant scolded us, "Girls, we have no more spare pants, don't ask." And our pants would dry and get stiff. They don't get stiff from starch the way they do from blood; you could cut yourself on them. There wasn't a single clean spot; by spring there was nothing left to turn in. Everything burned. On the Volga, for instance, even the water burned. Even during the winter, the river didn't freeze, but burned. Everything burned . . . In Stalingrad there wasn't a single inch of dirt that wasn't soaked in human blood. Russian and German. And gasoline . . . And grease . . . They all realized there was nowhere left, we couldn't retreat. Either we would all die—the country, the Russian people—or we would be victorious. That became clear to everybody, we had reached such a moment. We didn't say it out loud, but everybody understood. Generals and soldiers both understood . . .

Reinforcements arrived. Such young, handsome fellows. Before the battle, you looked at them and knew they'd be killed. I was afraid of new people. I was afraid to get to know them, to talk to them. Because they were here, and then they were already gone. Two or three days . . . You kept looking at them before the battle . . . This was 1942—the worst, the hardest moment. One time, out of three hundred of us, only ten were left at the end of the day. And when we were the only ones left, when things calmed down, we began to kiss, to cry, because we were suddenly alive. We were all family for each other. We became family.

Before your eyes a man is dying . . . And you know, you can see, that you can't help him in any way; he only has a few minutes to live. You kiss him, caress him, speak tender words to him. You say goodbye. Well, you can't help him any other way . . . I still remember those faces. I see them all, all those boys. Somehow, as the years passed, I might have forgotten at least one of them, at least one face. But I didn't forget anyone, I remember them all . . . I see them all . . . We wanted to make graves for them, with our own hands, but it wasn't always possible. We left, and they stayed. You bandage his whole head, and under the bandages he's already died on you. And he gets buried with his head covered in bandages. Another one, if he died on the battlefield, at least he was looking to the sky. Or he dies and asks,

"Close my eyes, dear nurse, but carefully." The city is destroyed, the houses. Of course it's terrible, but when people are lying there, young men . . . You can't catch your breath, you run . . . To save them . . . It seems like you don't have the strength to go on for more than five minutes, you don't have enough . . . But you keep running . . . It's March, there's water under your feet . . . We weren't supposed to wear our felt boots, but I slipped them on and went. I crawled around all day wearing them, and in the evening they were so wet that I couldn't take them off. We had to cut them. But I didn't get sick . . . Can you believe it, my precious one?

When the fighting at Stalingrad ended, we were ordered to evacuate the most seriously wounded on steamboats and barges to Kazan, to Gorki. It was already spring, somewhere in March or April. But we found so many wounded, they were in the ground—in trenches, in dugouts, in basements. There were so many of them, I can't even tell you how many. It was horrible! We kept thinking, when we carried the wounded from the battlefield, that there would be no more, that we had evacuated them all, that there weren't any in Stalingrad itself. But when everything was over, it turned out that there were so many, it was unbelievable . . . Unimaginable . . . On the boat I was on we had gathered those with missing hands, missing legs, and hundreds sick with tuberculosis. We had to treat them, to encourage them with gentle words, comfort them with a smile. When they sent us, they promised we'd finally get to rest from battle; they said it was even like a reward, like an encouragement. But it turned out to be even worse than the Stalingrad hell. On the battlefield, you pulled a man out, gave him some aid, and handed him over—you had confidence that he was all right now, they had taken him away. You go on, you crawl after the next one. But here they're in front of your eyes all the time . . . There they wanted to live, they were eager to live: "Quick, nurse! Quick, dear!" But here they refused to eat, they wanted to die. They jumped off the steamboat. We had to watch them. Protect them. There was this one captain, I had to sit by his side even at night—he had lost both arms and wanted to put an end to his life. Once I forgot to warn the other nurse, I went out for a few minutes, and he threw himself overboard . . .

We brought them to Usolye, near Perm. There were already new, clean houses there, all especially for them. Like in a youth camp . . . We carried them on stretchers, but they were in agony. I felt like marrying any one of them. I'd have carried him in my arms. On the way back, the steamboat was empty. We could rest, but we didn't sleep. The girls lay there and suddenly started howling. We sat and wrote them letters every day. We designated who would write to whom. Three or four letters a day.

Here is a detail. After that trip, I began to hide my legs and face during battle. I had pretty legs; I was so worried they'd be mutilated. And I worried for my face. That's the detail . . .

After the war, for several years I couldn't get rid of the smell of blood; it followed me for a long, long time. I do the laundry—and I smell it. I cook dinner—again I smell it. Somebody made me a present of a red blouse, and back then it was a rarity, there wasn't much fabric, but I didn't wear it because it was red. I couldn't stand that color anymore. I couldn't go to the shop for groceries. The meat department. Especially in summer . . . And seeing chicken meat, you understand, it's very similar . . . As white as human flesh . . . My husband would go . . . In summer I couldn't stay in town at all, I tried at least to get away somewhere. As soon as summer came, it felt as if war was about to start. When the sun heated everything around—trees, houses, asphalt—everything had that smell. It smelled like blood to me. Whatever I ate or drank, I couldn't get away from that smell! Even clean bedsheets smelled like blood . . .

May 1945 . . . I remember we took a lot of pictures. We were very happy . . . The ninth of May—everybody shouted, "Victory! Victory!" Soldiers rolled in the grass—Victory! They tap-danced. Ay-da-ya-a-a . . .

Fired into the air . . . Whatever we had, we fired it off . . .

"Cease fire at once!" ordered the commander.

"But there'll be ammunition left. What for?" We didn't understand.

Whatever people said, I heard only one word—Victory! And suddenly we wanted desperately to live! And how beautifully we'd begin to live now! I put on all my decorations and asked to be photographed. For some reason I wanted to be surrounded by flowers. They photographed me in some flowerbed.

The seventh of June was a happy day, it was my wedding. The unit organized a great feast for us. I had known my husband for a long time: he was a captain, a company commander. We swore to each other, if we survived, we'd get married after the war. They gave us a month's leave . . .

We went to Kineshma, that's in the Ivanovo region, to his parents. I went there as a heroine; I never thought a frontline girl could be greeted like that. We had been through so much, had saved so many children for their mothers, husbands for their wives. And suddenly . . . I learned about insults, I heard offensive words. Before that, all I heard was "dear nurse," "darling nurse." And I wasn't common-looking, I was pretty. I had a brand-new uniform.

In the evening, we sat down for tea. His mother took her son to the kitchen and wept, "Who have you married? A frontline girl . . . You have two younger sisters. Who will want to marry them now?" And today, when I remember that, I want to weep. Picture this: I had brought a record, I liked it a lot. It had these words: "and you sure have the right to go around in fancy shoes . . ." It's about a frontline girl. I played it, and the older sister came and broke it right in front of me, meaning, you have no rights. They destroyed all my photographs from the front . . . Ah, my precious one, I have no words for that. No words . . .

Back then, we had coupons for food, little cards. My husband and I gathered our coupons and went off to exchange them. We came, it was a special depot, there was already a line, we stood in it and waited. When my turn came, the man standing at the counter suddenly jumped over—straight to me, and started kissing me, embracing me and shouting, "Boys! Boys! I've found her. I recognized her. I really wanted to meet her, I really wanted to find her. Boys, she's the one who saved me!" And my husband was standing next to me. The man was a wounded man I had pulled out of a fire. While there was shooting. He remembered me, but I? How could I remember them, there were so many! Another time I met an invalid at the train station: "Nurse!" He recognized me. And he wept: "I always thought, if we met, I'd kneel to you . . ." But he had lost a leg . . .

We'd had enough, we frontline girls. And after the war we got more. After the war we had another war. Also terrible. For some reason, men abandoned us. They didn't shield us. At the front it was different. You crawl—a bullet or piece of shrapnel comes . . . The boys protected us . . . "Take cover, nurse!" someone would shout and fall on you, covering you with his body. And the bullet gets him . . . He would be dead or wounded. Three times I was saved like that.

We returned from Kineshma to the unit. We arrived and learned that our unit wasn't demobilizing, we were going to de-mine the fields. The land was to be given to the kolkhozes. For everyone else the war was over, but for the sappers it still went on. The mothers already knew we had won . . . the grass had grown very tall . . . But all around were mines, bombs. The people needed the land, so we had to be quick. Every day our comrades died. Every day, after the war, there were funerals . . . We left so many people there in the fields . . . So many . . . The land had already been given to the kolkhoz, a tractor comes along, somewhere there's a mine hidden, there were even anti-tank mines, and the tractor's blown up, the driver's blown up. And there weren't many tractors. There weren't many men left. To see those tears in the village, after the war now . . . Women howled . . . Children howled . . . I remember we had this soldier . . . Near Staraya Russa, I forget which village . . . He was from there himself, he went to de-mine his kolkhoz, his own fields, and died there. The village buried him there. He had fought the entire war, four years, and after the war he died in his native place, in his native fields.

As soon as I begin telling this story, I get sick again. I'm talking, my insides turn to jelly, everything is shaking. I see it all again, I picture it: how the dead lie—their mouths are open, they were shouting something and never finished shouting, their guts are ripped out. I saw fewer logs than dead men . . . And how frightening! How frightening is hand-to-hand combat, where men go at each other with bayonets . . . Bare bayonets. You start stammering, for several days you can't get the words out correctly. You lose speech. Can those who weren't there understand this? How do you tell about it? With what face? Well, answer me—with what face should I remember this? Others can somehow . . . They're able to . . . But me—no. I weep. Yet this must be preserved, it must. We must pass it on. Somewhere in the world they have to preserve our cry. Our howl . . .

I always look forward to our holiday. Victory Day . . . I look forward to it, and I dread it. For several weeks I purposely collect laundry, so that I'll have a lot of it, and I do the laundry all day. I have to keep busy with something, I have to be distracted for the whole day. And when we meet, we don't have enough handkerchiefs—that's how our front liners' gatherings go. A sea of tears . . . I don't like war toys, children's war toys. Tanks, machine guns . . . Who thought of that? It wrenches my soul. I never bought or gave war toys to children. Not to mine, not to others'. Once somebody brought a little warplane and a plastic machine gun into my house. I threw them out on the spot. Immediately! Because human life is such a gift . . . A great gift! Man himself is not the owner of that gift.

Do you know what thought we all had during the war? We dreamed: "If only we survive . . . People will be so happy after the war! Life will become so happy, so beautiful. People who have been through so much will feel sorry for each other. They'll love each other. They'll be changed people." We never doubted it. Not a bit.

My precious one . . . People still hate each other. They go on killing. That's the most incomprehensible thing to me . . . And who is it? Us . . . It's us . . .

Near Stalingrad . . . I was carrying two wounded men. I'd carry one for a bit, leave him, go back for the other. And so I carried them in turns. Because they were very badly wounded, I couldn't leave them. How can I explain this simply? They had both been hit high up on the legs; they were losing blood. Minutes were precious here, every minute. And suddenly, when I had crawled away from the battle and there was less smoke around, suddenly I realized I was carrying one of our tankmen and a German . . . I was horrified: our people are dying there, and I'm saving a German! I panicked . . . There, in the smoke, I hadn't realized . . . I see a man is dying, a man is shouting . . . A-a-a . . . They were both scorched, black. Identical. But then I made out a foreign medallion, a foreign watch, everything was foreign. That accursed uniform. So what now? I carried our wounded man and thought: "Should I go back for the German or not?" I knew that if I left him, he would die soon. From loss of blood . . . And I crawled back for him. I went on carrying both of them . . .

It was Stalingrad . . . The most terrible battles. The most, most terrible. My precious one . . . There can't be one heart for hatred and another for love. We only have one, and I always thought about how to save my heart.

For a long time after the war I was afraid of the sky, even of raising my head toward the sky. I was afraid of seeing plowed-up earth. But the rooks already walked calmly over it. The birds quickly forgot the war . . .

1978–2004

CHERNOBYL PRAYER

Svetlana Alexievich

On 26 April 1986 the worst nuclear reactor accident in history occured in Chernobyl and contaminated as much as three quarters of Europe. While the official Soviet narrative downplayed the accident's impact, Svetlana Alexievich wanted to know how people understood it. She recorded hundreds of interviews with workers at the nuclear plant, refugees and resettlers, scientists and bureaucrats, crafting their monologues into a stunning oral history of the nuclear disaster. What their stories reveal is the fear, anger and uncertainty with which they still live but also a dark humour and desire to see the beauty of everyday life, including that of Chernobyl's new landscape. A chronicle of the past and a warning for our nuclear future, *Chernobyl Prayer* is a haunting masterpiece.

'A searing mix of eloquence and wordlessness . . . From her interviewees' monologues she creates history that the reader, at whatever distance from the events, can actually touch' Julian Evans, *The Telegraph*

THE FEMININE MYSTIQUE

Betty Friedan

When Betty Friedan produced *The Feminine Mystique* in 1963, she could not have realized how the discovery and debate of her contemporaries' general malaise would shake up society. Victims of a false belief system, these women were following strict social convention by loyally conforming to the pretty image of the magazines, and found themselves forced to seek meaning in their lives only through a family and a home. Friedan's controversial book about these women – and every woman – would ultimately set Second Wave feminism in motion and begin the battle for equality.

This groundbreaking and life-changing work remains just as powerful, important and true as it was forty-five years ago, and is essential reading both as a historical document and as a study of women living in a man's world.

'One of the most influential nonfiction books of the twentieth century' *The New York Times*

IN AMERICA

Susan Sontag

The story of *In America* is inspired by the emigration to America in 1876 of Helena Modrzejewska, Poland's most celebrated actress, accompanied by her husband, Count Karol Chlapowski, her fifteen-year-old son, Rudolf, the young journalist and future author of *Quo Vadis*, Henryk Sienkiewicz, and a few friends; their brief sojourn in Anaheim, California; and Modrzejewska's subsequent triumphant career on the American stage under the name Helena Modjeska.

'A tour de force. . . . A magical accomplishment by an alchemist of ideas and words, images and truth' Michael Pakenham, *The Baltimore Sun*

THE FIRE NEXT TIME

James Baldwin

James Baldwin's impassioned plea to 'end the racial nightmare' in America was a bestseller when it appeared in 1963, galvanizing a nation and giving voice to the emerging civil rights movement. Told in the form of two intensely personal 'letters', *The Fire Next Time* is at once a powerful evocation of Baldwin's early life in Harlem and an excoriating condemnation of the terrible legacy of racial injustice.

'The great poet-prophet of the civil rights movement ... his seminal work' *Guardian*

WIDE SARGASSO SEA

Jean Rhys

'There is no looking glass here and I don't know what I am like now . . . Now they have taken everything away. What am I doing in this place and who am I?'

If Antoinette Cosway, a spirited Creole heiress, could have foreseen the terrible future that awaited her, she would not have married the young Englishman. Initially drawn to her beauty and sensuality, he becomes increasingly frustrated by his inability to reach into her soul. He forces Antoinette to conform to his rigid Victorian ideals, unaware that in taking away her identity he is destroying a part of himself as well as pushing her towards madness.

Set against the lush backdrop of 1830s Jamaica, Jean Rhys's powerful, haunting masterpiece was inspired by her fascination with the first Mrs Rochester, the mad wife in Charlotte Brontë's *Jane Eyre*.

'Brilliant. A tale of dislocation and dispossession, which Rhys writes with a kind of romantic cynicism, desperate and pungent' *The Times*

A SHORT HISTORY OF DECAY

E. M. Cioran

'History is nothing but a procession of false absolutes, a series of temples raised to pretexts, a degradation of the mind before the Improbable.'

A Short History of Decay (1949) is E. M. Cioran's nihilistic and witty collection of aphoristic essays concerning the nature of civilization in mid-twentieth-century Europe. Touching upon Man's need to worship, the feebleness of God, the downfall of the Ancient Greeks and the melancholy baseness of all existence, Cioran's pieces are pessimistic in the extreme, but also display a beautiful certainty that renders them delicate, vivid and memorable. Illuminating and brutally honest, *A Short History of Decay* dissects Man's decadence in a remarkable series of moving and beautiful pieces.

'To miss reading this book would be a deprivation' *Los Angeles Times*

SILENT SPRING

Rachel Carson

Now recognized as one of the most influential books of the twenti-eth century, *Silent Spring* exposed the destruction of wildlife through the widespread use of pesticides. Despite condemnation in the press and heavy-handed attempts by the chemical industry to ban the book, Rachel Carson succeeded in creating a new public awareness of the environment which led to changes in government policy and inspired the modern ecological movement.

'Carson's books brought ecology into popular consciousness'
Daily Telegraph